FOREST BLOOD

FOREST BLOOD

a novel by

Jeff Golden

Wellstone Press

Excerpts from *Be Here Now* copyright © by Baba Ram Dass. Reprinted with author's permission.

Book design and composition by Jonah Bornstein
Cover photo by Richard Hart, staff ecologist, Headwaters

FIRST EDITION

Printed in the United States

ISBN 0-9647066-7-9

Library of Congress Catalog Card Number
99-070771

For Jack and Lane. Thank you. I love you.

ACKNOWLEDGMENTS

I don't know much about the adventures of other fiction writers from first page to finished, glossy-covered novel. I know this about my own: what you usually read on pages like this — that the book that follows could not have reached your hands without the help of other people — is absolutely true. It took a loyal crew to navigate the waters of today's cold-blooded market.

The first two to sign on were Sheila Burns of Bloomsbury Books in Ashland and Terrie Claflin, who teaches and coaches writers with almost as much brilliance as she writes. From the first half of the first rough draft — "rough" almost seems too smooth a word — of a manuscript that was then titled *Jack,* they understood and honored my purpose. That was enough to fuel completion of the first draft, after which friends like Phil Keisling, Barry Peckham, Jon Lange and Steve Sacks took a shift at the oars. Their reaction helped me start slicing away the flab; some of it was pretty clever flab (you'll have to take my word for it), but the effort of carrying it almost brought the poor story to its knees before the finish line. Others thoughtfully cheered me on to make sure I got there: KC Golden, Kristi Skanderup, Diane Walton, Melissa Everett, Fred Mann, Kathy Bryon, Sally Ranney, Ashley Henry, Michael and Michelle Saul, and the unmovably loyal Michael Weber. And whenever I wanted I could lift my eyes off the screen, quiet my thoughts and remember that Gayle Killam, the bpomh, stood behind me.

Two particularly gifted readers offered ideas that I finally had the sense to hear. Thank you, Peter Sage. And thank you, Robb (Mr. Mblabbah) Moss, both for moving me out of my own way in the story's first pages and for revitalizing forty years of incomparable friendship.

David Ignatius generously knocked on big heavy doors on my behalf. My passion-nurturing friend Neale Donald Walsch, in the midst of more demands and celebrity hubbub than most of us can imagine, made time to read the manuscript with great care (and, at least for the two chapters he read in an airline seat next to me, with gratifying little noises). During this same period of time, Nancy Walsch showed me why she's Neale's hero.

Forest Blood was proofread by my new old friend Jan Killam, who hit a loud but gentle gong whenever she found clunkers (especially in the way the character Will expresses himself) that slipped by everyone else, and by Tom Barber, who wields a red pen with laser precision. I'm also grateful for the technical advice of doctor of medicine Andy Kuzmitz and doctor of flyfishing Michael Baughman. Jonah Bornstein of Wellstone Press showed me the blessings of working with a small publisher who cares about craft and quality.

My children Daniel and Sarah are, in the end, my reasons to care. I like each of you two best.

PART 1

1

MY GUESS IS THAT IF YOU HEARD BOB EDWARDS SAY *YOUR* NAME TO TEN
million public radio listeners while you were taking your morning pee
in a plastic hose, your heart would stop. It wasn't that big a deal to me.
That's the truth. After what's happened the last month and a half it
almost felt like the start of another normal day.

Actually the day started about ten minutes earlier when the radio
clicked and Bob said, "Good morning! President Clinton travels to Phila-
delphia today, the start of an eight-state campaign swing for Democratic
candidates in next week's Congressional election. I'm Bob Edwards,
today is Monday, October 31, and this is NPR's *Morning Edition.*"

Bob's theme swelled up into the trumpet fanfare that tugs me out of
sleep at the same exact second of every weekday morning. Every sin-
gle one. I cling to the habit by making sure the alarm stays set at 5 a.m.
on the dot, the same as when I was logging.

Once years ago, on a soaking cold April morning as we drank burnt
coffee in the Company truck and waited to see who'd make the first
move towards a chainsaw, I was actually dumb enough to mention that
I woke up to public radio every morning. For years after that nobody
on the crew called me Jack...I was Ballet Boy, then for a while just
"Double-B." Wouldn't surprise me if a few comedians around town
still call me that.

"The murder trial of anti-abortion extremist Paul Hill for the shoot-
ing of a clinic doctor gets underway in Pensacola today, while Israel
begins reopening Gaza Strip border crossings today that were sealed

3

after the Tel Aviv bus bombing." But I don't log anymore. Funny how this works, but in order to log you have to be able to walk, which I don't do anymore either. The truth is getting up this early only lengthens a day that's already too long.

I do it anyway. Some nights, the ones I stay up late writing, that leaves only four or five hours of sleep. Not enough. Doesn't matter. With the way my life has turned out I can nap anytime I want, as long as the pain's under control. If I want I could sleep all day long. Who could ask for anything more.

"Cowgirl legend Dale Evans is 82 today and today's the birthday of Colorado Governor Roy Romer. He's 66 years old. The news is next." Then came Carl Kassel's voice, gentle and official, for six minutes; for me, still drifting in the last wisp of sleep, it was only a few seconds. Then Bob was back, listening to Cokie Roberts explain that if Republicans could take control of Congress in next week's election, Newt Gingrich would be the new Speaker. Now I was awake.

I reached over the edge of the bed for the hose, slipped it under the blanket and started peeing. That's when Bob said my name. "Since becoming the first critical victim of the alleged 'eco-sabotage' designed to stop logging in the Pacific Northwest, John Gilliam, Jr. has been recuperating in his family home in the tiny town of Lewis Falls, Oregon, with a 24-hour security detail buffering him from media and public attention."

Okay, when I said this was a normal way to start the day maybe I exaggerated. I doubt if anyone could get used to this stuff. "Yesterday Gilliam made his first public comments in weeks. He told the Alternative Radio Network he doesn't think the FBI's main suspect in the incident is the right man."

Then three sentences came out of the radio that gave me the weirdest sensation I've ever had. They came in *my voice.* I lay there, the hose still warm in my hand, hearing myself say something I never said. I mean, I did say all the words but I didn't say what they had me saying. If this sounds confusing, maybe you'd like to see how sharp you'd be after listening to your words twisted into small-minded drivel for millions of people to hear as they shave or boil eggs or dress their kids for school.

I could write down the words, supposedly my words, right now, but they wouldn't mean anything unless you knew what led up to them. The point is I've been fooling myself by thinking this might blow over and let me go back to being nobody. That's not going to happen. Not when every bozo out there with a videocam or laptop thinks they know my story well enough to tell the world. They don't. Finally, finally I get it: the only way this story gets out into the world, and I mean the real story, is if I tell it myself. I have to.

It won't take much work. I just have to organize what I began writing in my spiral notebooks the first day I could sit up straight in the hospital. I had no plan. All I wanted those first few days was a steady task for my thoughts, a task to consume them so they couldn't hurt me more than I already was. I absolutely knew that my mind had to keep moving since my body couldn't. I knew that if I didn't move I could end up like Fife Burgess, who used to be the sunniest guy in Lewis Falls.

AND VERY FUNNY. ONE OF THE BEST MEMORIES I HAVE FROM WAY BACK was the time Fife Burgess went bass fishing with Dad and me up at the reservoir that the Company used to stock above town. I was probably four or five. Fife and Dad got to talking about this new Forest Service timber cruiser who'd just moved to town from college up in Corvallis. The Lewis National Forest has had a ranger station in the middle of town since before I was born and other than the Company they're about the only employer around.

Fife thought this new guy looked like Dudley Dooright in his green khaki uniform, all pompadour and chin. He'd come to Lewis Falls single and childless. Fife started running through the options for female companionship in Lewis Falls and what this guy must have thought of each one until both Fife and Dad were laughing so hard I started thinking about what I'd do if they fell out of the boat. It was the only time I ever heard Dad laugh out loud.

2

FIFE BURGESS WAS HOLLY'S UNCLE, AND I SAW HIM SOMETIMES WHEN HE came over to her house. Holly's back yard ran right up against mine with only a rough cedar fence in between. Even that wasn't there when she and I were little, about the time we started kindergarten. It was all just one big yard.

That changed after the Burgesses got Booger. I always called him Booger Burgess, never just Booger, which bugged Holly. Booger Burgess was a demented little mutt with a Scotty head and a wiener-dog body and he wouldn't stop digging up my mother's bulbs. While Holly's folks tried one plan after another to keep him away, Holly set out to train Booger Burgess. I didn't tell her so, but I thought it was hopeless. Looking into those two black marbles Booger Burgess had for eyes you knew that figuring out ways to get into Mom's flowers took every watt he had.

But if she was going to try, I wanted to help her. I wanted to do anything that Holly was doing. One Saturday morning we were in the yard halfway between her back porch and mine, trying for the twentieth time to get him to stay while we slowly backed away from him. "Stay, good dog…stay, puppy dog…stay, Booger puppy dog," Holly cooed as she moved away, her palm pushing air in front of her like a traffic cop.

Suddenly Booger Burgess' ears went straight up, his busy tongue disappeared in his mouth and his head swivelled towards something behind us. The next moment he leaped up and tore past us to where

Dad's lime-green Dodge Power Wagon was pulling around the kitchen side of my house, turning towards the swing set off a corner of our back porch. The first thing I noticed was that Dad had Rum (that's what my mother named the truck, after the baby sound she said I made when I heard it bringing Dad home from work) set in granny gear, the one that sounded like a Sherman tank climbing up the side of a bunker. I'd only heard the granny a few times before when we were coming out of the creekbed with a full load of firewood. The second thing that I noticed was that the running boards, which were usually so high that I had to roll a knee on them to climb into the cab, were down where I could step on them. Rum looked shorter all over than I'd ever seen.

Dad stopped Rum at the swing set, crunched into reverse and started backing towards Holly and me. As he did we were looking at the fattest log I'd ever seen, so wide it rested on the rounded top edges of Rum's sideboards rather than inside the bed. Later I realized that it couldn't have been thicker than the biggest Douglas firs that my Dad skidded with his cat towards the Lewsco log trucks, but those were thirty feet long or more. This honker pushing Rum into the ground looked stouter because it was only seven feet long.

Dad backed up to a laurel tree in the corner of the yard near where we stood and stopped the truck. We watched him wrap a dirty blanket from under the truck seat around the base of the tree, then circle it with a cable that he also wrapped around the log.

"You kids stand back now, hear?" Dad yanked on the cable to check the connections. Holly and I took three steps backwards. Dad took a last tug on the cable and started back to the driver's door. He stopped and stared at us, hands on his hips. "Is that what you call 'back', Jack? Look, you two go and get up on Holly's porch, *now*. And take that piece of grunt dog with you, too." Booger Burgess was sitting on Holly's ankles by now. She picked him up and we walked sixty feet away to her porch.

Dad slid into the cab and crunched Rum back into gear. We watched her slowly roll forward until the cable lost its slack. Then with a deep rumble the power wagon moved forward, three inches, a foot, two feet, while the log stayed just where it was, locked in its rectangle of space. Then the rumble became a roar as the truck lurched out from under the log. It fell to the earth with a *wumph* that I could feel inside my ears. Next to me Booger Burgess shivered in Holly's arms like he was freezing.

We ran to the log as Dad got out of the truck. "Unh-unh," he said, shaking his head. "You kids stay back now. This thing can roll easier than you can run, and I don't want you near it, you hear me?" We stopped and watched him unhook the cable and coil it to rest at the base of the laurel tree. "Now, Jack," he said to me, leaning for a moment on Rum's back fender and wiping his forehead with a forearm, "I gotta go get Fife and his saw. You two are not to be messing with this while I'm gone. You got it? Holly, you understand?" We nodded. Dad drove away.

Holly put Booger Burgess down and we walked straight to the end of the log, running our hands over the raspy flat surface. Standing on tip-toes and stretching my arm straight up I could almost touch the crust of bark on top. But that doesn't mean we were *messing* with it.

It was an old cedar with circular layers of reds, tans and golds like you see together in pictures of those Utah canyonland parks. The broadest zone was in the middle, where it ran brick-red studded with spots and half-moons and long beads of rich brown. We touched these scars and felt the dark pulpy nuggets move under our fingertips. I started scooping them out with my fingernail, catching spurts of the stuff in my other hand. I reached out to Holly and poured the little pile into her hand.

"Chocolate cake crumbs," she said, spreading the crumbs evenly across her palm.

"Eat it, then," I told her.

"No! You eat it."

"Don't you like chocolate cake?"

"*You* eat it," she said, pushing the pieces with her finger from her palm to mine.

So I did. I put them in my mouth and started chewing. They were spongy and chalky and didn't taste like much of anything at all. I turned straight to Holly as I chewed, trying to look like I ate the stuff every day.

"Eeeyyeewww!" she scrunched up her face. "*Worms* have touched that! Eeeeyeewwwww!" And she turned and ran back to her porch and into her house, the screen door slamming in Booger Burgess' face as he tried to follow her in.

That was the first of countless times I've realized that Holly knows more than I thought she did. The crumbs were the leavings of worms and other critters building their tunnels through the cedar. This log was laced with them, a whole highway system splotting the cut surface like a bad case of measles. It was too far gone for Lewsco to sell, which made it fair game for Dad or any other worker who wanted to haul it off. This was years before someone decided that worm-wood paneling was natural and rustic and belonged on the wall of every tavern and Original Steakhouse between here and San Diego, so that the wormy cedar logs started selling for more than the good stuff. The same decaying Lewsco logs, cut 20" long, split into triangular wedges and packed into the massive steel Ashley in the corner of the living room, kept us warm every winter.

I'd almost finished digging the crumbs out of both ends of the log with a crusty old screwdriver when Rum pulled into the driveway and rolled to a stop near me. Fife Burgess stepped out of the passenger side. "Yo-*ho,*" he said, clapping his hands once and rubbing them together. "Mr. Jack!" I barely noticed because I was watching Dad climb out the driver's side, looking at me with his head cocked. He walked straight to end of the log and ran a finger through one of the little hollows I'd made. Then he looked down at me, his head and old felt hat taking up a third of the sky. I couldn't see his expression behind the swirl of cigarette smoke.

"Mr. Jack!" Fife was right beside us now. "Man, what are you, some kinda beanstalk, way you're poppin up another inch every day? Nother year'r two, won't be a doorway in town you can fit through." He stepped between us, turning towards Dad and away from me. His hand slipped into the back pocket of his overalls and came out with a red-and-white swirled peppermint candy pinned between two long fingers. "John," he said to my Dad, rotating the little disk until it balanced on a forefinger where only I could see it, "I don know why you fetched me over when your own boy's got big enough to do the whole job hisself." I took the candy and slipped it into my back pocket.

"Uncle Fife!" All of a sudden Holly was flying by me in mid-air, landing on the back of Fife's legs so hard he staggered. Booger Burgess ran lassoes around their feet as fast as he could, barking his tiny brains out.

"It's my girl!" Fife said, pulling her around his body until he could hold her. "The one and only one for me of all the ones from A to Z!" Dad stood a few feet away, his eyes following the tight loops Booger Burgess was cutting around us. Then he went into the house.

"Uncle Fife, what are you and Jack's daddy going to do?" Holly asked after she stopped laughing.

"We're gonna saw up that fat ol cull log for boards, darlin."

"What do you want the boards for?"

"To build us a fence, darlin," Fife nodded past me towards the middle of the yard. "There's gonna be a new fence right between your house and Mr. Jack's."

"Why?"

Without setting Holly down Fife got on his knees and scooped up Booger Burgess. "Because of *you!*" The dog stopped cold in mid-bark. "Because you're a no-good eggsuckin rootdiggin dog!" Fife shifted himself around to sit with Holly on one knee and Booger Burgess on the other. Then he leaned over until his nose was half a foot from the dog's. "Now, Boog," he said gravely, "I think it's time you n me had a little heart to heart. Seems to me you're not gettin any younger, son, you just are *not.* You're…how old is he?" he asked Holly as she crumpled up his shirt sleeve in delight.

"He's *two*, Uncle Fife!"

"You're two now, Booger, which means if you were a boy person you'd be stealin smokes and terrorizin girl people by now. My point bein that it's about time for givin thought to your future, seein as how if you don't, no one else will, seein as how it's a human-eat-human world out there. Am I right, or am I right?" Booger Burgess was vibrating with guilty confusion, looking everywhere but at Fife. "Am I right?" he asked Holly.

"Uncle *Fii-eye-ife!*"

"You know I am," he said, turning back to Booger Burgess. "It's only your true friends who care enough to tell you the truth about this, Boog, and I'm a true friend," and on for another two minutes easy until he set the poor mutt down. The instant his paws hit the ground, Booger Burgess' distress fell away and he was back into Fife's lap, covering his coarse beard and nose with a hundred tongue strikes. Fife collapsed backwards in laughter, the dog clinging to his chest without missing a lick. When Holly leaned into the chaos they became a ball of giggling fur and cloth, rocking side to side right there on the grass while I watched. I almost jumped on, too.

That picture's the very first thing I thought of, that and the little peppermint candy he snuck to me, when Dad came home one night when I was in high school with the news that Fife had been crushed. He'd been checking the pulley on a self-loading truck when an old cable snapped. The log it was hoisting came crashing down on the side of the bed, twisting over end-to-end and slamming Fife to the ground. It shattered his ribcage and pelvis and broke his back just above his tailbone. He's been in the chair ever since.

Back then the Company was completely different. It cared for its people. When Fife was as healed as he was going to get, they made a job for him organizing the dailies at the log scaling station. That didn't work. It was too painful for Fife to sit at a desk for more than an hour or two. I didn't see Fife again until I was 21 and could go into Sam's Spot. That's where he more or less lives. Sam cut away a few feet of his bar to make a notch just big enough for Fife to fit his wheelchair. If you walk into the Spot this afternoon you'll find Fife Burgess there mixing V-8 juice into a glass of Blitz beer and nodding at whatever someone happens to be saying.

That's what I meant. That's how I won't end up.

IF I WAS IN HIGH SCHOOL WHEN FIFE WAS CRIPPLED THEN IT HAS TO BE at least 25 years ago, and it still gets me. When I think of him I'd rather think of who he was before. That's why I want to get down all the details from the day the fence started going up, back when he strode lean and tall across our yards, stronger even than Dad.

When Dad came back out of the house it didn't take them long to start cutting. They set two heavy planks up on sawhorses on either side of the big log to give themselves twin scaffolds to walk on. Then they went back to Rum and pulled out Fife's Alaska chain mill out of the bed. This was a chainsaw three times longer than anything you see today, with a handle on the far end that a second man could hold. Attached to the long chain-bar and parallel to it were a pair of pipes that rolled freely. Fife took some measurements of the log and then set the pipes an exact distance from the chain-bar and tightened four nuts to lock them in place. Then he stepped around to the engine side of the machine and pulled hard on the cord.

It gurgled for half a second and was quiet. Fife pulled again and the gurgling lasted two seconds. On the fifth pull the old saw erupted and Fife squeezed the trigger until the sound was a furious roar, pushing everything else out of the air. Fife eased the throttle back to a loud idle, tweaked a couple of screws on the engine housing and poured into it a thick amber syrup from an old dishwashing bottle.

They picked up the trembling saw and set it on the ends of the knee-high planking that flanked the log. They each stepped onto a plank, Dad with his back to me and Fife facing him on the other side of the log, and picked up the saw again. They strained to lift the saw higher until the guiding pipe rested on a plank they'd fastened to the top of the log. Then they slowly started walking down the length of the planks with the log between them, Fife holding at shoulder height an engine that would run a Harley and, six feet down the bar with a new Prince Albert dangling from his lips, Dad leaning against a silvery iron handle with both hands.

When the chain first touched the end of the big cedar log the engine's pitch rose a little. Dad and Fife walked the saw easily down the length of the log. When the saw was all the way through Fife shut it off. It spluttered and stopped and the silence was jolting.

They carefully stepped down from the planking and carried the big machine back around to the other end. Dad pulled off the plank they had used to guide the saw through its first cut, and a broad arch-shaped slice of bark fell to the ground. They wouldn't need the plank anymore, because now the pipes could roll across a flat surface on top of the log, right about where the dusky bark met the honey-colored wood.

"Start with one-by boards, John?" Fife yelled over to Dad.

"Set it for two-bys," Dad yelled back. "Want to make sure we get enough out for all the horizontals first."

"First *two*-bys," Fife nodded. He locked the pipes in place exactly two inches from the chain-bar. Then he fired the saw back up and they stepped onto the planking again.

Before they began this pass I saw Fife yell something to Dad and laugh. Dad shook his head and flicked the butt of his Prince Albert towards the truck. With this cut they were into the solid part of the wood. The sound moved up another notch towards a whine and they had to walk slower. The whirring chain left behind it in the log a perfect horizontal black seam as thick as my finger. Dad turned his head from the log and scrunched his eyes almost shut against a fountain of tan dust that shot out sideways from inside the log. It stuck to patches of sweat on his neck and his cheek, filling in between the stubble.

When they reached the end this time they had a two-inch slab of cedar two feet wide on the top and a few inches wider on the bottom. It looked like any board except for the roughness and the bark on the sloping edges. I remember the edges, because when they were trimmed off later to make the boards square they became long whippy strips that I'd break into short lengths when Mom sent me out back to fill the kindling bucket. We used that stuff to start up the old Ashley for probably three winters before we ran out.

As they were starting the third cut Holly shuffled up and sat down next to me on the grass. She turned to face me with her hands pressed tight against her ears, playing the scene for all it was worth. She arched her eyebrows high and pursed her lips until her eyes and mouth were three perfect circles. I figured she'd been practicing with a mirror; the winter before, on a rainy Sunday afternoon just after Mr. Burgess had brought home their first TV, I sat in their overheated parlor and watched two Shirley Temple movies with her.

When they had enough lumber for the main framing pieces Fife changed the adjustment to make the boards that would be the fence's skin, and we watched him and Dad slice the log down an inch at a time. Every couple of minutes Holly turned her surprised Shirley face towards me. I shrugged and kept my attention on the men. I didn't want to be sitting there. I stood and hitched up my jeans, crossed slowly in front of her and walked with great purpose over to Rum, which I reached before figuring out what I was going to do. I vaulted onto the tailgate with a spring to make it look easy, then turned around to watch the cutting, one leg hugged up to my chest, the other dangling carelessly off the back of the truck.

What if I just walked over to my Dad as they were starting a new cut and just reached out for the handle? And he gave it to me and stepped back, so that I'd be climbing up on the planking with 100 pounds of saw and Uncle Fife on the other end. And Fife revs it up again and it's him and me pushing the chain through the wood, Holly watching every moment as I lean forward on the handle, squinting and sweating with sawdust blasting me, slowing down for nothing as I march like part of the machine to the far end of the plank...

Then Mom was right next to me, setting a big platter of roast beef sandwiches and a cluster of pop bottles on Rum's tailgate. She looked up with a smile and rolled her eyes to share with me alone the knowledge all sanity had been left behind. Then she turned and waved to the men as they were stepping down from the planks. Fife switched off the saw. They walked to the side of the house to hose off their hands and headed towards lunch on the truck. Mom was right behind them. She'd gone back to the kitchen to get the turquoise clock radio she kept above the sink, carrying it out now with a long extension cord trailing behind. She set it on top of Rum's cab, and I heard the bouncy theme that always started the Portland Beavers' broadcast. Dad nodded to her as he sat down on the tailgate and lifted a sandwich off the pile.

3

I SHOULD EXPLAIN ABOUT DAD AND THE BEAVERS. HE LOVED THEM. TO the day he died he thought baseball reached its peak in the Pacific Coast League, the place where big business and big money didn't get the chance to poison it. I remember a winter night soon after the summer Dad and Fife sawed up that log, when Dad came home with the *Oregonian* and read to Mom how the Dodgers and Giants were moving to California. "Here we go," Dad said. "That ain't baseball they play. It's show business. You see if they don't screw everything up." If he'd lived to see the Big League strikes they probably would have killed him.

When the Beavers played day games Mom sometimes slipped the kitchen clock radio into Dad's big lunch bucket, and he'd combine all his breaks for the day together for a late lunch. That gave him time to find an outlet to plug into, maybe in a garage or ranger station near the cut or just the sharpening shed, if it had power, to catch a couple of innings. It didn't matter where they were playing, San Francisco, Los Angeles, Seattle, San Diego, home in Portland.

Night games he plain didn't miss. He tied an antenna high up a huge old spruce, a hundred feet at least above our back yard, to pull the Portland station in more clearly. Then he'd twiddle with the tuner in the middle of a coffin-sized hi-fi system he'd bought at the Auction Barn in Port Douglas until the lacquered voice of Ted Perskelli filled the living room, sometimes with crackles, usually clear as could be. I wasn't supposed to speak or make any noise when Dad had the Beavers on.

You have to understand that for Dad the Beavers were a lot more than Oregon's team. He was born in Lewis Falls in 1929 to parents who'd both been born in Lewis Falls. Grandpa had taught himself reading by reading everything he could find on American History, especially the Revolutionary War. When their first son was born, Grandma, who lived every hour of every day for Grandpa, suggested naming him George Washington Gilliam. In the story Grandma told me one bedtime forty years ago, Grandpa looked in the fire for about an hour thinking it over while she nursed the baby. Finally he shook his head and said no, old George had already gotten more credit than he deserved (though he deserved a lot), including naming a whole state after him to pretend it was as important to history as Oregon was, and it was time to recognize it took more than one man to get this country going. So on his second day Dad became John Adams Gilliam. My whole name, never used, is John Adams Gilliam, Junior.

Dad almost never came off the hill, the span of Coast Range where Lewis Falls sits just west of the summit, until he was ten or twelve. That's when he got serious about baseball. There was no Little League then, but there were ten open acres in the center of town. Today it's thick green lawn that we call the Square. Back then it was shrubgrass tended by the Company. Dad played on that field for ten years or more.

The whole wall of the Spot over the shuffleboard table is a gallery of the Company teams over the years. The first photo is from 1927, the same year the Babe hit sixty home runs. Then they go in order, one for every year into the mid-Fifties except 1942, '43, '44 and '45. Every one was set up the same way, a clump of eleven or twelve young guys in two rows on and behind the same exact metal bench, with someone older in street clothes sitting in the middle of the front row and a couple of batboys sitting cross-legged on the ground in front of them all. Except for the older guy, they all had on serious uniforms, and I mean the whole nine yards: caps with flowing ornate Ls over the beak, heavy wool jerseys with LEWSCO flowing diagonally from right shoulder to left hip in fancy-curved script, big baggy wool pants giving way just below the knee to heel-less baseball hose, white undersocks, black cleats. The teams from the '30s look exactly like the major leaguers looked in the '30s. The teams from the '50s also looked exactly like big leaguers in the '30s. The Company got full mileage out of that old fabric.

They were kids, intense, dead-serious kids glaring out from those photos. You can look at every Lewsco player from 1927 to 1955, and I have a few times when the conversation at the Spot got too stupid and I wasn't ready to go home, without seeing smiles on more than five faces. Three of them are in the first row in 1938, which set off a looney-tunes argument one night about what the joke might have been.

None look graver than Dad, who stands on the far right of the upper row in 1946, 1947 and 1948. Habit was important to him. He's glaring at the camera like he's considering whether to snap the lens off with his bare hands. I've tried to imagine behind the stare to what it felt like to play on those teams, which Dad almost never talked about. All I know is that he played third base and he was good. Mom says nothing got past him on the ground, even when he was playing shallow for the bunt, and that he hit as well as anybody on Sam's wall.

The Lewsco team covered a lot of territory in a ten-week season every summer, when the light was long and the woods were too hot and dry for prime cutting anyway. What I know most about is the 1948 season, when they were visiting Yakima for a four-game series. On the first morning Dad strolled downtown with Ray Byrnes, a welder at the mill who played first base, and some other guys. They stopped at the Crispy Creme Dairy Bar and plopped down on five bar stools at the counter for breakfast.

The waitress set five mugs in front of them and poured coffee. She tried to take their orders but Ray Byrnes was making it hard. First he had to tell her who she was waiting on, how they needed a big breakfast so they could crush the local mamas-boys into the dirt like they did in every town in four states, the punishment he'd personally be giving the outfield fence that afternoon, and how pretty she was.

The last part was true. She was Lois Enderdahl, eighteen years old, a big girl with a broad open face, dark gold hair and green eyes. Her parents were wheat farmers from North Dakota who got tired of getting squeezed between the militant socialist Grangers and the brokers who bought the harvest, so they moved west where they could mind their own business.

Not that Yakima was tame. It was a raw farm town, full of swaggering roosters looking for excitement and finding little. Lois served customers cruder than Ray Byrnes every day at the Crispy Creme. She flirted straight back at him and cranked out their breakfasts without losing a step. As she was clearing their plates, Ray told her she couldn't deny herself, or the grandchildren she'd want to tell stories to, the pleasure of seeing him beat the tar out of the Yakima boys. He wrapped a dollar bill, which covered his breakfast and a nice tip, around two tickets to that afternoon's game.

Lois called up a girlfriend and they went. Ray went 0-for-5, three strikeouts and two errors at first. Dad went 3-for-4 with a three-run double and a game-winning backhanded stab of a Yakima line drive that was on its way to the left field corner.

The next morning Dad got up earlier than the rest of the team and walked downtown alone for breakfast at the Crispy Creme. He did the same thing the next two mornings. Eleven months later Dad drove Grandma and Grandpa up to Yakima to watch him marry Lois. Then he drove them right back to Lewis Falls, the two women in the back seat and the two men in front. Grandma and Grandpa got out and Mom and Dad drove straight on to Prineville in central Oregon to join the team. Mom followed the Loggers that summer to the Dalles, Walla Walla, Moscow, Everett, Centralia, Roseburg, two homestands in Lewis Falls, Eureka and Redding. She could have stopped anywhere along the way and gone back to Yakima until the season was over — she says Dad told her that was fine, if she wanted to — but she didn't. Dad was on a tear, playing the best ball he ever would, and she wanted to see it.

Right before the season ended on Labor Day, Dad got a telegram in Eureka. It was from Portland. The Beavers had heard a lot about him, and if he could find the time, they'd like him to come up to try out for the team. I've seen the telegram. Mom has it in a plastic cover in the trunk at the foot of her bed.

John and Lois Enderdahl Gilliam showed up at Civic Stadium in Portland on the afternoon of September 8, 1948, an hour before the start of a game against the Hollywood Stars. They invited Dad into the dugout to watch the game. Mom sat in a section behind home plate reserved for the players' wives. The Beavers lost, 7-3.

After the game Mom and Dad walked two blocks to the Mallory Hotel, where the team had a sixth-floor corner room reserved for them. Mom can describe that room to you as if she were in it last week. They stayed for six days, with Dad working out with the team every morning and a couple of afternoons when there was no game. Then they drove back to Lewis Falls. Other than playing catch with me half a dozen times I don't think Dad ever put on a glove again.

Mom's version is that Dad had a great tryout, that they could have stuck him in the lineup then and there and finished the season at least as well as they did, which (Mom doesn't mention) isn't saying much. She says the only reason Dad didn't get snapped up was that they had only one infield slot to fill and they gave it to the son of some bigshot Portland guy, a rug dealer who had his store's name all over the outfield fence in Civic Stadium.

Dad had almost nothing to say on the subject. Once when I was little I heard him tell somebody he couldn't get around the bases fast enough for Pacific Coast League ball. It wasn't true. I was in the woods with him twice when he had to get away from trees that didn't fall where they were supposed to. I never saw anyone move faster. I didn't know the truth until the very end of his life, and I mean the night before he died: it wasn't slow feet that kept him out of the big leagues. It was the inside curveball, the pitch that sails straight for your head as it leaves the pitcher's hands and somehow ends up on the edge of the plate sixty feet later. He couldn't make himself hang in.

He paid every day for the rest of his life for failing. I watched it, I could feel it. I just never knew why, until it was too late. It didn't have to be like that.

WHEN MOM AND DAD ARRIVED HOME TO LEWIS FALLS FROM THEIR Portland trip, Grandma and Grandpa surprised them with a 50-year lease on a two-bedroom Company house. I grew up in that house, and strangely enough sit writing in it at this moment. It's strange to me anyway. For Lewis Falls, it's about right. Some folks up here live in houses their great-grandparents moved into when Woodrow Wilson was president, back when the Company built an eight-block grid of them, one almost exactly like the other, for anyone who'd been working in the woods or the mill at least five years. I'm guessing the wives started comparing notes back then and decided that barracks life wasn't going to cut it anymore.

The Company leased the homes for four bucks a month at first. I think the going rate was up to about $25 by the time I was born. About the same time the Company started giving folks the option to buy their homes outright. The ground underneath the houses still belongs to the Company, and if you decide to sell you have to sell back to them. It's simple and predictable. People who don't like it leave.

4 🌲

LEWIS FALLS IS JUST ABOUT THE LAST OF THE DOZENS OF COMPANY TOWNS that once studded the Coast Range from Northern California to Canada. When Holly and I were growing up it officially had 840 residents. That was the number on the hand-carved sign on the west edge of town, the first landmark you see if you come up from the Port Douglas side. The other corner of the sign said the elevation was 2035 feet. Underneath the numbers was a slogan:

"WELCOME TO THE HOME OF THE LOGGERS"

The quotation marks were part of the slogan, carved there with everything else. It didn't seem to bother anyone but me. In sophomore English I wrote a paper about it. The title, typed with letters that jumped up and down a tiny bit the way all my school papers did, was "Do We Really Need the **"s** Before and After?" Next to it in Mr. Cartaino's red pencil it says "D+.... Perhaps you could ask yourself, Do We Really Need the *Sarcasm?*" That pretty much ended my adventures in writing until now.

Drive half a minute past the sign and you're in beautiful downtown Lewis Falls. On your right is the Square, ten acres of grass bordered on two sides by the L-shaped high school, LFHS, and on another by the combined elementary and middle school.

On your left side, straight across from the Square, is Lewis Falls' single block of commerce. The first half of it, maybe 200 feet of street frontage, is Sam Abbott's. Then there's the garage and tiny office of the volunteer fire department, then a two-room unit that the county's

19

road deputies use when they're up this way. The back room was a jail cell when I was a kid. The wall of black iron bars is still there, preventing a set of filing cabinets and a few dozen cardboard boxes from escaping. The last building is a low-slung stretch of white cinderblock, one of five District Ranger Stations scattered across the Lewis National Forest.

That's all of it. At the corner of the Ranger Station you can turn left and head down a mile of gravel road that switches back and forth into the canyon and ends up at the Falls, or you can head straight on and start the 45-minute drive over the summit and down the hill to Grants Pass. That's the Sherman County seat where the east-west Highway to the Sea crosses Interstate 5. By Southern Oregon standards Grants Pass is a big city. It's also the business and commercial axis of the Rogue Valley, a sheltered expanse of silty farmland and old orchards that are disappearing under Walmart and Costco parking lots built for the Californians retiring or trying to set up small niche businesses up here. We call them equity refugees, among other things. You don't need me to get started on that subject.

To understand Lewis Falls you have to know about Sam's business, which contains just about every activity in Lewis Falls you need money for. It's kind of a prehistoric mini-mall under a rusty Texaco Star: two gas pumps that used to cover the corner by the flashing light, a grocery and barebones hardware store, the tavern — Sam's Spot, or just the Spot, Lewis Falls' premier social and cultural institution. Behind all this is a cluster of three cabins he rents to the cushier deer hunters, or the wayward sons and daughters who'd come back for holiday visits but weren't about to stay under their childhood roofs, or lost or peculiar tourists.

The gas pumps are gone now. Sam couldn't afford the new double-walled underground tanks that the Legislature demanded ten years ago, so he dug up the old ones and filled in the hole. Now anyone driving over the top from Port Douglas on the west to Grants Pass on the east better start with half a tank. And if you live here in town you have to remember to keep a couple of gallons around in a spare can. This is one of the reasons Lewis Falls folks are so fond of world-saving environmental laws passed by politicians who've never set foot up here.

Sam Abbot, owner, bartender, store clerk, back-up chef and janitor at Sam's, is old now. He was old then, in the mid-1950s, at thirty or so. I passed him in height before I was twelve and he pretended to cuss me out for it. Since then, too slowly to notice, his barrel chest fell into a duffel stomach. Stretched over it like a sausage skin is a blue and green flannel shirt. He must actually have a few of them, because it's always the same and always clean.. There's a tiny wiry thatch of yam-colored hair that spills over the top button, and below his rolled-up cuffs a mat of orange fur covers both meaty forearms. As kids we used to make up stories of what he would look like naked. We called him SN, pronounced "sin," for Strawberry Nose. That would sound more clever if you could see it. It's pink, folded in on itself, studded with tiny holes that look exactly like seeds. It's too small to hold up glasses, so he's always pushing his half-round rims back up or peering over them like Ben Franklin. More the second as the years go by.

For forty years the top half of his head has been bald as the famed billiard ball in his coin-operated table. But the fringe has gone through several editions. The first one I remember was the Julius Caesar look, when he kept it just long enough to comb over the top like dark shiny corduroy. In the late '60s he cut it back to a nondescript Joe Garagiola style. I think he was trying to mark some distance from the longhairs who were starting to show up around then to settle and garden little pockets of land folded into the hills outside of town. They weren't what you'd call welcomed with open arms at first.

Ten years later, when it got hard to tell rasty town loggers from the outlying flower children, Sam felt okay letting his fringe dribble down below his shoulders. Sometimes he gathered it back in a pony tail so tight it seemed to make his head shine brighter. Then four or five years ago he just shaved it all off. The sides aren't bright and shiny like the top, but fuzzy about like the surface of a tennis ball. I guess he decided to seize the initiative and turn baldness into a creed instead of something that just happened to him. All along he's kept his killer mustache, a fat red snake that crawls leisurely from the middle of one cheek to the other. Sometimes he's asked if Sam is his given name (it is) because who he reminds most people of is Yosemite Sam from the old cartoons.

Sam loves quotes and knows some good ones. He's a little weak on attribution. Go into Sam's and start talking about how somebody got lucky and I guarantee you he'll say, "Seems to me the harder I work, the luckier I get." A few years ago I found out it was Ben Hogan who said that, though he said "practice," instead of "work." I almost pointed it out the next time Sam said it, but someone else jumped in with a comment and as he was talking it came to me that it didn't make any difference.

A lot of the quotes end up on the FUNNIES. That's a corkboard about the size of a car door out in front of the Spot that Sam nailed up before I can remember, along with a hand-carved wooden sign on top that says SAMS FUNNIES. Today it's gray and decaying from the moisture of years, but it can still hold a pushpin.

The FUNNIES includes anything Sam feels like putting on it. He tolerates postings on the edges, usually index cards selling old cars,

TVs and free kittens or flyers about what the Lions or the Church is up to. But most of the space is usually covered with clippings from exotic publications. For years, maybe still, he had Lewis Falls' only mail subscription to the Sunday *New York Times* and the *Atlantic Monthly.* Whatever he thought we needed to see ended up on the FUNNIES. Only he knew what that was. For a while he had a thing about Ronald Reagan at his ranch. Every clipping and picture he could find of Reagan chopping wood or mending fences ended up on the FUNNIES. I asked him about it. "The way I see it," he said, looking over the top of his glasses, "the measure of a man is how he does his chores. And this man doesn't do his chores for shit."

Which doesn't necessarily tell you what his politics are. The only image Sam was trying to project on the FUNNIES was that he doesn't fit into an image. A few years ago a little poster showed up on the upper left-hand corner with a rough drawing of the globe and the words "EARTH FIRST! (WE'LL LOG THE OTHER PLANETS LATER)." Maybe he put it up himself or maybe someone else did, but if Sam hadn't liked it it wouldn't have stayed up on the FUNNIES. It was there for more than a year.

Sam is also a patron of the arts. There was always a free pitcher ready for anybody who made a sincere attempt to add to Lewis Falls' legendary heritage of verse. This sometimes made the Spot a rather creative place, maybe along the lines of a Paris salon in the 1920s. The undisputed Poet-King was Humph Rodgers, a thick sullen guy who drove logs to the Grants Pass and Port Douglas mills all day. Some thought that gave him an unfair advantage, all that monotonous time behind the wheel to ponder the intricacies of rhyme and rhythm. He denied it fiercely, swearing his poems came to him as a whole and instantly as he sat on one of Sam's creaky stools. Either way, whenever someone clinked a spoon against a beer glass and Humph stood up, the tangle of conversation stopped. He would look around until everyone was quiet and then, serious as Robert Frost, recite his new creation. They were classics the second they came out of his mouth. Like any good Lewis Falls kid, I used to know a bunch of them. Right now only a couple come back to me word for word. There was

> *We're mountaineers*
> *With hairy ears*
> *We live in caves and ditches.*
> *We wipe our ass*
> *With broken glass*
> *And laugh, because it itches.*

And who could ever forget

Ole Casey said
Just 'fore he died,
"There's four more things
I want to ride:
A bicycle, a tricycle,
An automobile
And a bowlegged gal
On a Ferris wheel."

Then Humph would solemnly turn his gaze from one end of the bar to the other, Sam would plunk down a thick-headed pitcher in front of him, and the Spot would rock with cheers that Mom claims she could hear from our house. Humph would sit back down and melt into the conversation until the spirit seized him again a day or six months later.

THE OTHER PLACE YOU NEED TO KNOW ABOUT TO KNOW ABOUT LEWIS Falls is the Falls. They're no secret, but we're not keen for everyone in the world to know about them either.

Down in the canyon below town the Lewis River drops twelve feet over a shelf that runs its whole width. The shelf is volcanic rock, much harder than the granite around it. Over millennia the river wore down the granite into a gentle grade, but it couldn't make a dent in the volcanic material. Below that another lava glob must have hardened, because the pool at the bottom of the Falls, our swimming hole in the summer, ends at a wall that forced the west-flowing river to take a hard right to the north. Then it turns hard to the left towards the west and then a little further, so that it flows southwesterly away from town. The twisting and the turning carves out a little peninsula of land two-thirds surrounded by the river, a bluff that takes seven minutes to climb if you start at the pebbly mud beach at the pool below the Falls. At the top of the bluff are the Elders.

I don't believe anyone has ever written about the Elders before. I didn't mean to be the first, but I can't tell the whole story if I leave it out. The Elders were a grove of eleven trees, six cedar, three Douglas fir and two spruce. They formed a circle so round that they looked planted, and the space between every two of them was almost the same. Standing on the edge of the Elders looking west you could watch the Lewis gather full speed again after the pounding of the Falls and surge through a narrow canyon towards the coast. If you walked halfway around the circle to face east you were looking across the swimming hole and down into the Falls.

We would go up there to sit inside the circle with the Elders all around us. The ground was flat and soft with the duff of decayed needles, moss and twigs, so that you just wanted to lie flat on your back on a summer day and stare up through the tops of the Elders to the jagged crown of blue sky between them. When the wind blew it looked like they were leaning their heads closer to whisper to each other.

We were quiet at the Elders. Without thinking about it we just left the shouting and braying down at the Falls when we hiked up. I can't remember any of us getting really rowdy up there even once, tossing axes or skinning off bark to leave our names or anything else. Once I found two beer cans and a little flurry of fast-food debris up there. *Once.* I packed it out and that was that.

The people at the South Coast Museum think the Elders was the site of a Medicine Circle. It was a place that the Shasta Costa, a fishing tribe from the coast, would come to meet the Galice, who came up from the Rogue Basin, to trade and celebrate together every Spring. The Elders was probably reserved for the chiefs and their medicine people to meet and smoke together, about like the Penthouse Suite for the big dogs at a trade convention today. Over the years all kinds of pipes and points have been found up there, some buried and some just under the duff.

I don't know any Lewis Falls adult who spent as much time up at the Elders as Fife Burgess. He told me about it in a ghost story way back when he used to visit Holly's house, so I wasn't sure at first that it really existed. It was Fife who found the musket shot there, six spheres the size of green grapes. Today they sit in a little pyramid in a glass case at the South Coast Museum as the centerpiece of the main hall. You can't grow up around here without going on a school field trip to see them two or three times. Considering what a big deal they seem to be they don't look like much.

5

THE LEAD BALLS WERE ALMOST DEFINITELY CARRIED THERE BY BENSON
Lewis or one of his men. Benson Lewis was the nephew of Meriwether
Lewis, the youngest son of the Great Explorer's older brother.

Benson Lewis envied his uncle's fame and wondered out loud why it
hadn't made his family rich. From the age of twenty Benson ran a
bootleg fur trade up the lower Columbia and Willamette Basins, pay-
ing no attention to the exclusive licenses that the eastern companies
had won from the federal government. Benson traded with inland
tribes that the licensed guys barely knew existed. He piled up and
shipped out mountains of pelts in return for whiskey and sugar, travel-
ing back home to Virginia every other year to count his money.

In 1833, in a draw in the eastside foothills of the Coast Range south-
west of where Portland lies today, Benson Lewis came across the most
gorgeous fur he'd ever seen. It was thick and glossy, so black it shone
almost blue in the sun, and covered the back of a Churok chief who
was the honored guest at a celebration for the return of the salmon.
Benson spent two full days bargaining for that fur. He offered every-
thing he had with him. The chief just stared at him. Benson promised
to bring back wagonloads of new merchandise on his next visit. The
chief stared. The conversation got less and less relaxed until the Indian
translator told Benson where the fur came from. They had traded for
it with a Cow Creek band from the south that claimed it was the pelt of
a large man-shaped beast that stayed near a cluster of caves in the
mountains above the ocean. If Benson would sail down the coast until

25

he came to a rock formation that looked like a woman shouting at the sky, he would see a large stream emptying out of the foothills and across the beach. If he followed that stream up into the mountains, he would find the caves and perhaps the beast with the beautiful fur.

Benson left that day. Three days later his ship spilled out of the mouth of the Columbia and turned south. Five days after that he was fuming, certain he'd been had by a bunch of greasy savages. Then the shouting woman appeared.

The rocks created an inlet calm and deep enough to anchor the ship. Benson and three men went ashore and started climbing up into the Range alongside the river they found. His notes, much sparser than the ones his uncle kept years earlier, hum with amazement at the size and thickness of the forest he found as he gained elevation. "Rough-swathed giants as have never been dreamed of allowed us entry all day" was the beginning, middle and end of one entry.

One afternoon Benson and his men came to a sharp right-hand bend in the river where they heard a muffled roar. It got louder as they picked their way along the water's edge along the inside of the curve until they lifted their eyes to become, almost definitely, the first white men to look at Lewis Falls. Benson Lewis first called it Broad Falls in his notes but apparently had a better idea later.

He doesn't mention the Elders at all, though the musket balls are strong evidence he was up there. It may be that he found goodies from the Indian potlatches up there that he didn't want to mention. What he left behind for Fife Burgess to find over a century later was such good stuff that you wonder what kinds of things Benson took home.

But archaeology wasn't Benson's thing. Business was. And what he saw around Lewis Falls after a summer of surveying and mapping fired up his business imagination so much that when the rains came he raced back to Virginia to figure out how to own it. Here was a whole temperate mountain range, as full of lush resources and empty of people as the Appalachians must have been when the Mayflower landed. When people talked with glassy eyes about the Oregon Territory they meant the Columbia Basin and the broad valley of the Willamette River that flowed into it. That part of the territory was already spoiled as far as Benson Lewis was concerned. But the coastal range further south, *his* range — nobody but him even knew it was there, or if they did they weren't doing anything about it.

The South Coast Museum has a small permanent exhibit on Benson Lewis' adventures. It has folders full of his papers after his return from Oregon, including letters to his family about the "Virginia of the West" where they could live like rustic nobility. He figured there were three ways to make that happen: he could go back and squat, holding off any newcomers who challenged his claim, which would be almost impossible in that terrain without bringing more settlers than he wanted to share with. He could throw in with the infant railroad enterprises that were starting to draw their lines into the northwest. Or he could help Oregon become a state and make sure he was at the front of the line when its new Lands Office opened for business, which is what he decided to do.

He took advantage of the fiftieth anniversary commemoration of the Lewis and Clark Expedition at the White House for some nose-to-nose lobbying. The museum has a copy of a letter from Benson to President Buchanan where he gives flowery thanks for the honor of being included in the "magnificently historic occasion." He goes on to say that if Lewis and Clark were still alive they would surely be working tirelessly for Oregon statehood as an "appropriate and reverential continuation of President Thomas Jefferson's abiding vision of a united nation joining one ocean to the other." Then Benson really laid it on: the addition of Oregon to the union "must needs be accompanied by the addition of a fourth name to the trinity of American heroes that we so recently met to honor, the name of the man his countrymen know with affection as 'Old Buck': the name President James Buchanan."

In the margin of the letter is a comment scribbled in another hand: "Respond per Protoc. No. 8." The museum folks think Buchanan scribbled it to instruct his secretary which boilerplate language to use in a letter back to Benson. Lower technology than today, but the same game.

The exhibit also has a deed, stamped on top with the Seal of the State of Oregon, describing by latitude and longitude the block of land to be held in fee simple from that day forward by Benson Lewis, Esq, and his designated heirs and progeny. It's dated March 21, 1859, one month and one week after Oregon became a state. Benson Lewis was the owner of 400 square miles of the finest cedar, spruce and fir forests in the world, with a center point almost exactly where I'm sitting right now.

Benson did nothing else on this dream or any other. After staking the claim he went back to Virginia. Then he moved to a cousin's plantation on the Georgia seacoast to get distance from the Civil War. He disappeared when Sherman marched to the sea.

Benson Lewis, Jr, his only child, volunteered for the Confederate Army as soon as the war began. He was a Captain by the time an artillery shell blew his right arm off at the shoulder at the Battle of Manassas. His interest in Oregon came on suddenly when the Union confiscated the family's Virginia property. After the war he rode a train to the end of the line near the Colorado/Utah border — the Golden Spike wouldn't be driven for another few weeks — and found a wagon and packer to take him across the Rockies and into Oregon. His father's maps helped him find his way to the settlement of Port Douglas. There he built his compound right at the mouth of his river, a long stone's throw from the shouting woman that pulled his father to shore more than thirty years before.

There he gave shape to his father's vison. What Benson Junior saw in the forests that began near the edge of his compound and carpeted the Range all the way to the inland valley was the chance to build the New West in the most literal way. He looked at the river pouring out of the Range and saw the bottom end of a perfect delivery chute for logs that grew twenty or thirty miles away. On the north bank of the river just above the high tide mark, Benson Junior built the first sawmill in Southern Oregon.

The mill and the jobs it offered were the spark that lit Port Douglas. More and more drifters who'd come west without real prospects or a plan found their way to the little village to give fishing a try. The rumor of a new mill with a blade the size of a cow, a flow of logs to its back door that would never end, and a boss ready to pay decent wages to any able-bodied man who was serious about work, probably sounded too good to believe. But it was true.

By the 1870s little Port Douglas had more going on than any coastal town between Eureka and Coos Bay, mostly because Benson Junior couldn't sit still. He started a bank, a dredging company, a general mercantile, a street-light company and an opera hall, home of, that's correct, the Port Douglas Opera Company, est. 1872. Somewhere in there the river officially became the Lewis River and the town's name was changed to Port Lewis. When Benson Junior wore out and died in 1892, the burghers who'd been answering to him for twenty years brought back the name Port Douglas.

Benson's oldest son Benson III was the obvious choice to take over the company, but he'd had a massive blowout with his father over the prostitute he had married and taken away to Los Angeles. That left two more children: Sarah, who went off to college at Bryn Mawr and never came west again, and Fletcher, the little brother no one had much noticed. That would change.

By the time Fletcher Lewis took control in 1893, the best trees near the coast were all cut. The yield decreased as the crews moved to higher elevations, because the Lewis was too narrow and winding for logs to float down. Fletcher spent years wading the upper stretches of the river, looking for ways to deepen or straighten it so that his abundance of higher-elevation timber could slide down to the Port Douglas mill.

He had a lot of dirt pushed from one side of the river to the other with no good results.

Then one day — maybe a hot afternoon, sitting on our beach and staring at the Falls with a big bottle of homebrew — Fletcher had a new idea. If the logs were too hard to get down the mountain to Port Douglas, maybe logs didn't have to get down to Port Douglas. His customers didn't want logs. They wanted lumber.

It took Fletcher a week to finish the basic design of a mill that used the Falls' hydraulic force to turn its blades, and less than a year to build it. The town of Lewis Falls, nestled in the middle of a high mountain valley with enough timber to feed its hydro-mill for a generation, was born. My favorite pictures at the museum are the ones of horses drawing narrow wagonloads of lumber through the trees, down to the shipping docks in Port Douglas.

Then as the century turned, Fletcher had another unruly idea. He looked to the east of Lewis Falls, up over the Coast Range summit and down to the Rogue Valley, where a new north/south railroad line was hooking Oregon to California and Washington State. It was the shipping lifeline to a nation under construction. If he could tap into it, the demand would be there for every stick of lumber Lewsco could produce.

Fletcher wrote to the Oregon & California Railroad, trying to describe the deluge of timber and lumber it could haul if it built a spur line up the eastern slope of the Range to Lewis Falls. The O&C bosses wrote back to congratulate him and assure their full cooperation when he was ready to connect the spur he was building to their main line. Fletcher wrote back to guarantee he'd spend hundreds of dollars a day using the spur as soon as O&C built it. O&C wrote back guaranteeing him priority access to their main line as soon as he finished building his spur. The paper flew back and forth for three years, a thick file now in the museum archives. Towards the back part of it is a letter from President Teddy Roosevelt declining Fletcher's invitation to pay for the project. It runs three paragraphs and the middle one says

> While your kind words regarding the government's efforts to date to assist the settlement of the West are appreciated, the construction of a commercial railway many miles into a heretofore undisturbed forest wilderness would not conform in every respect with the priorities of this Administration.

or nice try, Fletcher.

He would have probably given up on the eastside connection altogether it if it hadn't have been for the San Francisco earthquake. The internal parts of the city's grandest houses, the Victorians that popped up like morel mushrooms after 1906, are packed from basement to roof with Lewis County lumber.

Fletcher's hustle simply overcame geographic logic. Dozens of mills much closer to San Francisco were already operating back then, producing ample supplies of perfectly suitable lumber. But they weren't operated by anyone like Fletcher Lewis, who took the first southbound train he could find when he heard about the earthquake. With the city still smoldering, Fletcher ran through the streets cutting deals with shell-shocked business owners and landlords, promising to have loads of framing lumber stacked wherever they wanted as soon as they were ready to rebuild. With the mass of ruins that had to be burned off, hauled off and dumped into the Bay, Fletcher figured he had a few weeks to start delivering.

He went home and borrowed, bought or stole every flatcar and freight car he could move to Grants Pass. He parked them on a siding in the midst of his thrown-together mill and rented a locomotive to shuffle them out of the way as soon as they were loaded. Then he assembled the longest train ever pulled through the Northwest, every car stacked high with green rough lumber. They told him it was too much weight to get over the Siskiyou Mountains that separate Oregon from California. He made them add another engine to the front and rear of the train and personally ordered the engineer to move it out of the Grants Pass station. He did, slowly, and made it as far as Devil's Slide, ten miles into California. There the weight stopped his four engines cold. For half a day the train coasted slowly back into Hilt, right at the border, where two dozen overloaded flatcars were unhitched and rolled onto a siding. Three days later over a million board feet of Southern Oregon lumber pulled into the freight yards of San Francisco, where a hundred empty wagons were waiting. Every week another train groaning with lumber arrived until San Francisco was framed up again.

Every piece had come together exactly the way Fletcher had planned except for one: without a river flowing down the east slope of the Range, he had to spend three times more than he'd figured to get the logs to Grants Pass. He'd commandeered every draft animal and wagon bigger than a buckboard in Southern Oregon to do it, and it didn't take the packers and drivers long to see they had a highly motivated customer. The daily rate for a wagon and driver tripled overnight.

He didn't forget. In 1910, a wealthy man with a wealthy company now, Fletcher Lewis went ahead and built the lateral rail line that the government and the O&C Railroad wouldn't. It crossed steep drainages on narrow trestle bridges and tunneled twice through granite ridges on a 29-mile climb from Grants Pass to the loading arena on the edge of Lewis Falls. The engines and flatcars Fletcher bought hauled logs down that line for twenty years, until maintaining the track and bridges became more expensive than buying the box-shaped Diamond-T trucks that were coming on the scene. The Lewis Falls Railroad, the only project Fletcher Lewis ever took on out of spite, was his only failure. It cost Lewsco about half the fortune he'd made rebuilding San Francisco. It cost Fletcher Lewis his fire and sense of adventure.

Fletcher never married. When he died the only family member still active in the business was his sister's son Walter, who'd come west to work in the mill as a teenager. Walter Tyler turned out to have some of his uncle's imagination and more skill at spending other people's money. It wouldn't be too much to say Walter opened Oregon's southwest corner to the world. He organized the dredging of the inlet at Port Douglas into a channel deep enough for big freighters and the construction of a two-lane state highway connecting Port Douglas, Lewis Falls and Grants Pass. Finally you could get to Lewis Falls without launching a full-scale expedition. They say the highway changed everything up here. But if it's true that the town was an outpost for loners and misfits when its purpose was to run Fletcher Lewis' hydro-mill, then not everything has changed.

After running the Company for thirty years, Walter Tyler died in 1950, the year before I was born. When Oregon historians call him a great man they usually miss what I think was great. Like his uncle, he took on one big project that didn't pan out, a flakier project than the doomed Lewis Falls Railroad. Walter Tyler was a complete freak for baseball. As work was finishing on the cross-Range highway he decided that Port Douglas needed a Pacific Coast League team, and he did his best to start one. People warned him that it was too remote, but people had said the big port and highway would never be built, too.

For a year Walter put all his might into the project. He brought a barnstorming team of major leaguers to Port Douglas to play three games against a Lewsco all-star team, just to fire up the local imagination. The museum has a picture of Walter shaking Babe Ruth's hand at the main gate of the mill. The Babe's puffing on a cigar and smiling at the camera like the complete pro. His team beat Lewsco 10-2 in the first game in a steady downpour and left the next day before the second was scheduled to start. The next spring the Port Douglas Seahorses opened their first season. They played until July, when the rest of the League's teams refused to come down anymore.

After that Walter Tyler stuck strictly to the timber business. If he thought he'd be remembered at all, he surely didn't think it would be for baseball. As it happens, that's exactly the reason the kids I grew up with remember Walter. His son Ben, who took Lewsco over when Walter died, is responsible for that.

6

AFTER I SAW "FIELD OF DREAMS" I REMEMBER SOME REVIEWER SAYING "Yeah, yeah, I'm sure, this farmer in the middle of nowhere climbs up on his tractor one day and starts knocking over his corn and a minute later he's got this big-league baseball field with grass like the surface of a billiard table and infield dirt that looks like brown baby powder." Something like that.

It didn't bother me. In 1957 it happened in Lewis Falls. The Lewsco Loggers, Dad's old touring semi-pro team, had put down the bats two years earlier, probably victim to one of the Company's first budget moves. They shifted their energy into youth baseball. Working every spare hour they could find they took two weeks to stake out a 2/3-scale ballfield and build the most amazing diamond you've ever seen. I remember them circling their pickups at night to shine the head-lights on the grandstands and bleachers they were building. Mean-while Dad worked the field smooth with his cat. He scraped the old shrubgrass off until the bare surface was perfectly flat, then spread and contoured the rich red clay they hauled in like fine soft sculpture.

No one had the touch on a D-6 that Dad did. I could tell how proud he was of that diamond. The voice that moved him didn't come whis-pering out of the corn, though. It came from his boss, Mel Raines, Ben Tyler's right-hand guy in the company. That field showed Mel's clout in the Company. It was the only project Ben ever funded, Dad told me later, with no re-used materials and no bitching from Ben about the size of the bills. Ben even approved a full set of professional-grade lights around the perimeter, which brought night baseball to Lewis Falls before it reached any Oregon town outside of Portland.

Mel had been smart enough to suggest naming it after Ben's father Walter. Newspapers from all over the state came to the opening ceremony, where Ben cut a ribbon that brought down a sheet to reveal a huge bronze face of the old man, the kind they have at Cooperstown, mounted high on the backstop where you could see it from most of the grandstand seats. Walter Tyler Memorial Field was hands-down the best ball diamond between San Francisco and Portland. In 1960 it became the permanent home of the annual Northwest PONY League championship tournament, which brought fleets of busses full of players, coaches, and later RVs full of parents to the South Coast Range every year. We loved that tournament. It was the longest and most exciting party of the year for us. For the band of hungry motel and cafe owners between Grants Pass and Port Douglas it was Christmas in July.

The best one of all was 1964, when I was 13 and we made it to the finals. We were the South Range Timber Wolves, a combined team of kids from Lewis Falls and Bounty, a tiny hamlet fifteen miles away that started as a health spa sixty years before. Neither town by itself had enough able-bodied 13- and 14-year-olds to field a team. There we were, two tiny podunk specks on the map with a combined population 1/10 the size of Port Douglas and 5 percent the size of Grants Pass. We didn't even think about that then. We had the fans and we had the field. We had the fever. And we had Steve.

It was Steve, not the memory of some dead Company boss, that drove Mel Raines to build that field. Steve Raines, Mel's middle kid and only son, was a month younger than me. Mel had him pushing baseballs around before he could walk. Basketballs and footballs, too.

The way Steve moved was different. Every step and gesture flowed from the one before and towards the next with no flinch or friction. Sometimes when I walked next to him I noticed that my feet were making all the noise. At higher speed his grace was more obvious, on the court or field where nothing was ever hard for him.

No matter what sport or how old we were it was the same story. He set the pattern in first grade when he kicked the kickball nearly twice as far as anybody and then roamed the center part of the field playing three kids' positions at once. That sometimes meant snatching a ball out of the air just before it fell into your outstretched arms. But it was hard to get mad at Steve. It was impossible to stay mad.

He had this smile. He still has a trace of it, though now it's rare to see. It was so wide open, so goofy cracking across his face, that you didn't care how he used it to work people. You just wanted to see it.

He was also bigger than anyone else when we were kids, with a sculpted shape that none of the rest of us had until we started lifting weights to play football. He was something to grow up around, this beautiful little giant with a cockeyed smile that put him back on your level.

Steve pitched that championship game in 1964. We were playing the team from Boise that won the tournament the year before and nobody gave us much of a chance. That didn't keep people from coming. The stands at Walter T were overflowing and the whole Square from the high school to the grammar school was covered with blankets of people who wanted to be near the game even if they could hardly see it. The moment I'll never forget was running out to second base to start the game, hearing the roar of the crowd — it really was a roar, that's how many people there were — and scanning the edges until I found Mom and Dad in an upper row way down the right field line. Mom was standing, waving like a shipwreck survivor at a rescue plane. Dad, one hand resting on her back, just watched.

Waiting for Steve to finish his warm-up pitches I saw his dad Mel sitting in the second row behind home plate, the same seat he used for all of our home games (he'd usually be in the exact same spot for all of our away games, too, bringing along a folding chair for the fields that didn't have bleachers). Both knees were jiggling up and down and he was rubbing his hands nervously. Even when he turned his head to say something to Ben Tyler on his right, his eyes never left Steve.

On Ben's other side was a tan lean man with sharp features, square black glasses and a high sloping forehead. He wore a gray sweater of some light silky material that buttoned up the front. I knew him but I didn't know how. Odder yet were two guys in black suits who stayed close to Ben's guest. And behind their bleacher at the curb was a shiny black Cadillac, longer and much fancier than we saw up here. Any other day our curiosity would have stopped us cold, but that day the thrill of the game was stronger. I'm getting a little jolt right now just writing about it.

Boise was bigger than us and a lot more experienced, but they couldn't hit Steve worth a damn. We weren't doing any better. Their pitcher was even bigger than Steve and threw harder, nothing but fastballs. I was on the on-deck circle in the bottom of the second when he struck Dougy Ferrin out on three pitches, so I had half an inning out in the field to think about stepping up to the plate against this guy.

Bottom of the third. I waited ten feet off the plate as he took four warm-up pitches. God, they were even faster at close range. The catcher stood and threw the ball to second base, the umpire yelled "Play *ball*," and I stepped heavily into the batter's box.

My stomach was frozen. I knew only one thing for sure as I took my stance: Dad, two hundred feet down the foul line, was watching my left foot, the one closer to the pitcher. What that foot did in the next few seconds was all he wanted to know about this game. He wanted to see it move straight toward this big kid on the mound as his fastball approached me, so that all my weight and nervous energy would surge into the ball as I made contact. What he expected was to see it shuffle minutely towards third base, the first move for bailing out of the hot zone in case the pitch came inside. He expected it because that's what I'd done against every fast pitcher I'd faced since I was plunked in the helmet by a fastball on Opening Day the season before. No matter what I told myself I couldn't (wouldn't, according to Dad) take control. I'd wiggle my front foot to sink my cleats into the batters box. As the pitcher wound up my mind chanted *hang in...hang in...hang in.* Then the ball left his hand, my brain went dead and my left ankle was pulled as if by an invisible rope towards the third-base dugout. That's what Dad watched for when he came to my games. It's all he watched for.

"Let's play BALL!" the umpire yelled. I wiggled my foot like I was snuffing out a cigarette to plant it deep and looked out to the big Boise kid on the mound. On the chance I could get a walk — no one had yet — I decided not to swing until he got a strike on me. He started his wind-up. *Hang in...hang in...hang in.* He let fly and the rope jerked my ankle a foot's-width sideways. The ball skidded down in the dirt, way too low. The second pitch split the plate for a strike.

One-and-one. A walk wasn't unlikely at all. He wound up his third pitch. *Hang in...hang in.* This one was coming closer, much closer. My left foot hopped to the left and my right stepped back to catch my weight as the ball popped in the glove over the inside edge of the plate. Strike two.

Terrible. I stepped out of the box to breathe. I lifted the sole of one shoe to tap the cleat, twice slowly, with my bat. Then the other shoe. Ballplayers did this. I looked up to see the Boise pitcher waiting. "Son?" said the umpire. I stepped back in. *Hang in. Hang IN!* The pitch sailed and the feel of the rope was overcome by a spasm of energy as my bat flailed a circle around my body. The pitch missed the outside edge of the plate and the end of my bat by almost a foot. A little hum came from the crowd.

I watched the red dirt in front of my feet the whole way back to the dug-out to keep from looking towards Dad. No one said anything when I got to the bench except Randy Barnett, a squirrelly bench-warmer who always did. "Bitchen swing, Gilliam. The wind almost knocked me over."

Another strike-out in the fifth inning felt a little better, because the second strike was a healthy foul grounder five feet to the right of first base. By the seventh inning the starting pitcher was replaced by another kid, tall and thin and about 3/4 as fast, and I grounded out hard to the second baseman. That would have been okay, except that it ended the inning with two men on base and Boise leading, 4-1.

We'd made it 4-2 by the time I came up in the ninth inning. Dougy Ferrin had walked to start off the inning, and the first two pitches to me were balls. My left foot twitched outward with each one, but not much; most likely only two of us in the whole park noticed it. My life at that instant fit into two wishes. I wanted to get on base and I wanted my left foot to keep still. In return I would have given Satan anything he wanted.

Hang in. The third pitch came over the center of the plate. All that moved was my foot, a tiny hop to the left. Two-and-one. This wasn't going to be free. I tapped the outer corner of the plate with my bat and laid it back over my shoulder. *Hang IN!* I heard the Boise pitcher grunt with the effort of the next pitch. The white blur grew fast along a path that looked like it would end at my ribcage. I crumbled to the dirt faster than gravity, waiting to hear the umpire's call before starting back up. Three-and-one.

This called for a very thorough cleaning of my cleats. I stood outside the box and tapped each one with my bat three times. I wasn't about to look anywhere else. Not at the pitcher, not at the Coach and especially not down the rightfield line. To be safe I tapped each shoe one more time. I stepped slowly back towards the plate and took a stance. *Please...just hang in.* As the ball left his hand my bat started a diagonal chop through the air over the plate while my chest and shoulders leaned away from the plate like one of those bottom-heavy rubber clowns that always bounces back upright. A buzz ran through my hands as the ball hit the knobby end of the bat and spun erratically just over the second baseman's glove into right field. When I could think again I was standing on first base, watching Dougy wriggling with excitement across the diamond on third.

The crowd was screaming. We still had three outs left with the top of the order coming up, two guys on base and two runs to make up. Unless there was a double play, that meant Steve could come to the plate representing the winning run.

Matt Conley stepped up to the plate and in almost the same motion lashed at the first pitch. It was the hardest ball he'd ever hit. Steve's comment after the game was that it would have made the third baseman a girl if the kid hadn't jerked his glove up to catch it. Then he dove towards third base touching it with his glove a thin instant after Dougy's foot returned to avoid a second out.

Watching Mike Smeltzer step to the plate I realized that a double play would end the game and the best season we would ever have. I pictured how I'd have to go into second base if Mike hit a ground ball, screaming and pumping like a freight train the way Billy Martin or Johny Logan did and hoping not to get creamed in the forehead by the relay throw. On the third pitch Mike did hit a grounder, a soft one to the shortstop, and I ran like hell. Halfway down the line I could see from the second baseman's floppy pose that the play wasn't coming our way. The play was to first base for the second out, while Dougy stayed carefully on third.

From across the diamond I watched Steve walk to the plate and straight into the exact situation we'd imagined a hundred times in make-believe hero games: bottom of the ninth, two out, two runners on base, the championship on the line. He looked like his mind was far away as he walked towards the plate, slowly swinging the bat back and forth. The roar from the crowd was steady now, as if nobody needed to inhale.

Steve took a strike and then a ball. When I saw him stride into the third pitch I started running. He whacked a line drive about six inches above the pitcher's head, an easy out if it had been traveling 1/3 as fast, right through the block of space I'd been occupying an instant before and into center field.

My eyes were on Buck Ferrin, Dougy's dad coaching at third, who was windmilling his arms to send me home. I rounded the base wondering where the ball was. If the centerfielder played it clean and made a strong throw, I was heading for a gladiatorial smash-up at home plate. The panic stoked me to a speed faster than I could run, and as I tried to straighten my curving path for a dash to the plate, one foot tripped over the other. I stumbled forward two or three more steps before crashing to the dirt, landing on the three points of both hands and the bill of my helmet.

The crowd sounded like a hurricane. I pushed myself up and started running before I was really on my feet, gaining ten or twelve feet of ugly progress towards the plate before falling again. This time I lifted my head first and saw the catcher standing twenty feet away on the plate, staring out past the pitcher with arms spread wide and quaking with hunger for the ball. I got most of the way up and cut the distance between us in half, stumbling to my knees one more time. It was exactly like the worst dream I've ever had.

I covered the last ten feet in a lurching crawl. With a final lunge I stretched to slap both hands on the edge of the plate. The crowd's screaming and catcher's frenzy told me Steve was right behind me, so I started to roll to one side to make room. Then a blast of weight fell on my back as Steve's hands and mine and the catcher's shoes wriggled together like flopping fish on home plate. A second later the ball, delayed because the center fielder let it skid through his legs, finished its round trip. It bounced off the catcher's shinguard and rolled off to the side.

South Range 5, Boise 4.

I can't describe the next five minutes. It felt like half the gross human tonnage of Lewis Falls and Bounty, first uniformed boys and then whoever else was close, piled onto Steve and me on the plate. I couldn't breathe but it didn't matter. When I did wriggle free I immediately jumped back on the top. I dug down for Steve, and as I pulled him up someone grabbed one of his legs and two other people grabbed the other until he was sitting on a mixed set of shoulders. I was caught in the moving surge that carried him around the edge of our dugout to the grandstands. His butt bounced up and down five feet in front of my eyes.

Through the mass of people I could see Mel Raines jumping over people in the grandstand to get to his son. When he did he pulled Steve across shoulders and heads to hug him like a giant teddy bear. Two rows behind him Ben Tyler watched beaming. Next to him the other man, the one with square glasses and the fancy sweater, was smiling, too.

As I strayed to the edge of the crowd Mom and Dad appeared next to me. Mom was actually jumping up and down in place and squealing, just like someone making fun of the whole thing would do, but she wasn't. She hugged me and pressed both hands on both of my cheeks and then hugged me again. As she held me I turned to Dad. He was nodding his head slowly, squinting against the smoke from his Prince Albert. "Damn, Jack," he said.

"COULD I HAVE YOUR ATTENTION FOR JUST A MINUTE, PLEASE?" The garbly sound came from a bullhorn that Ben Tyler was holding fifty feet away in the grandstand. Mom and Dad and I turned towards him. Ben's free arm was around Steve's shoulders, intertwined with Mel's arm draping Steve from the other side. Steve looked blissfully goofy. "THIS IS...THIS IS WHAT IT'S ALL ABOUT," came Ben's amplified voice. "NOT JUST A GREAT VICTORY—" a little whistle in the circuitry flared into a nerve-frying squeal. Ben shook the bullhorn over his head without clearing it. Mel stepped in front of Steve to grab it. He made a quick adjustment and handed it back to Ben.

"THIS ISN'T JUST A GREAT VICTORY," Ben went on. "IT'S PROOF OF WHAT CAN HAPPEN WHEN A WHOLE TOWN, A WHOLE CO*MMUN*ITY OF PEOPLE, BELIEVE THAT THEIR BOYS CAN DO ANYTHING THEY SET THEIR MINDS TO. *ANYTHING THEY SET*

THEIR MINDS TO." Ben let the bullhorn dip and turned to Steve, squeezing his far shoulder towards him so that Steve's head flopped back and forth like a dashboard gremlin. Mel's face twitched with emotion.

"AND PROUD AS I AM, PROUD AS ANYBODY STANDING HERE TODAY, THERE'S SOMEONE WHO'D BE EVEN PROUDER. I KNOW HE'S LOOKING DOWN RIGHT NOW WITH A SMILE ON HIS FACE. PROUD AS I AM, THAT THERE,"and Ben pointed up meaningfully to the big bronze image of Walter T on top of the backstop, "IS ONE PROUD MAN." Walter did look proud, but it was hard to imagine the smile.

"AND IF HE WERE HERE, YOU KNOW WHAT HE'D SAY? HE'D SAY, 'BOY, QUIT YOUR YAPPING AND INVITE THE FOLKS OVER TO CELEBRATE RIGHT.' SO I WANT TO SEE ALL OF YOU FOLKS OUT AT THE RANCH IN ABOUT THIRTY MINUTES TO HELP ME SHOW THESE BOYS WHAT WE THINK OF THEM. AND BY THE WAY, WHAT DO WE THINK OF THEM?"

That almost started a riot. Ben handed the bullhorn to someone below him and Mel snatched it away. "LET'S HAVE THE TEAM ON THE BUS," he said. "I WANT TO SEE THE 1964 PONY LEAGUE CHAMPIONS OF THE NORTHWEST UNITED STATES OF AMERICA ON THE BUS IN THREE MINUTES FLAT!" Mel put down the bullhorn. Like parts of a single body, he, Steve and Ben started a wave of movement towards the cars and busses.

"Can we go?" I asked Dad. I turned to Mom. "I want to go."

Mom looked at Dad, who was carefully grinding his cigarette butt into the grass. Then she said, "You go, Jackie. You be polite at Mr. Tyler's and you remember to thank him, too."

The bus was full of teammates by the time I got to it. They pelted each other with gloves, hats, shoes, whatever came to hand. Mel boarded the bus last and for the whole two mile ride to Ben's ranch he pranced the aisles like a clown making fun of ballet, grabbing different kids in hammerlocks around their heads or slapping their shoulders. "You actually made the throw from third base without a bounce today, Ray! Twice! And Andrews! I take back what I said before, you *can* get down the line to first as fast as my grandmother. Oh, man!" With every pass up and down the aisle he'd stop behind Steve in a middle row and lay his hands on his son's shoulders, kneading the meat of his muscles. His manic patter never stopped. "Oh manohm-anohman! Jerry! Clutch hit in the eighth, mister, you *clocked* that one!" Steve looked straight ahead and beamed.

Then Mel saw me further back in the bus. He pointed at me and his head burst back with laughter. "Jack!" was the only word he managed to get out, twice, smothered by a wave of crusty laughter. He held onto kids' shoulders to stay upright. Finally he just shook his head and pulled himself back towards the front on wobbly legs.

The bus turned off the road and through the woods to stop in a gravel clearing next to a huge log house with wide porches on three sides. The sleek black Cadillac from the game was parked next to the porch stairway. We climbed off the bus to the cheers of grown-ups and moved on to a grassy yard between the main porch and an open bed of flaming coals. The half-Indian who wrangled Ben's horses was slowly turning a whole skewered calf over the fire. Every couple of minutes he'd pick up a 4" paint brush and slather on a soupy bronze sauce. The coals sizzled as glops of the stuff dripped off the beef, and I can't remember anything before or since that smelled so good. I picked a Dr. Pepper out of a horse trough filled with ice and went over to stand with Will Tyler, Ben's grandson about my age who lived in Grants Pass. He was staring at the calf's roasting head as it slowly rotated. The eyes were open, blank and glassy as black lightbulbs. Once I noticed them I could hardly look away either.

I came back to the sound of Ben's voice. "Okay, just once more, everybody, I promise," he shouted from the porch above where we were gathered, raising his arms for quiet. "Just a minute or two, I promise, and then we get to the grub. I *pro*mise." The hum of talk and laughter around me faded.

"To celebrate this wonderful day," Ben said, leaning on the porch railing, "we have the honor of welcoming a wonderful guest." To Ben's right and just behind him stood the stranger who'd been at the game, lit up now with a warm smile. "You all know who he is, if you were watching the news last week about that Convention down there in San Francisco." I looked at him harder, almost knowing. "He and I have been friends for twenty years or something now, so I called him and told him if he really did want to land himself a Lewis River steelhead like he was always saying he'd better come get it now, before he's too high and mighty for the likes of us." Ben looked to his side to check his friend's expression. "Just to show you how smart he is, he took me up on it. He's taking a few days before heading into battle to float the last stretch of the canyon with me into Port Douglas, starting in the morning."

Now Ben turned to his friend with a gesture inviting him forward. "In the meantime, it just tickles hell out of me that we got to show him how the game of baseball is played, South Range style. So I just want to introduce the finest bunch of young ballplayers in the world to the finest politician in the world." Ben pulled him with one arm around the shoulders to the railing. "Meet Senator Barry Goldwater, and starting next year, *President* Barry Goldwater."

The grown-ups all around me on Ben Tyler's lawn began to clap, then some of the kids. My teammates slowed down their assault on the food tables. I saw Dougy Ferrin look up with a 1/3-eaten hot dog in each fist. Mike Smeltzer put down the blackberry pie he'd started eating straight out of the tin. They looked like puppies aroused by a high-pitched sound, sensing the moment's importance but not its meaning. I knew more than they did because Mom, the girl who'd grown up listening to her parents' stories of Grange rallies and midnight barn-burnings on the North Dakota plains, kept up with events. I had actually been listening to the kitchen radio with her the week before when Goldwater was nominated.

It didn't seem odd that he stood above us on Ben Tyler's porch now, nodding warmly as the applause died down; like Ben, he was one of the special guys who ran things. "Oh, I'll tell you," Goldwater began, "I've seen a lot of baseball games in my time. Even played in one or two of them. But I've never seen one to beat what you boys did today." The crowd cheered and whooped around me, and Goldwater joined the clapping. "Where's Steve Raines?" he asked, looking around him on the porch.

The noise swelled as someone pushed Steve up the porch steps. The glowing smile filled his face as he walked slowly towards Goldwater. "What do you think, folks?" Goldwater said, wrapping an arm around Steve's shoulders. The folks thought it was the best thing in human history. The noise climbed to near where it was at the end of the game, and I looked around me to register the whole picture. There had to be three or four hundred people making that huge sound together on Ben Tyler's lawn. As my gaze panned across those familiar happy faces I felt a certainty, like a signal received from somewhere outside, that this was one moment that would carve a clear notch in our lives. The last place my gaze touched before returning to the porch was the far corner of Ben's lawn, where a heavy plank picnic table and two benches were set. Standing on top of the table, two feet higher than her Dad on the ground next to her, Holly Burgess was clapping her hands fiercely above her head.

"If I do succeed in the months ahead, with God's will and your help," Goldwater said, loud enough to throttle down the end of the cheering, "you can bet I'll remember what I saw here." He turned to take something from behind him and raised a notebook-sized photo into the air. "Ben was kind enough to give me this picture of the team that you all had taken when the tournament started. Now, I'd like each of you boys to sign it, and then I'm going to put it in a frame to take with me. Then when next year comes I'm going to put it on my desk in the Oval Office, where I'll be sure to see it every time I sit down. And every time I see it I'll remember what this country of ours can be." The cheering exploded again. I turned around to look at the bench in the back corner. Holly wasn't there anymore. I didn't see her again that day.

Goldwater told us to dig into the mountain of food. We did. The afternoon passed into a blur of sweet rich food and music — Ben had brought a square dance caller from Grants Pass who commanded the movement of three dozen grown-ups fanned out across the yard — and talk, the collective inning-by-inning re-creation of the game, a first draft that would be improved a dozen times through the years. As dusk started softening the daylight, I saw Bobby McInteer off to the side, flapping his hand for me to join him. I followed him behind Ben's tractor shed. Dougy Ferrin and Matt Swerdlow and someone else I can't remember were sitting there, still in their uniforms, working on a fifth of Wild Turkey that must have been fresh from Ben's pantry. I sat down to swallow half a slug just so they'd ask me again next time. The talk was about Steve. They sounded half-sarcastic and half-awestruck. I didn't especially want to hear it and slipped away after a minute.

Most of the crowd and the sunlight were gone as I walked into the main entry of Ben's lodge. The team picture lay on a table by a big carved newel post at the bottom of the stairs. I added my signature to the ones already on it. That's when Will Tyler found me and said his grandpa had told him he could have a friend stay overnight with him. Will took me to a telephone so I could call home. Mom answered and told me it was all right with her; if it wasn't with Dad, who was off in Rum somewhere, then he'd come up and get me.

People drifted home after the sun set. Steve and Will and I stayed on in the den at the top of the stairs and turned on the television to watch *The Twilight Zone*. It was about a man who found a magic stopwatch that could make time, along with everyone in the world but him, stand still. He was having a great time manipulating things and people in little ways until the day he decided to rob a bank. He was wheeling a cart loaded with cash out of the vault towards his car when the stopwatch fell to the ground and smashed into pieces, leaving the world around him frozen forever.

When it was over Will was asleep on the couch and Steve and I could hear the murmur of Ben, Mel and Goldwater talking below us in the living room. We went out into the hallway and sat at the top of the steps near the massive rock chimney that rose through the middle of the house. Goldwater was directly below me, deep in the lap of an old overstuffed leather chair with arms of shellacked wooden planks. I saw the top of his head, and sticking out like the hand of a watch at 12:00, a straight-necked brown pipe.

Mel was doing most of the talking. He was pacing around the room, words pouring out of him in a rush. He was saying that by the time Steve and the rest of us were starting families of our own, Lewsco would have to be different. If it didn't get bigger, he said, it wasn't going to make it, because what people care about is how much they have to pay for a 2x4 stud, and if you weren't the biggest you wouldn't be able to make it for the price they want to pay.

The blue smoke from Goldwater's pipe rose towards me and spread out to nothing halfway up. "Bigger," he said. "What does that mean?"

"Well, two things, maybe," Mel said. "They're the only two ways we can go. We either rig up the Port Douglas and Grants Pass mills with the newest gear we can find, and I mean *all* of it, from barkers to planers to loaders, never mind the cost. If we don't want to do that then we have to get somebody else to saw the logs for us, somebody with crews that aren't bitching and asking for more all the time. Somewhere where they're grateful to have the work at all, like they were when my Dad was starting out. Remember, Ben? And you know what, Senator? I don't think there's a place like that in Oregon anymore. Or maybe in the whole country, from what they tell me. So maybe," he said, stopping still to look straight at Goldwater, "maybe we mill logs somewhere else."

"Mmm," Goldwater said. A little circle of orange flared and faded in the bowl of his pipe. "Like ... ?"

Mel's look flashed to Ben, then back to Goldwater. "Could be lots of places," he said. "Where I keep hearing we ought to look is over in the Orient."

They went on for a while, Mel pacing again, stopping short to make the points he really wanted heard, Goldwater asking questions, a grunt and a few words each time, slowly filling and burning and refilling the sweet-smelling tobacco in his pipe. The last time Mel paused expecting a question he got only a soft grunt.

He waited almost a minute, watching one older man and then the other. Then he brought his hands together in a muffled clap. "Well!" he said. "I better be getting on my way. I got a crew starting over at Grinder Lake tomorrow with a chief that's greener than snot. They're gonna need some lining out to get started. Stevie! Let's go, boy!" Steve hurried to his feet, gave me a little nod and started down the stairs. Below us his Dad stood up, too, and stepped towards Goldwater. "Senator, pleased to meet you. I'll be pulling for you, and so will everybody I talk to."

"Well, I appreciate that, Mel," Goldwater said, standing to take his hand.

"That's good, sir," Mel said. "I hope you remember us, like you said, when you get up there. I hope you remember who's out here doing the real work."

"I always remember who does the work, Mel."

"Right. Good. Ready, hot-shot?" Mel said to Steve at the bottom of the stairs. I watched the tableau of thanks and handshakes and goodbyes from my high perch, heard Ben praise Steve again and Goldwater urge him to keep working and playing hard. Then Mel and Steve were gone.

Goldwater and Ben sat quietly for a minute. Each lifted a stout glass of amber liquid from the wide arm of his chair and sipped. They watched the small fire in the rock hearth. I saw the toes of Goldwater's cowboy boots, one crossed over the other, sway back and forth. "Impressive fellow," he said. "How old is he, Ben?"

I saw the top of Ben's head tilt for a moment's thought. "Thirty-five? Thereabouts."

Goldwater nodded. "Well, he's bright. Knows what he thinks. Not too shy about making sure you know, too. He'll keep you busy, won't he, pulling back on the leash?"

Ben chuckled. "Oh, yeah. Mel's a hard-charger. He's brought me a lot of fresh energy when I needed it."

"Energy, yep. That part's plain." Goldwater sipped his drink. "What are your plans for him, Ben?"

"My plans are that I'll start catching me a lot of steelhead because of that boy. He knows almost all there is to know about the woods and the mills. Next year I want to bring him into the office, teach him sales, monitoring the numbers, so by about the time you're running for re-election you come back here and we'll spend all our time on the river."

Goldwater tapped his pipe in a big glass ashtray on the arm of the chair. "That's soon, Ben. I don't know if that boy sees what you've done here. He sees a lot of forest, a lot of trees to cut, lots of boards to sell. But I wonder if he knows why it's all here, going this smooth after your family's been at it, what, a hundred years? More? He sounds a little to me like Cortez, discovering all you've got like it wasn't here before he showed up. The way you all first went about this, learning when and where you could cut so there'd always be more to get later, the way you figured where to set up the mills and then brought people in and took care of them, so that they'd take care of the Company, too, so they'd always be there when you needed them, same as the forest. It doesn't sound like your boy sees it."

Ben shifted in his chair. "Well, I appreciate it, Barry, but I don't know that my family thought it all out that careful. You know, all those years back to when we first got here, there was an awful lot of trees and not too many people. It didn't much matter how you cut it, it was going to grow back. It's only been the last bit of time since about when the war ended, with the gas saws getting light enough so one guy can easily pack it and everybody wanting to build their own home, that we've had to be careful."

"That's right, and that's my point." Goldwater paused to light up a new bowl. "You *are* being careful. You're thinking about it. That's more than I'll say about a lot of them out there. I could tell you stories about what some of them want to do, what they tell me, when they're writing out checks for the campaign, they expect *me* to do. They sound a lot like that boy you're bringing along so you can go fishing, Ben. This country would be a lot better off if everybody ran the way you run Lewsco, Ben. But that's not what I'm seeing."

Ben got up and picked a cut-glass bottle off a side table. He dribbled a stream into his glass and then walked towards his guest. "It used to be simpler," he said, pouring a larger portion into Goldwater's glass. "Used to be you sold to markets close by, or concentrated on special outlets like we did in San Francisco. You built your relationships, and if you stayed straight and fair with them, they stayed with you. Now it's a free-for-all. The brokers and wholesalers I knew breaking in are all gone, now it's smart guys from New York doing the buying, and if you're a nickel high on one bid they'll tell you Sayonara and you'll have a hell of a time getting them back."

Ben had made a tiny tour of the room as he talked, over to the hearth to look at the fire for a moment, now behind his armchair, leaning his forearms on its back. "That business Mel was talking about, shipping logs across the ocean instead of milling them first? It's just about starting to happen. Those fellas over there, they're figuring out how to put out a product a lot cheaper than we can if they can get the raw material from us. It's just a matter of time. Pretty soon when I drag the log down to Port Douglas, I can either spend 40 cents making a 2x4 that I'll sell for 50, or just put the whole log on a boat for Japan where they'll give me 80 cents or a dollar. If I can keep it here my people get the work instead of the Japs, but how long can I do that?"

"What is it that they have, better machinery? That's where they beat you out?"

Ben nodded. "Starting to. That, and they don't pay the fellas on the line what we do."

"Well, how big a problem is that?" Goldwater said. "What's to keep you from setting up machines better than theirs?"

Ben held out his hand and rubbed his fingertips back and forth with his thumb. "It's millions, Barry. We've got good land, and a good work force because we pay 'em right, but we don't have that kind of money."

"Well, sure, but how about the banks? You can borrow what you want, right?"

Ben shook his head. "They see the changes coming too. Makes 'em nervous. I've been dealing with Oregon Bank for 35 years, but this one they don't want to hear about."

"Well, come on, Ben. You've been around over a century making a profit, right? And you've got, what, a quarter-million acres of prime timberland?" Ben moved his head in a figure-8, a semi-nod: not exactly, but close enough. "So you can raise the money, right?"

"I can." Ben was back by the fireplace now, one arm on the mantle and the other jabbing life into the flames with an iron poker. "I can go public. I can sell shares of the company and use that to build up the mills. That's what Mel says to do. Two, three more years, he figures, a family operation won't be able to survive." Ben put down the poker, backed away from the hearth and dropped back into the chair. He watched the flames for a while before turning to Goldwater. "Could be he's right. Maybe the only way to do this is the way everybody else is doing it."

The top of Goldwater's head bobbed back and forth once, twice. "Could be. Could be you do have to sell. But goddamn, Ben, don't do it just because everyone else is. I don't think your dad or his dad or grand-dad put all this together by doing what everybody else did. When a company like this passes from the hands of someone like you, some-one who knows everything about it and loves it like a living thing, like it was his child, and becomes a factory with managers and accountants and experts who all have their own little piece that's about as big as their desk . . ." He stopped. Slowly he swirled his drink and sipped from it. "I'm not sure it's progress, Ben."

I slumped down on the coarse carpet that covered the second floor landing, my head next to the carved newel post, close to the edge so I could hear what Ben thought of that. The next thing I knew two thick furred arms were scooping me up and setting me gently on the TV-room sofa that formed a right angle with the one Will was sleeping on. They had to be Ben's arms.

7

NOT QUITE A YEAR LATER, JUST BEFORE SCHOOL ENDED, I TURNED fifteen. That's what I'd been waiting for. Finally I could go into a timber show. I'd visited before a few times, coming along with Mom when she took Dad a special lunch or something he'd forgotten at home. I wanted to stay after Mom left, but he wouldn't let me. He said I had to be 15 before I could be there on my own. He said it wasn't his rule but the Company's, though I never heard anyone else mention it.

On my birthday Mom put together the dinner I asked for: fried chicken, peas, french fries and a double chocolate cake that she topped with red candles. She turned out the lights as she brought it from the kitchen and they started singing happy birthday. Mom held the glowing plate in front of me until they finished, then set it down. I looked around the table. Steve was there, and so was Dougy Ferrin. They were both looking at the cake. Mom and Dad were watching me.

"Come *on,* Jack," Steve said.

"Make a wish, Jack," Mom said.

"This is about the woods, Dad," I said.

"I didn't ask," he said.

"Wishes don't come true if you tell what they are," said Mom.

But he let me go in with him. The night of the 4th of July, when we were walking home from watching fireworks at the Square, he told me to hit the sack as soon as we got home, because we were getting up early. I managed not to ask him a single question; if he started thinking about it he might change his mind.

I probably got two hours' sleep that night. Every creak I heard in that old house starting about 2:00 a.m. had to be Dad coming to wake me, just to get an extra-early start to teach me what I needed to know. At 4:30 on my clock radio, the old turquoise one from the kitchen that Mom gave me when I started high school to get up on time, Dad came through the door and sat on my bed. There was just enough indirect light from a big pre-dawn moon to see his outline and the canvas vest he always wore to work.

"Here," he said, touching my hand with the rim of something hard and cold. I turned on my bedside lamp. It was a hardhat, a dull tin helmet like a small flying saucer with finger-thick ridges running across the top. I turned it around in my hands until I came to a little plastic strip above the rim, a Dymo label with embossed white letters on it that said JOHN JR.

I ran my fingers across them as he stood up. "Get moving now," he said. "Meet me in the kitchen, and be *quiet*. Your Mom's still sleeping, and you're not waking her, got it?" I nodded, but he was gone. Three minutes later I was dressed in clothes I'd kept together in a bag in the closet for weeks, waiting for today: black gorilla jeans, a brown T-shirt torn under the arms, a green and white flannel plaid shirt to wear over it, heavy grey cotton socks, Red Wing boots I'd found in the top of a garbage can the year before — other than some yellow paint stains, they were in fine shape, just a little too big for me — and a Beavers ball cap Dad had given me for Christmas.

Crossing the dark living room I caught one leg of the ottoman with my foot, a thump in the silence that earned me Dad's glare when I reached the kitchen. He was pouring tar-colored coffee into a dented Thermos. I saw his loaf-shaped lunch pail, a brown bag for me and a frozen jug of water on the end of the counter. As he capped his Thermos he jerked his head once towards the back door. I tiptoed towards it like a cartoon cat burglar and opened it as slowly as I possibly could. The hinges squeaked and I looked over my shoulder. Dad looked ready to kill me.

We walked silently to his truck. I held the door ajar, figuring to close it once we were down the street. Dad pulled himself in and used the center of the steering wheel to roll up a Prince Albert. He lit one with a safety match struck on the bare metal ceiling. His face looked tired in the orange burst of light. Then he started up the truck with fifty times more noise than I'd made in the house. I closed the door with the smallest adequate slam as we rolled into a slow turn around the corner of Holly's house. The moonlight was flashing off her darkened windows. *What if,* I thought, *what if she's up and happens to glance out the window?* In one motion I tried to toss off my ball cap, put on my new hard hat and lower the truck window so I could stick my head part way out of it. *Probably not, she probably wouldn't, but the truck started loud, she could get up and look out to see what it was, even the moonlight could wake her . . .*

"What are you doing, boy, having some kind of seizure?" Dad said. My hard hat was knocking against the window and my arms tangled together in the hurry to get the glass down before we passed Holly's. "It's too early to get yourself hurt, okay? We're supposed to get to work first." His smoky cough was almost a chuckle.

The sky had the color of a dying fluorescent tube when we reached the landing at Rocky Top. Seven or eight pickups were already parked there close together. One in the middle had a cluster of heavy silhouettes leaning over its bed. I could see the ends of half a dozen cigarettes like fat orange fireflies among them. Dad parked to the side of the cluster and rolled one more smoke before stepping down from the cab. "Thermos," he said, and slammed his door. I picked it up off the seat and followed him.

"Morning, John," one of the dark forms said.

"Ray," Dad said. Three others said his name, and he theirs.

"Today's the day, huh?" said Ray, the first one. "That you, Junior?"

I nodded, then in the pause realized they probably couldn't see. "Yes, sir."

"We-hell," another man said. "How come you didn't warn us, John? We would have planned the boy a little welcome party, huh?" A couple of others snickered.

"Thanks the same anyway, Marv," Dad said. He'd unscrewed the Thermos cap and was pouring steam and coffee into it. The mix of strong smells — the rich sourness of the coffee, the burnt-nut scent of tobacco, a little gasoline from the trucks, the biting freshness of cut fir and pine, all wrapped in new morning air — was even better than I'd imagined going to Dad's work would be like. Nearly every time I've smelled that blend since, and it's been thousands, I've thought of that morning.

"Oh, come on, John," Marv said. "Me and Ray're working the rock pile this morning. Dontcha think Junior deserves to see the rock pile?"

More snickers. They waited for Dad to swallow some coffee and light a smoke. "No," he said.

"We're just talking the first hour, John," Ray said.

"Yeah," said Marv. "We just want to see if he has the Blood."

"Blood" meant forest blood. When I was growing up people in Lewis Falls would talk about who did and didn't have forest blood. If you had the Blood, the only place you could spend your working life was the woods. You didn't have a choice any more than you could choose to live without breathing.

"No," Dad said. He twisted the cap back on the Thermos and pulled hard on the cigarette. "He's staying with me."

The group moaned like a chorus, awwwwwwww, pretend disappointment. "Hopeless," Dad said, shaking his head and turning back towards the truck. "Hopeless." It was a softer tone; he was telling them things were okay. I didn't find out until much later what they meant by the rock pile. I'm not sure it's worth describing, but I'll think about it.

Just as the crowns of the tallest trees around us started taking on a broth-colored glow, the first chainsaw crackled to life and revved up. On those hot summer days the idea was to get the saws running by 5:30 a.m. so the work day could be finished by two in the afternoon. That's when all mechanical work had to stop during the fire season, to keep down the chances that the heat of a truck muffler or sparks from a chain grazing a rock would find dry grass.

Dad started up his Cat, a D-4 Caterpillar compact enough to maneuver through dense growth. With the controls set right to warm it up, he stopped and looked over at me. He scraped a match on a metal strut to light a Prince Albert. He pulled deeply on it and released a triangle of gray smoke, still watching me. Then he patted a plywood ledge rigged up next to the seat, just one little tap. I ran over and hopped up.

Dad's job was to make the work easier for everyone else to do. He moved that tractor all over the show, pushing brush, rootballs and small hardwoods together into piles for burning when the rains came. What he left was cleared working spaces where a man could safely ramble with a viciously sharp chain whirring at his hip.

Dad's other task was to skid logs, once they were on the ground and bucked to standard length, to the landing where trucks could load them. The choker-setters, who weren't much older than me, would wrap one end of thick braided steel cable around the logs and hold the other up with a red bandanna when they saw Dad coming. He'd back up the Cat until they could slip the cable's tear-shaped loop over the tow-ball, then off he'd go. The weight and mass of the log ploughed a furrow through the forest floor as Dad pulled it along, until by the end of the show a whole area would be criss-crossed with new soft brown trails.

Late in the morning Dad put the Cat in neutral and leaned over to me. "Right there," he shouted over the engine clatter. He was pointing to a root ball that was hung up between a white oak and the corner of the Cat blade. He'd taken two passes to pull it clear and push it towards a slash pile, but it was still stuck. "Wear these," he said, handing me a pair of rough leather gloves. "Get that clear."

I hopped to the ground hoping I knew what he wanted. It took me a few seconds to find where a root was wedged into a metal seam on the blade's edge, another few to pull at the right angle to get it loose. It would have been faster if I weren't rushing. I stepped back when I was done to look at Dad. He was glaring at the rootball. In an instant it was on the slash pile. He backed the Cat away without a glance my way and turned it towards a little knoll that needed brushing. I stayed on the ground until lunch, pulling woody tangles away from rocks and stumps towards the coming path of the Cat's blade. When Dad paused at the controls and leaned back in his seat it meant there was something for me to do on the ground. It wasn't always obvious. I scurried around until I figured out what to do.

We sat on the ground leaning against the Cat tracks to eat our lunch. After a few quiet minutes he said, "You like jumping straight out of bed every morning like there's nothing to it?" I was quiet, wondering. "Then lift with your legs, not your back. Whenever you're lifting stuff with your back arched over, so there's a pull in those little muscles way far down, you're chalkin' up another morning of woe when you get to be my age. I know you don't feel it now, but you will." He looked up at me from the cigarette he was rolling. "You believe me?" I started to nod. "No you don't. You don't believe that things change. Neither did I. Neither does anybody." He flicked the head of a safety match into flame and lifted it to the cigarette, breathing in deeply. "It don't matter. Just keep your back straight when you're lifting and try to do the work with your legs."

He was right, both about how to lift and that I wouldn't seriously listen. From that first summer, through all the years in the woods until I quit, even into the first few years of repairing appliances, I lifted with my back. I'd start out the way you're supposed to, crouched down like a catcher to grab something. Then I'd begin to stand up. If the cargo was light, fine. If not, I'd raise up to the limit of my leg strength and then quickly talk to myself. *I can't lift this just with my legs. Guess I should put it down and figure out another way to get it done. But it's halfway up, maybe more, and the first half is the tough one and there's no one around to help and I have to get it done, so just this once, I'll just use my back for this one lousy 3-foot lift, that's not going to hurt anything, next time I'll do it right, just this once, HUNNHHH!* I'd jerk it up with my back and shoulder muscles and figure nobody's wiser.

A couple hundred just-this-once lifts over the years and the web of muscles between the center of my back and the top of my butt was like custard pie. I wouldn't notice it much in the morning, but by afternoon I had to find ways to keep my back ramrod straight. That's why I used to cut trees higher on the stump than other fallers. I couldn't see that it really mattered, even in later years after the buy-out when Mel and his pals kept screaming at us to cut on the blue dot, which seemed to drop closer to the ground every month. It's money, they said. Cut too high and you're leaving money on the stump. Easy to say for guys who ride around in a Company pick-up all day and haven't touched a saw in years. Their backs are fine no matter how low the stump gets cut.

You can bet ten dollars to a dime that Mel and them have been talking about my bad habits. I can hear them saying I'd still be walking today if I'd only followed instructions like a good boy and made my cut at the goddamn blue mark. They'd never say it straight to me or the media, but they're saying it. What gets me is that they're right.

8

IF I CLOSE MY EYES RIGHT NOW I CAN EASILY GO BACK TO THAT VERY FIRST
day and see Dad as his hands danced across the levers and controls,
pushing, pulling, turning and twisting in one unbroken day-long move-
ment. He made his Cat a fine efficient athlete. I kept watching his
face. The only moving parts were his lips, which pressed together and
back every minute to pull another hot charge of Prince Albert into his
lungs, and his neck, which swivelled constantly to keep everything to
both sides of us in view. His eyes never changed.

It was that calm watching he did, not his few flat words, that taught
me about the woods. And it wasn't really *watching*. I don't know the
exact word for what he did. The cliche about growing eyes in the back
of your head comes pretty close. Something happens to your brain
when saws and machinery start humming around you. It's like that
sonograph they have below decks in navy movies, where a monoto-
nous tone burps out a tiny circle of perception that quickly grows out
towards the horizon, wrapping around and revealing any object that
gets in its path. You're at the center, hearing and feeling whatever's
intruding from any direction, calculating with your instinct which way
and how fast all the pieces are moving.

Not everyone out there has it. I learned that quickly, when they gave
me the job of shuttling oil, gas, and sharp chains out to the crew on
the ground. The guys on the crew greeted me all kinds of ways. On
hot days nobody minded seeing me because I also carried a couple of
plastic jugs of drinking water that had sat in a freezer all night and

slowly melted throughout the day. The water was so cold it stunned your throat. It was the first thing they wanted when I walked up.

But not everyone wanted a fresh chain. Some guys took one every chance they got. They'd start spinning loose the retaining nuts on their bars before they'd even finished chugging the ice-water. Sometimes the chain they gave me in return wasn't really dull; the teeth didn't have the shiny edge of a freshly-sharpened chain, but they probably could have run through another tankful of fuel okay.

But these were guys who did everything in the woods just right, not just okay. When they were falling trees they took extra time to set a fall-path that would do the least damage to the younger growth that could become the new dominant trees. When they were bucking fallen trees, cutting them to the exact length the mill wanted, they'd stretch and twist themselves to cut from a distance rather than stomp over a green seedling that was in the way. If a truck radio was blaring during the lunch break these guys were the ones who'd wander off by themselves to listen to the forest instead of the Oakridge Boys or Waylon Jennings. I figured these guys took a new chain from me every time because they wanted to make the work easier. It also had something to do with respect.

Other guys had a different idea of what was easy. It takes an experienced logger three minutes or so to swap and re-adjust his chain, but some guys saw that as three minutes lost from the work, a three-minute delay from getting the damn tree on the ground, and they couldn't be bothered. These guys would grudgingly take one new chain for every two or three that my regular customers took, and the old chains they traded in had teeth about as sharp as a pencil eraser. These were the guys you really had to look out for in the woods, because they weren't conscious of the dozens of moving parts, mechanical and human, around them.

Being conscious the way Dad was is what makes logging so exhausting. The raw physical output is hard enough, but what really sends you home whipped is the effort of six or seven hours of unrelieved concentration. I'm not complaining. That electric feeling of being at the center of so much energy is mostly what kept me in the woods all those years. The 360-degree scope of how you work has a stunning wholeness to it. You see it *all*.

When you're first starting a show and come into an area that hasn't been cut since before Dad was born, it's all forest, fir, spruce, cedar, madrone, hemlock and alder scattered among each other up the gentle sweep of hillsides and tiny valleys. Old dead trees lay among them across the forest floor, *becoming* the forest floor. These are the host logs, discarded because of their defects when the last round of cutting took place or else knocked down by wind or lightning since then. What they host are complex societies of bugs and plants, luxurious bright-green swatches of drenched moss on the surface that are like full-scale forests for ants, beetles, grubs, no-see-ums and even smaller tenants that slowly pioneered their way to the central core. Over the years their tunnels multiplied, intersected and fractured one another until the mass could no longer hold its form, so that tiny avalanches of dark brown chunks began to fall away from the log. You could reach into some of the older ones and pull out handfuls of wood like fibrous pudding. Trees turning back into earth.

When you looked with enough care to notice, you could see how it all fit together, all parts of a whole. It might sound strange but for years I thought we were parts of the whole, too. It was the way we fit together with each other, fallers, buckers, slashers, choker-setters, skidders like Dad, loaders and drivers meshing like odd-shaped gears of an efficient clock. We were a bustling man-made system within the vaster God-made system and it felt like we belonged there.

I know logging's not pretty. It's loud and abrupt. *Violent* is probably a fair word. It leaves scars. Violence and scars are part of any forest, sometimes from fire, sometimes from windstorms or lightning, sometimes from machines making roads and cutting trees. But scars don't break a forest. They mold it in small ways, moving material and the patterns of growth from here to there so the contour changes from what it would have been otherwise. But that's kind of a fuzzy thing to measure with anyway, because who knows how the other forces would have shaped it if man hadn't walked into the picture? Ten years after we finished a show and blocked off the skid roads, back when we were doing things right, you'd barely know we'd been there. All the rough edges would be softened again by rain, snow, moss, the debris of down-fall, so that only the stumps, graying into the general landscape, might give us away.

Back then we left more than we took. When I started cutting for Lewsco we picked trees not just for their mill value, or even because they were old and past their growth peak, but also because taking them would free up space and sunlight for nearby trees that were hitting their stride. We left thousands of trees that would have brought big mill dollars, partly because they'd bring bigger dollars in twenty or forty years, and partly because — I swear this is true — Lewsco used to believe in forests. From everything I heard Ben Tyler say as I was growing up, and all the times I heard Dad tell Mom about him, I don't think he ever thought of trade-offs between profit and good forestry because to him they were the same thing.

This light-handed selection wouldn't produce enough timber volume today to keep a company up there with the big boys. Lewsco pulled it off for a century because it had so much forest. You could send a show into any one of the hundreds of draws and subdrainages in the South Range, take out three or four dozen trucks of logs, leave for a couple decades of healing and then do it again. Usually you didn't have to replant like everyone does today; by leaving the big old cone trees to scatter their seeds and shade the undergrowth, new generations were always on the way, tiny seedlings that would become sawlogs and elderly breeder trees for more seedlings long after we're all gone.

That's how it went on Lewsco land right through both World Wars and the housing boom that followed the second one. They ignored the fast money dangling in front of timber producers back then. You have to respect that no matter what you think of what the Company turned into. When people argue whether or not the change was inevitable, I know what I think. It was Ben Tyler who made the first big decision, and from being around him I just have this faith that if there were a way to keep Lewsco on its old careful unhurried path he would have found it.

9

I THINK I KNOW WHEN BEN STARTED LETTING GO. DAD AND I ACTUALLY heard him talk about it, not directly to us, but to Mel Raines, who was sitting next to him at the time flying the Company plane back from Portland in the late summer of 1966. It was a 4-seater, and Dad and I were sitting in the back. Saying it like that makes it sound like we jetted around with the big boys all the time. The truth is it was the only time I've been in an airplane, except for flying to Portland the day before, and I'm almost sure the same was true for Dad.

We were sitting there because Dad had just passed the 20-year mark with Lewsco. The Company used to make a big deal when that happened. Ben would usually recognize the employee with a deluxe weekend for two in Portland, all expenses paid. That doesn't sound like much today, but back then when the state was somehow bigger it was like a Paris vacation. Most guys took their wives, who came back with souvenirs and sacks of gifts and a month of sparkling stories. But Mom said no. When Dad told her the Beavers would be playing at home in Portland Civic Stadium that weekend, she told him to take me instead.

So early on a Saturday morning we drove to the edge of Ben's ranch, where he had an airstrip with a little corrugated hangar and two planes. We crawled into the back of the twin-engine and Mel and Ben climbed in front. Mel fired her up and bumped her down the hardpan strip until it lifted up and over the fringe of fir trees that marked the edge of the ranch. Two hours later we were in a station wagon, an old Ford that Ben kept parked at the Portland Airport, headed for downtown.

In another half-hour Ben and Mel were dropping us off at the Mallory. "You do *not* let your father pinch pennies here, boy," Ben said as he handed me my overnight bag. "They aren't his to pinch." Everything all weekend long, including the Beaver tickets waiting for us at the box office, was on Lewsco.

Just before the 2:00 game time Dad and I walked through a concrete passageway and into the sunlight of Civic Stadium's interior. A wave rushed through me like adrenaline with the edge smoothed off. It was so green. Growing up where I did I thought I'd seen every shade of green there is. But the way it was here, smooth acres of grass shining in the sun, bordered by an arc of bright commercial wooden signs attached end-to-end (Mobil's red flying horse, the Hamms bear, a 20-square-foot chocolate Hostess Cupcake with the white squiggle on top, the Lucky Strike bull's-eye and a stretch of auto repair, real estate and insurance businesses I never heard of) and studded with sharp geometric shapes of brick-red earth at the pitcher's mound and between the bases — it was a whole different color. All across the field, shagging fungo flies out in center, snagging ground balls in the infield, just playing catch or stretching their hamstrings in foul ground, were clusters of Portland Beavers and Spokane Indians, easy and casual right to the edge of looking bored. They were gods. What gets me is that now, today as I write, I could have sons as old as they were then.

The moment we found our seats, eight rows up from first base, Dad started talking. He pointed to Frank Civiletti, the Beavers' manager, hitting practice grounders to his infield. He told me Frank — Chub, Dad called him — caught for the Beavs back when Dad had his tryout, and had been friendlier than most. I asked Dad if he thought Chub would remember him. If so, I thought but didn't say, maybe we could get invited into the dugout or the clubhouse after the game. Dad rolled a Prince Albert as he thought about it. He lit it and looked back towards home plate. "Don't know why he should," he said.

That quieted him until the National Anthem ended and the first Indian stepped to the plate. Then he had more to say in two hours than I ever heard from him in a month. He wanted me to notice what the smart defensive players were doing away from the ball, how the first or third baseman would protect the line, or try to make the hitter think that he was, how you could guess fastball or curve depending on where the centerfielder was leaning. He'd point sometimes with his finger, sometimes with a nod of his head, but his eyes never left the field. Even between innings as he talked about who was coming up or who was left in the bullpen, he never looked directly at me.

The game was tied 3-3 in the top of the ninth when the Indians put runners on first and third with two out. The batter was the eighth guy in the order, Juan somebody from Puerto Rico or Venezuela or somewhere who had a magic glove but couldn't hit. All game Dad had me watching Juan's front foot. It skipped an inch away from the plate and towards third base every time he swung. "Even if he connects, where's he gonna take it with that swing?" Dad said after his second strikeout. I wondered for an instant if he was talking about my late baseball career, but then I got back into the game.

When Juan stepped to the plate in the ninth, Dad let out a little cough of surprise and looked at the program on his lap. "Oh, really?" he said. "They still got Madison and Blake on the bench, and they're batting this guy? Well, Christmas comes early to Portland, Oregon. They must think they need this guy for defense, nice work if you can get it, but come on, letting him hit now? Thank you, Lord."

Juan took a ball and a strike and on the third pitch took his little stutter-step and swung. We heard the thin click of wood hitting the bottom third of the ball and watched it rise in a lazy arc two feet beyond the first baseman's glove. The ball touched the fair edge of the chalk and skittered across foul ground and toward the Beavers bullpen. That's where the right-fielder caught up with it, and his throw to home plate was too late to catch the second runner scoring all the way from first. "Ka-RISTE!," Dad said, rising to his feet as what turned out to be the winning run rounded third. "Ka-riste, Mary, Joseph, Peter and Paul! Hang in there, why don't you? Hang *in* there, why don't you?"

Twenty minutes later we spilled out of the Stadium amidst a quiet crowd and strolled down Burnside all the way to the waterfront. A tanker was steaming up the Willamette, and from the Burnside Bridge we could see two other bridges raise and then lower to let it pass. When we were hungry, or as close as we'd get to it that day, we walked back uptown to Jake's Famous Crawfish House on Stark. It was loud, smoky and packed. We slithered around the thicket of backs lined up at the huge golden oak bar to a heavy oak-sided booth in a rear corner.

I didn't have crawfish, but I did eat some weird creatures in a stew served in a huge white bowl. Dad had a well-done steak and a brick-sized baked potato. I asked him if he'd been to Jake's when he had the try-out. No, he said, he pretty much kept to the hotel and the ballfield. Mom might have, he said, because she'd had time to wander while he was practicing. I meant to ask her when we got back, but I forgot.

I topped off dinner with a thick slice of cheesecake with berry sauce and then we walked up Broadway. Downtown was in the clustered shadow of buildings now, under a sky still full with the light of a summer evening sun. I couldn't believe how many people were out and about, moving in all four different directions with definite purpose, at seven on a Saturday night. How many places could there be to go?

Ahead of us I saw a massive creme-colored building with ornate plaster edges. A cloth awning over the entrance said it was the Benson Hotel. Half a dozen limousines hovered at the curb, waiting like steelhead circulating at the mouth of a side creek to unload their passengers on a red carpet. Men in tuxedos would pop out first, then lean back in to help women, hobbled by long tight gowns, get themselves upright and on the sidewalk. We crossed the street with the signal and would have walked right past them if Dad hadn't cut me off with a cross-step that turned us up the side street. I was thinking about it, testing out a question for Dad in my head, when we passed Ben's Ford station wagon. It was parked at the curb five spaces off Broadway.

"Look who's here, Dad," I said, slapping the front fender. "Where do you suppose they are? Want to look for them?"

Dad took out a pack of Camels — he'd picked it up in the hotel lobby, writing our room number in a notebook on the counter. He lit one. "Problem is," he said. "if we did, we might find 'em."

We circled the block and returned to Broadway on the other side of the Benson. Another block down was a huge theater facade with an elaborate neon PORTLAND flowing vertically down the front of the building. The removable letters on the white marquis said THE SAND PEBBLES. Right there, in downtown Portland, we were walking straight towards a theater that was playing *The Sand Pebbles*. With plenty of time to see it and somebody else happy to pay for tickets. As we walked I wondered what reason Dad would find for passing it by.

"Feel like a movie?" Dad said. "I could stand to see a movie."

We bought tickets and headed straight for the candy stand. Dad bought two foil-wrapped tubes of Flicks, the chocolate wafers I always got when we saw a movie in Grants Pass every few months. Then we passed into the auditorium. Though the film hadn't started it was so dim it took a few seconds before I could see. The only light was soft glowing pools of gold and red outlining oddly gorgeous shapes: the heavily pleated curtains on either side of the blank screen, the tiny curtained alcoves high on both sidewalls that made you think of Lincoln's final evening, the curving gilded balcony that hung above the rear third of the room. Forty feet straight above us the light haloed the edges of a gigantic scallop-edged disk, something like the base of an antique chandelier that was bigger than my bedroom at home. There was enough light to know that the ceiling was bursting with elaborately sculpted shapes, but not enough to see what they were.

When my eyes adjusted I was looking at a field of plush seats, aligned as neatly in each direction as headstones in a military cemetery. They just kept on going. "If everybody in Lewis Falls came here," I said to Dad as we took two seats in the middle section, "and Bounty, too, do you think they'd all fit in here at once?"

He turned around in his seat to scan the theater, then turned back to the screen. "Including Maude, too?" he asked. Maude Smith was Sam's cook at the Spot, talkative and friendly all the time, with a heft to her that inspired an ongoing line of sexual jokes so scuzzy they almost embarrassed some guys in the woods. It was about the third time that day I almost felt like I was watching the two of us from a distance; Dad's telling me Maude jokes now?

Then the strings of an orchestra swelled up, the lights dimmed out and *The Sand Pebbles* began. I don't think either of us moved again until the lights came back up three hours later. They were the best hours I've ever spent in a theater.

The next morning Ben and Mel pulled up in the station wagon at noon, right when they said they would and ten minutes after we'd started waiting. The trip hadn't been good to Mel. His eyes were blurry and sunken in puffy grey sockets and the little talking he did sounded painful. But Ben had enough to say for both of them. His main reason for coming up, it turned out, was to go to a big glittery dinner (yes, at the Benson) for Governor Mark Hatfield, who was running for the United States Senate. As we rode to the airport I heard for the first time how well Ben knew the Governor, how they got together just about every time Hatfield came down south.

It didn't sound like bragging the way Ben said it. He was just telling a story to pass the travel time. Ben had held a party for the Governor at the ranch two months before, which was news to Dad and me but not Mel. As Hatfield left that party he asked Ben to be sure to come to Portland for the main fundraiser of the campaign; a surprise guest was expected, the Governor had said, that Ben would love to meet. Scheduling the gift trip for Dad and me on the same weekend was Ben's economical instinct in action.

Ben stretched his tale out with descriptions of the Benson, the banquet, the small talk the Governor was trading with his supporters, to build a little suspense about the mystery guest. We were in his little plane taxiing on the Portland runway before he told us. Or told Mel, really.

"...so we're finally all sitting down and they're bringing us our salads, and up high at the head table there's the Governor sitting next to the podium, and to his side Francis Cooke, that's the banker, and Tom McCall, who the Governor trusts about as far as he can throw, and the Congressman, what's his name. But next to the podium on the other side the first seat's empty, and then there's Charlie Cameron who's the state Chair, and a couple of $25,000 guys. Then Charlie gets up and hits the microphone a couple of times, pow, pow, and says 'Ladies and Gentlemen, it is my privilege and honor to introduce to you a man we all know and admire, a great American who visited us here six years ago.'" He stopped as Mel lifted the plane off the runway towards a cruising altitude.

I was watching the compass. When we found a southward heading, Ben went on. "Who do you think walks on the stage then?" he asked Mel.

"Wilt Chamberlain," Mel said.

"Richard Nixon," Ben said. "Richard Nixon walks out, the Governor stands up and they shake hands. Then Nixon holds the Governor's hand up like a boxer and everybody cheers." I looked at Dad, who stared out the window as if nobody was talking. Mom would be impressed, though, and in a couple of hours I'd tell her. What I found out years later reading Nixon's biography was that we were one stop on his marathon rubber-chicken circuit. He spent that whole year, 1966, pumping the congressional campaigns of Republicans likely to remember him two or six years later.

Over the drone of the plane Ben described Hatfield's speech and Nixon's ("'My friends,' he says, 'you can go all over this great country without finding a young man as honorable and honest and dedicated to keeping this great country great as your very own Governor Hatfield'"). It was obvious from Ben's tone that he agreed.

After the banquet Ben took the elevator up to his room, locked the door and took off his coat and shoes. He said he was pouring a glass of brandy when the phone rang. "It was Davis, the Governor's man, asking me if I'd come to the Governor's room. I said when, he said right now, so forget about the brandy, on goes the shoes and jacket, and I go up there. When I knock, Davis lets me in and sitting in the living room are Will Baxter, you know, Baxter Studs, and what's his name from Blue Mountain Lumber, the young one."

"Bill Stevenson," Mel said.

"Stevenson. So I say hello, shake hands, and just as my rear touches the sofa this other door opens and in walks the Governor and Vice President Richard M. Nixon. I'm up, everybody's standing up, and he walks around shaking hands, and when he comes to me and the Governor says my name he says 'Ben? Well, you and I have a mutual friend. Senator Goldwater told me to give you his greetings.'"

Mel laughed, a couple of quick snorts. "I'll bet he did."

"I'll bet he didn't. Barry wouldn't give Nixon the time of day. But it tells me, here's a guy who doesn't miss a trick."

For the rest of the flight Ben gave Mel just about every word of the conversation. Nixon was asking all kinds of questions about the industry, what the big costs were, how they set prices, how they decided when to cut their own lands and when to bid on government timber, what they thought about markets and competition in Asia. "Then he asked me how I planned to capitalize to keep up with cheaper product coming in from Canada and the South," Ben said, "things I wasn't that keen to talk about in front of Baxter and, mmm..."

"Stevenson."

"Stevenson. But he was asking me because I was the only one in the room who still owns my company."

Mel snorted again. "You're the only one in goddamn *Oregon* who still owns a company with more than six trucks and a buzzsaw to its name. Washington, too, probably."

"That's what Nixon asked. The four of us, the Governor too, thought about it and came up with ten that are still family-owned, but none bigger than us. So Nixon asks if I'm thinking about selling." I looked over at Dad. He looked like he was still studying the wing of the plane. "I hum and huff around, pretty soon he figures out he's got too many people in the room for that kind of talk, so he stops asking questions. From then on, he does all the talking." Ben stopped and took a map from under his seat, looking from it to the control panel and back.

"What'd he say?" Mel asked.

Ben put the map back. "He says 'Look, you are the kind of businesses that this country is built on, for us to be strong, you have to be strong. And you're only going to be strong if you're willing to change with the times.' And he's looking at me mostly now. 'Now, when I grew up people could do it all on their own. My father worked for himself his whole life, and he worked hard, mother too, they never had to answer to another soul in the world. We didn't have much, and that made us prouder than anybody is today of what we did have,' then he looks straight at me and says 'That was fine back then, we worked as soon as we were old enough and that took care of the whole family. But your family, Ben,' he says, 'there are hundreds in your family, today it takes more than hard work to take care of them all.' He says, 'The old ways were the good ways, there's nobody respects the old ways more than me. But the way we did things, my father, mother, all of us, we had to be practical. That was the thing. *Practical.* If you weren't, you weren't going to make it. We have a lot more today,' he says to me, 'much, much more today, but it's still true if you're not practical, you're not going to make it. Not very long.'"

There was a pause, a few moments of engine noise alone, as Mel turned his head towards Ben. "Is that supposed to be big new news to me, boss?" he asked. "What has your ace pilot been telling you all along?" Ten minutes later he set us down on Ben's landing strip.

I was right about Mom being interested in the weekend. She had all kinds of questions that night about the Beavers game, about downtown and the movie. She wanted to know way more details about the room at the Mallory than I noticed. When I came to the part about Ben and Nixon she just listened.

10

TWO MONTHS AFTER THE PORTLAND TRIP, AFTER THE BEGINNING OF school ended my first season in the woods, an extra piece of paper showed up in Dad's paycheck envelope. Sam also posted it on the FUNNIES.

NOTICE TO ALL LEWSCO EMPLOYEES

Beginning on October 1, 1966, all full-time employees of the Lewis Corporation will have the opportunity to become owners of the Company.

By that date we expect to have all necessary permission to sell shares of the Company to qualified buyers. If you have worked more than 1500 hours for us in three of the last five years, and you are working for us on October 1, 1966, you are a qualified buyer.

Shares in the Company will first be sold for $10 each, and the price will be adjusted every two months according to independent expert opinion of the total worth of the Company. Dividends will be paid at the end of every year that the Company makes a profit, in an amount that will be set by the amount of the Company's profit.

There are two ways to purchase shares. An employee can do so with an agreed-upon amount taken out of every paycheck, or can make a purchase with a personal check or money order at any time. Employees who later choose to sell their shares back to the Company will be able to do so on the first business day of any month, for the offering price of the share for that month.

I intend to make shares available until 45 percent of the total value of the Company has been purchased. I reserve the right to end sales at any time.

The law requires that you receive more information about the details of this offer before you invest your money. For a "prospectus" that has all the legal language you may call the central office.

This is a very important and historic step for the Lewis Corporation. I am very pleased to know that the future of the Company will rest in the hands of the finest employees in the world.

Ben L. Tyler, President
The Lewis Corporation

It was the longest stride towards economic reality that Ben could get himself to take. There were simpler things he could have done. He could have sold the Company to a bigger corporation, somebody already invested in the necessary gear. Or if he wanted to play seriously himself, a full-bore public stock offering with a bank and brokerage house in charge would have raised the capital. Instead he came up with this home-grown proposal to a bunch of loggers and mill workers who probably thought they were living on the edge if they moved a savings account from a bank to a Savings & Loan for an extra interest point. I doubt if it was what Nixon had in mind when he told Ben to be practical.

Not that I knew what he was thinking. Somehow Ben never got around to finding me in the woods for a personal consultation on his business strategy. But limiting sales up front to 45 percent of the Company's value tells you he wasn't ready to let go. Of course he could have held onto majority control in a regular public stock offering, too, but he probably didn't relish the idea of flying off to some New York skyscraper every year to argue with a bunch of lawyers and accountants who'd want to chew up the forest for higher profits. Much better if his junior partners were people who grew up in his woods. People who understood. Maybe the amount of change would be tolerable if the Company could be kept in the family.

Mom found Ben's announcement when she opened Dad's paycheck envelope, which he always brought home to her sealed, and read it twice before she spoke. I was sitting on the other end of the kitchen table finishing the bowl of cereal I'd poured the minute I got home from school, just like every day.

"John?" she said. I heard Dad grunt. He was a few feet away in the service porch, changing into cleaner working clothes. "Do you know about this?"

"Yep." His voice was muffled by a towel. "The guys was talking."

"What do you think about it?" She watched Dad walk in and cross to the stove to pour a mug of coffee from the tin pot. He came back and sat down heavily in the chair between us and rolled a Prince Albert. A hot rinse in the laundry sink had pinkened his cheeks above a week's worth of dark stubble, and his thin wet hair spiked out in ten directions. He looked tired.

He reached towards a clean ashtray in the center of the table and picked a book of matches out of it. "It's for people with extra money to spend," he said, "who don't care what happens to it." He slowly opened the match book, bent and tore out a match, struck the match and lit his smoke.

"It says ten dollars for a share," Mom said. "That's not very much."

Dad let loose a funnel of smoke and raised his eyebrows high. "No? Well, that's something to know, because I thought it was. I thought we watched out for every dollar in this household. In fact I thought this was the household, maybe I remember it wrong, where I brought you home that silky yellow shirt with the pearl buttons from PD, and you kept asking me what it cost, then you took it back down the hill yourself and got a refund and bought the same kind of material and the same buttons to make it yourself to save a few bucks. To save less than ten dollars, I'll tell you, 'cause the damn thing only cost fifteen to begin with. That's what I thought this household was."

He didn't sound mad or upset. He sounded tired. Mom pressed her lips together and looked down in her lap, then back up. "I'm sorry, John. It was a beautiful blouse, really, much nicer than the one I made. I wish I kept it. I just thought, what's the difference, why should I get a blouse so nice when you don't get anything for yourself, and you're working so hard every single day to keep us going..."

"Which we're not going to do so good if they start gouging another hole out of my paycheck," Dad said. "I don't notice lots of money lying around after you pay the bills, so what would we do with a check that's ten bucks shorter?"

"We could do it, John," she said. "I could find ten dollars every two weeks in here. Maybe a little more." She reached over to a little odds-and-ends alcove and pulled out the black ledger book where she accounted for every household expense. "It's in here. I could find it."

Dad's glance bounced off the book and down to his hands. It looked like an emergency repair to the wet end of his cigarette suddenly needed all his attention.

Mom opened the ledger. "Do you want me to try?"

"What's the point, Lois? Say you could squeeze it out of there, what would the point be?" Dad looked hard at her now. "First of all, you know the Company's in trouble or why would they be doing this in the first place? Do you remember them wanting to sell us shares during the good times? I don't. I don't remember that at all. So in other words, we do all the work, then say to them 'skim off our paychecks, please and thank you', so that when things go to crap because of all the stuff going on that we don't even know about, we're the ones holding the bag?" He took a drag and broke off a tip of ash on the edge of the ashtray. Mom waited. "Maybe we don't have a lot, but it's enough. Isn't it enough?"

"Of course it is," she said. The ledger was still open beneath her hands. "You do fine for us, John."

"So why do we want to mess with it? When a workingman tries to be more than that, somebody gets screwed and who do you think it is? You remember your folks in Dakota? What did they go through when all of a sudden the farmers were going to be their own boss? Who was it who got screwed then?" Another drag, another thin triangle of smoke. He shook his head. "So what would the point be?"

We both looked at Mom. I don't know what she was thinking. What she said was "What are the other men going to do?" For her that was pushing things. Especially since we all knew she could find out what other families were thinking better than Dad could. In his circles he'd be hearing God knows what pile of bullshit about who'd be buying and how much. When it came to money those guys never stopped playing poker. Mom could get the straight story, and probably did starting the next day. My guess is she traveled her whole kitchen circuit, ten homes or so within a four block radius of ours, to get the lowdown from the Lewsco wives. Some of them must have been excited, because she asked Dad twice more (that I heard) whether she should fiddle with the ledger to find a way to buy a few shares. If Dad had said yes, or even shrugged like he didn't care one way or the other, we might have ended up with a sliver of the rock. We didn't.

Most of my friends did. Holly brought it up a couple of days later as we were eating lunch at our spot behind the chemistry lab. She said her folks had talked about it on payday, too, probably at the same time mine were. "Right, right," I said to her when she told me. "Just get this picture. Pretend you were in a big balloon floating over the middle of town that day, and you could peel back all the roofs, and in every single house, at every kitchen table, there's this couple having the same conversation, 'What do you think?,' and some are going 'Why don't we give it a try?', and some are saying it's the stupidest thing they ever heard of, all happening at once like this huge beehive of noise and arguing, as big as the whole town. But everyone in it thinks they're the only ones trying to figure it out." Images like that seemed to tickle Holly. I thought them up for her when I daydreamed.

The decision was different in her house. The Burgesses didn't have much more money than we had. Her dad was a front office guy who made more than Dad did, but the difference was probably eaten up by the way they'd help out Fife when he needed it. She told me they were nervous about buying in, but they were more scared they'd look back and kick themselves for not taking the opportunity. They ended up deciding to buy one share the first month, two shares with the second, and to just keep adding one each time until they couldn't squeeze any more. That seemed pretty smart. I thought about suggesting it at home, but I didn't figure it would improve Dad's outlook on the whole thing. Now I wish I had, because as far as I can tell Mrs. Burgess ended up in pretty decent shape.

That same week Mr. Overland pushed off three days of his lesson plan in American civics to have us talk about the Lewsco offer. Mr. Overland was the first teacher I ever had with a mustache. The high school's full of them now. He was the *relevant* teacher at LFHS, and he was gone one year later. He told us *this* was what civics was all about, the dynamic interplay of forces pushing their own agendas at cross purposes or some such. He was excited about it.

Holly told the class about her folks' escalating plan. A couple others said their parents were doing the same thing. When Mr. Overland asked what we thought the most important "dynamic" was, Holly raised her hand. "I think the most important part is that the people doing the hardest jobs will get some of the rewards for a change, instead of all the extra going to the people who have the easiest jobs and are better paid in the first place."

"Okay," Mr. Overland said, smiling. "Good. Who else?" No hands went up. "Who else thinks it'll make things fairer?" Nothing. "Steve?"

Steve Raines beamed his smile and sat up a little from his slouch. Usually he had plenty to say in class, but this week he'd sat quiet. "Fairer? Than they are now?" He shrugged his broad shoulders. "Beats me."

"You think things're fine the way they are," Mr. Overland said.

Another shrug, the same smile. "I don't see anybody suffering." He looked from one side of the classroom to the other. "All those suffering, please raise your hand?"

A titter and two-thirds of the hands went up. Mr. Overland ignored it. "So what *do* you think about this, Steve? Will it be good for the

Company? How about for the town?"

"Well, it'll be good for the people in the town who go for it," said Steve. He unfolded his arms and sat up straighter. "I think people like us finally have a chance to make something of themselves, and if they don't do it now then they won't have anyone but themselves to blame."

From the desk diagonally in front of Steve's Holly turned to look at him. I was trying to read her expression so hard I squinted. But her mouth and chin were cupped in her hand and her eyes showed nothing.

Steve was warmed up. "You know, some people who don't have money think people who have it are just lucky. It's not luck. It's guts. The people who make it are the ones who flop it out there—" he smacked his desk with a flat palm "— right *there*. Right where it can get chopped off. Then if things pan out they have to listen to all the whining about how lucky they were." He shook his head, swinging his big smile from one side to the other. "Well," he patted his desk three quick times, "it's flopping time now."

That was the moment, and this I remember like I was in that classroom right now, when I wondered how much of this was Steve talking and how much he was passing on straight from his dad. I do know that Mel jumped on the opportunity like nobody else. He hocked half of what he owned and gave the bank another mortgage on their house to buy more and more shares. Mel flopped it out there. That's how he got to be who he got to be.

11

STEVE COULD TALK RIGHT IN CLASS ABOUT FLOPPING IT ON THE TABLE because he was Steve. He could skate right through the boundaries that held in the rest of us on the strength of that smile. He knew it. He knew that anyone he turned it towards felt appreciated and included in his charmed world. He told me as much a couple of times as we grew up. But even when I knew he was turning that smile on like a lamp, it looked absolutely natural.

Often it was. I wish people who see him today as a Company stooge could have seen him thirty years ago. At recess or lunch he'd sometimes stroll off to the edges, seeking out the kids who kept to themselves. He'd walk right up to the geekiest kids and sit down for a little talk. They'd be wary at first, probably thinking he was point man for some trick we'd cooked up to make them look silly. But he kept going back to check in with them and there was never a trick. After a while you'd look over and see the geeks were doing most of the talking. Steve would be listening carefully. After a while his geeks got less geeky, gradually moving in from the edges towards the rest of us. Those of us in the middle changed, too. We didn't start racing each other to reach out to unpopular kids, but we didn't make fun of them anymore.

I asked Steve about it once. We were camping at Whiskey Creek, one of the first times our parents let us overnight on our own. We'd had hot dogs on a stick and beans in a can and a pack of hot black bubbly marshmallows each. Everything sticky or greasy had been stuffed into a plastic bag that we hung from a high tree branch. Steve had snuck one can of beer, a 16- ounce Hamms, into the bottom of his pack, and he cracked it open as we crawled into our sleeping bags. It was sour and warm but we finished it. We lay quiet for a minute, ears full of the creek's gurgle and eyes full of stars. I asked Steve why he spent time with losers. Weren't they weird? Why not just hang with the solid guys, me, Dougy, Ray, Ray, Bobby, all of us? "I already know what you guys are like," he said. A minute later he was snoring.

It was just raw curiosity, like a smart puppy's. I think it's the part that kept Holly hooked to him for so long. The outward packaging didn't hurt, especially through the soap operas of high school when every kid's watching and measuring. He was the first-place trophy and she had him. But by itself that wouldn't have held her.

They were together from whenever it was we stopped hating girls until we graduated high school. There were times, and this is true, when that felt good. They were the two people closest to me and when they came together the world fit together with more sense. There was a tiny place for me that wouldn't have been there otherwise.

Then there were the other times, the times I churned in pain about how things were, imagining different ways they could have been. If it had been anybody but Steve, I would have wondered *why him instead of me?* and fixated on life's stupid unfairness. With Steve, I knew why. Anyone would. Still there were times I worked myself up into thinking he was all flash and if she bought it she wasn't much better. She *had* to know that puppies aren't just about that adorable bubbling joy of life. The bubbles go all over the place, fizzing up and then disappearing. What was so compelling one minute doesn't exist for them the next.

A perfect example was when Steve and I were finishing a long Saturday of flyfishing in a favorite hole on Whiskey Creek just above its entry into the Lewis. There wasn't more than an hour of sun left in the afternoon. I knew he'd promised to take Holly to the Port Douglas drive-in that night for something she wanted to see — I think it was *Lion in Winter* — and if we didn't pack it up and hustle back to town there was no way they'd make it.

"We should probably get going," I said. He didn't answer. His eyes were fixed on a little shiver of water between a rock and a grass paddy, where a steelhead had cracked the surface a few minutes before. He'd just laid his fly there for the third time.

I waited and watched him false-cast twice before laying the line back down. "What do you say, Steve? You're gonna be late, man." No answer. He couldn't spare an atom of attention. A minute later he gave the rod a jerk and counted a few silent beats. Then he shook his head once with a sour face and looked up at me like I was a surprise visitor. "Okay?" I said.

"Just a couple more," he said, nodding towards the little patch of water. "That's all it'll take. I can feel it."

"But weren't you picking up Holly at 7:30? It has to be after 6:00 now, maybe 6:30. We gotta go."

He waved his rod back and forth and dropped the fly in the same square foot of water. "We will," he said. "Just a couple more."

"What are you going to say to Holly?"

"I'll figure it out when the time comes." He was quiet for another two minutes, tickling the hole with his fly. He looked at me and smiled. "He's right here. I *feel* him."

"So you'll just cruise up an hour late and say 'Hi, honey, I decided to blow off the movie?'"

"The movie'll be there next week, or another will." The fly sailed through the air again and touched down three inches from where the fish had broken water. "He won't." Two minutes later he was reeling in and talking again. "Hey, I don't make the rules. I just play by 'em." He pulled a plastic box out of his pocket to pick another fly. "Don't worry about Holly, Jack. I'll take care of Holly."

On the third cast with the new fly he hooked his fish, a four-pounder, and brought him in. As we hiked down the creek in early dusk I wondered what he'd be telling her an hour later. I'd be so different to her and I ached for her to know it. God, if she could just *hear* how he talked about her when she wasn't around. I looked at Steve's thick back as he hiked in front of me humming a Ventures' surf tune. What if I brought along a little tape recorder one day and got him going, then dropped the tape off in her mailbox in a blank envelope? I imagined a picture of Holly in her kitchen, looking down at the tape recorder as Steve's voice came out: "Don't worry about Holly, Jack. I'll take care of Holly."

Of course I didn't do it. I don't even remember badmouthing him to her once as we grew up. The funny thing is that I ever thought I had to. The idea that I'd understand Steve or anyone else better than Holly did is pretty funny.

He did it to me, too. I'm thinking of a time that same summer, after I bought my first rig with savings from my two summers in the woods. Dad wasn't wild about the whole thing. He thought one of the reasons to live in a town like Lewis Falls was so kids didn't need a car. We knew that living in Lewis Falls was exactly why we needed a car.

With nine $100 bills in my pocket, almost my whole stake in the world, I thumbed a ride one Saturday down to the annual Highway Department surplus auction in Grants Pass. I had a picture of myself rolling back home behind the wheel of a monster, maybe a Power Wagon like Rum. At that time Rum was still around, up on blocks hulking and engineless, in a corner of our back yard. Power Wagons were the original wall-climbers. They said something about their owners that I wanted said about me. It's probably not too different from the Hummers kids like today. But I also knew a rig like that would top out at about 40mph cruising speed, which wasn't going to give me the range of travel I wanted.

When he realized he wasn't going to keep me away from the auction, Dad sent me off with one rule: figure out your price limit for anything you bid on and stick to it. I did. The first rig I bid on was a one-ton Ford with dual wheels and waist-high running boards. My limit would be $750. Somebody started the bidding at $500. The auctioneer asked for $600, then fell back to $550. I raised my paddle with my blood pumping so hard I could hear it. Someone else bid $600, then the first guy bid $650. I waved a paddle at $700 and waited for five hour-long seconds while the auctioneer kept pointing at me. "Seven hundred once," he said. "Seven hundred *twice...*"

"Seven fifty," a new guy said from behind me. A rush of cold air went all the way through me. I watched drained and a little nauseated as somebody, I think the guy who bid first, bought my truck for $900.

Three trucks later I was breathing normally. The auctioneer asked for a minimum $400 bid on a 1958 Dodge half-ton, Highway Department-orange, with a swirling crack in the windshield. He got it and asked for $450. I raised my paddle and set my ceiling at $600.

"...four-fifty, do I hear five hundred? Four-fifty, do I hear five hundred? No? I got four-fifty going once...four-fifty going twice...SOLD to the feller trying to grow whiskers for four hundred and fifty dollars."

I was a truck owner. And at that magical moment of passage for American males, all I could think was *Oh, shit. I've bought a complete lemon and everybody but me and the chump who started the bidding knows it.* Actually I ended up driving it hard for three years and selling it for $500. It ranks among my top two or three all-time bargains.

But it didn't quite pack the punch back up the mountain that I wanted. I wasn't ashamed of it — it wasn't a VW or a Falcon — it just wasn't the kind of truck guys asked to borrow. Until Steve did one day. He drove a big International Travelall back then, a monster station wagon that used to take Lewsco crews up into the back-country. Mel had it retired into his garage and spent a year spiffing it up, then gave it down to Steve for his birthday. It was big, the most important thing, and had a classy gold-and-bronze paint job that Mel and Steve had carefully applied. It turned heads my rig wouldn't. Steve called her the gleaming dream, or just GD.

The summer I'm remembering GD was out of commission for opening night of the Lewis County Fair. She'd blown a head gasket the day before, and by Saturday afternoon Steve and I were surrounded by more engine parts than were going to go back together that day. Steve and Holly had tickets to see Porter Waggoner and Dolly Parton that night on the main stage at the fairgrounds. At about 4:00 he looked across GD's wounded engine at me and asked if he could use my truck. No problem, I said without any thought.

I started to think about it as I laid a tarp over his engine and picked up the tools. I didn't have tickets for the show but I'd been thinking about cruising down to PD to find some. As Steve talked on about his engine and what else he should probably do as long as it was opened up, I sorted out and weighed things. How much did I want to see the show? More than I did the minute before Steve asked for my truck. If he hadn't, would I have actually gone? I didn't know. Did I want to ride down there with the two of them? I knew the answer to that one: no. Early into my six block walk home, my keys and truck left with Steve, I was feeling okay about things.

The first thing I did the next morning was walk out front to look for my truck. It wasn't there. I figured it would be soon, which was okay. My big plans for the day were mowing the back lawn, listening to the Beavers and maybe loafing down at the Falls later.

It didn't show up all day and I didn't hear from Steve. At dinner time I called him. Battery problem, he said. He'd used the dome light in the cab and tried to turn it off when they parked, but it was still flickering (I knew what he was talking about; a ticklish switch was one of the quirks I hadn't fixed yet). By the time Steve and Holly came back to it the battery was dead.

He told me he was getting set to roll-start it when some older kids swung by, invited them to jump in their van and head out to the Breakwater, a dancing bar on the highway north of PD where they didn't check IDs. Holly wanted to go, so Steve wasn't going to bother them to help get the truck started. They hopped in the back of the van and took off. Then the end of the night came, Holly fell asleep in the back of the van as they were coming up to the junction where the Lewis River Road heads up east from the Coast Highway, and Steve just figured he'd mess with the truck the next day. It'd be safe overnight at the fairgrounds.

The next day, the day we were talking, he'd slept in, then got called for a game of hoops, then remembered he'd promised Mel he'd clean up the shop, which he'd just finished doing an hour before I'd called. The time just got away from him. I asked if he'd get his Dad's rig and drive me down now so we could get it. He'd like to, sure, but Sunday evenings had to be family time. Mel's rule. We'd do it tomorrow.

He was already out of the house when I called the next morning. No, Mrs. Raines said, she didn't know where. I hitched down the hill with my spare key and jumper cables and brought the truck home myself. On the ride up the hill I wrote a little speech to him in my head. I thought about calling to deliver it when I got home and decided to wait until the next time I saw him. It'd seem more natural that way. He'd probably expect it less and maybe listen more.

Two days later in the late afternoon I heard GD's horn out front. Steve wanted to tell the gory details of getting her engine back together, and he wanted to do it on the way to a pig roast out in Bounty. I went back in to tell Mom and grab a sweatshirt. He jumped into the story the second I was in the cab and had me laughing before we hit the town limits. Neither of us said anything about my truck then or since. I wonder what he'd say if I brought it up today.

12

WE WERE BOTH IN THE WOODS FOR MOST OF THAT SUMMER BUT NOT ON the same job. Because I'd shown them something setting choker the year before, they gave me a saw. I quickly got comfortable with it and started clearing brush away from where the fallers and buckers had to work. By the end of that summer I was a bucker myself, cutting downed logs to the exact length the mill wanted.

Steve didn't get a saw. They didn't have him out on the ground at all. By then they were thinking of him as a town treasure, too important to LFHS sports to take a chance getting hurt. While I was learning to cut, Steve was learning to work the machinery, D-6s, D-7s, high-lead cranes. You can guess how good he was at it.

I remember a morning lunch break on a fire-shortened day in July. Dad, five or six full-timers and me had pulled out our lunch boxes in the parking area. One of the truck radios was blaring out a story from the riots that were filling the streets of Chicago. The broadcaster's soothing voice gave way to the bull-horned shouts of a protestor from Brooklyn or somewhere like it: "AND WE'RE HERE TO TELL LYNDON *bleep* JOHNSON AND HIS BOOTLICK HUBERT HUMPHREY, MR. *PRES-*IDENT, YOU CAN TAKE YOUR WAR AND YOUR ARMY OF PIGS IN VIETNAM AND YOUR ARMY OF PIGS IN CHICAGO AND FUHRER RICHARD DALEY, SIEG HIEL, AND THE TEAR GAS AND BOMBS AND THIS WHOLE *bleep*ING CONVENTION YOU WIRED FROM THE START AND STICKEM UP YOUR HAIRY REDNECK *bleep*." The roar of cheering from Chicago stopped cold as someone shut off the radio.

"That would take a very large ass," said Peter Thomas, sitting on a short stump near the truck. I heard one big laugh and a couple snickers. Dad didn't react. He sat leaning against a tree, his feet crossed in front of him. His jaw muscles were working hard on a sandwich.

"Shit," said Ray Swerdlow. "You believe those guys? Little pukes." The words fought their way around a melting mix of Wonderbread, mayonnaise and meat. "Beat their damn heads in 'swhat they oughta do."

Ray Swerdlow wasn't smart, but he was clear. He was the pure voice of one of the primary colors of Lewis Falls, angry and blaming. He'd blurt out what was on other minds, stripped of the cross-currents and complexities that kept others quiet. People listened to him hold forth more than you'd expect, until he crossed a line of sloppiness, somewhere near the bottom of his second pitcher at the Spot. I think the sound of those raw opinions exposed to open air helped people focus what they really thought. Listening to him talk also made people feel smarter and more civilized. Sometimes they'd roll their eyes at each other when he slowed down. You could say Ray Swerdlow brought people closer together.

Peter Thomas definitely appreciated him. Like Ray — like all of us eating lunch by the trucks that morning — Peter grew up in Lewis Falls. He was halfway between Dad's age and mine, and halfway through thirty years or so of setting choker. He'd had most of the responsibility for teaching me how. I never saw him with a saw in his hands, though he would have handled one fine. Pete's voice was another of the town's colors, more muted than Ray's. He was challenging and skeptical. Like Ray, what he had to say helped people think. But he didn't make them feel smarter. Pete borrowed so many books from the county library van that came up from Port Douglas that people called it the Petemobile. He pointed me towards most of the good books I read growing up. He usually brought a book into the woods for lunchtime and breaks, but today he seemed to feel like mixing it up. "To a bloody pulp, huh, Ray? Just whale on those little fuckers 'till their brains squirt out their ears."

"You got it," Ray said through his food, a little wary.

"Why, Ray?"

"Cause they're snot-nosed punks," someone I couldn't see said from a pickup bed above and behind me. "Cause they'd rather live off Mom and Dad then work a goddamn day in their lives."

"Or off you and me," another voice tossed in. "We're the ones pay the welfare."

"Yeah," Ray said, pumped up with support. "Snot-nosed punks. Living off welfare and then screaming their snot-nosed heads off about how the world's screwing 'em. Fuck, ya talk about biting the horse that feeds you."

Peter laughed. "Ray, I haven't worked one single day with you that you weren't bitching about how the world's screwing you. You're the biggest horse-biter going. Those kids out there, they're your comrades-in-*arms*. They are, Ray. Maybe you ought to go out to Chicago and get in those marches with them."

Laughter, hoots, agreement. "Yeah, Ray, you gotta get to Chicago!" "Take my truck, Ray." "No, here, here's my keys." Dad's mouth quivered for an instant as he rolled a smoke.

"You could help make things better, Ray," said Peter, trying hard to look serious. "Less shitty, just like those kids want to do."

"What are they making better, Pete?" someone asked.

"What are any of us making better?" Peter said. He looked at each of us for a moment. His eyes went to Dad last.

"Shelter," Dad said. "Buildings. Without us, people don't get the new houses they need."

"The forest," Ray said. "Without us the forest'd blow down and burn up and just go to rot." Somebody snorted. There was another pause as Peter kept looking around.

"What about families, Pete?" the voice in the pick-up bed behind me said. "We're raising kids. Good kids."

"Mmm-hmm," Peter said. "Okay. That's good. So what are we doing to make things better for them than they've been for us?"

More quiet. Dad was holding in a gust of his Prince Albert. He let it out slowly, his words breaking up the smoke. "We're not running around making all the noise. We're doing what you do, Pete. We're living with it."

"Is that what to do, John?" Peter said. "Live with it?"

"We're not the ones making all the fucking noise," Ray burst in. "That guy there?" He pointed to the cab where the radio had been playing. "He was talking about the *President.*"

A snicker came from up behind me and then, in a mocking hushed voice, a song. "Oh Beautiful, for Spacious Skies," like a film sound-bed for John Wayne looking off into a red sunset, "for Amber Waves of Grai-ai-ain..."

"Sright," Ray said. "That guy was talking about the President of the United States of America."

"For Purple Mountains' Majesteeee..."

"Yes, he was," Peter said.

"Well, you don't do that."

"Well, what do you do, Ray? That's what I'm asking."

"You mind your own fucking business like I do," Ray said. "You go to work, you mind your own business, and if I ever catch one of those little pukes running down the United States of America, you cut off their nuts with your filet knife."

There wasn't a man-made sound, not a snicker or crackle of lunch wrappings, for a long moment. I glanced at Peter and then at Dad, who looked like he was biting the inside of his mouth. He broke the silence. "It's awful damn hard," he said, "to argue with logic like that."

"Fuckin' Ay," Ray said.

I REPLAYED THE CONVERSATION THAT NIGHT FOR HOLLY. I WAS OVER AT her place on an errand for Mom. She'd borrowed walnuts from Mrs. Burgess that morning, and as thanks sent me back over with a dozen brownies. Most survived the journey.

Holly answered the door with a big smile and stepped back to invite me in. Across the living room Walter Cronkite was saying goodnight. Holly went over to turn him off while I crossed to the kitchen to hand Mrs. Burgess the cargo. She looked in the bag and made a hissing noise and a fond crack about Mom's sneakiness. She asked both of us if we wanted a brownie and milk. Holly didn't and I did. Holly steered me to the dining room table, where a minute later Mrs. Burgess plunked down three brownies on a flowered dessert plate.

Holly leaned forward with her mouth slightly open as I described the day's lunch break. "Poor Ray," she said, her head shaking. She pushed me to recall the exact words they'd used about making things better. The end of the story cracked her up. "That's *funny*. Your Dad is funny!"

"Oh, he's a riot," I said. "Keeps us in stitches 24 hours a day."

"*No*, you know what I mean. He just has his own way of seeing things. It's funny, it's different from anybody else, and you don't usually know it because he's so quiet." With nothing to say I waited for a new subject. "And Peter Thomas! Did he really say all that?"

"Well, more or less." He'd said every word of it, but the admiration in her voice made me pull back some credit. Next time there was a lunch-time debate I'd have to speak up so I'd have something to tell her about afterward.

"It's about time. I look at what's going on in Chicago," she said, nodding at the blank TV, "and I look at what's going on here, and I think 'I'm in the wrong place.' Things are really happening, the whole *world* is changing except for Lewis Falls, Oregon. Do you know what I mean, Jack?"

"Sure. You're right. Except I think it's maybe starting to change here, too."

"Why? Because somebody's willing to tell Ray Swerdlow out loud he's a dinkus?"

"It wasn't just that. I wish you'd been there today. I can't really describe it." Then I tried to. I tried describing the silent gaps between what they said, how they watched each other, the looks on their faces. I wasn't trying to prove any point; it didn't matter much to me if Lewis Falls was changing or not. All I wanted was to be as fascinating for her as somebody from Chicago or wherever else she thought she ought to be. The more intently she listened, focusing on my right eye one second, my left the next, nodding tiny nods when I completed a thought, the more I wanted to give her.

I walked home that night in a glow, warmed by the feeling that Holly and I were together. I don't mean a couple. That was her and Steve. But in a bruising world we were on the same side. We understood it the same way and we didn't need to explain ourselves or convince the other one of anything. We were part of each other's little sanctuary. We could charge each other up with extra energy instead of draining it off the way that most people and events would.

Without noticing the steps in between I was standing at my own front door. I let the screen slam behind me. "How'd Isabel like the brownies?" Mom asked.

13

THE BONDING OF OUR TWO HEARTS FOR ALL ETERNITY LASTED ABOUT three days. I was coasting down to the Falls on a hot afternoon when I noticed it was gone. With work shutting down at 2:30 during fire season I'd often be driving down the Falls Road to join the crowd before 4:00. It took three minutes to get there from the middle of town over the graveled washboard surface, and I spent them wondering if Holly was down there and how I should enter in case she was.

I pulled my truck onto the shoulder and got out to scoop up a little dirt and rub it on my face and arms. I'd be the Sweaty Virile Logger, the solid guy who toils in the woods while others fritter the day away with suntan oil and beer. Most of the crowd was down at the Falls when I got there, but Holly wasn't. I got stares and a hoot as I reached the water's edge. I dove in and scrubbed myself off with quick hard swipes. As I stepped back out I massaged my scalp hard so I didn't have to make eye contact with anyone. Bending yourself around what you guessed Holly would think about things was hard work.

She'd be down there about two days a week. Whenever she was, Steve was, too, though usually not right next to her. She liked to float on an air mattress in the calm part of the pool, either reading a paperback or lying on her stomach with her chin on her hands, talking and laughing with a little flotilla of girlfriends. Steve and the guys mostly hung out in the cavern, a broad ledge of rock that stretched behind the Falls. Filtered by the thick clear wall of water, the light in there wavered and glistened. It was the choice spot to get loaded. Then we'd watch each other crawl to the edge and sit directly under the Falls, letting it pound our head and shoulders as long as we could. For a stretch of time I held the record at one hour and forty-one minutes. Holly was there when I went in but not when I finished.

Hanging out at the Falls was supposed to be a daytime activity. Up where the Falls road starts in town, two swinging metal gates were brought together and padlocked early each evening by a Forest Service ranger. A big yellow sign said that entry from 6:00 p.m. to 5:00 a.m. was strictly forbidden and that violators will be prosecuted (about once a year, some midnight editor with a heavy black marker would make that "prosecutors will be violated"). You can guess the exacting care we took to follow that rule.

The only thing that kept us away from the Falls most nights was the hike, a mile down from town and more to the point a mile hike uphill to return to town. To tender teenagers like us it felt like a chore. We probably averaged two or three nights a month down there in the summer, usually close to the full moon. Most melt together in my memory, but I clearly remember some. Like the one with Steve and Holly and Angela Ledbetter. Angela was on cheerleading squad with Holly, blonder, more pixie-ish, with more to say and less worth listening to.

I was Angela's human development project through most of high school and she was devoted. Sometimes that made me feel like a stud, since along with Holly she was the best-looking girl in town. Other times it made me feel jumpy and mean, especially when she talked about the future. I knew there wasn't any. That didn't stop me from doing the deed, the first time for both of us, three weeks after graduation. It was in my orange truck in the parking lot of Bowman Beach State Park, just above the California line, June 28, 1969, about 9:30 p.m. That was it. She called me almost every night for a week, and we went to somebody's birthday picnic in July, but I didn't want to take her out again. Six months later she married Tim Slater, a kid from Bounty who's a big-time roofing contractor in Grants Pass now. They have a slew of kids. The last I heard of her was when she visited Mom last year to pitch some Mary Kay products. Mom says she still looks great.

But I'm talking about way back when she first looked great. It was a full moon in late July before our senior year. Venus was just coming out as we started down the road and the trees sliced the moon into bright slivers. All the way down we listened to Angela's story of her mother's story of her mother's sister's story about the wandering hands of the manager of Lewsco's nursery, where the Company raised seedlings for replanting. Holly made a couple of friendly exclamations and Steve laughed. I was quiet.

When we reached the parking area we heard a burst of laughter cut through the roar of the Falls, then some whoops and more laughter. "Come on this way," Steve said, and he veered left to avoid the beach, towards the base of the hill that formed the downstream boundary of the big pool. He passed between the two thin firs that marked the start of the narrow path up to the Elders. As we zigzagged upwards between trees and boulders Angela kept talking about how enchanted it all was, how maybe we should leave bread-crumbs like Hansel and Gretel, about something from Norse mythology we were studying in school, until the effort of the climb took all her breath. We were all quiet for the last fifty yards.

Then we weren't climbing anymore. We were in the small circular opening that capped the hill, amidst the ring of straight massive trees on a duff of twigs and crumbling needles so thick it felt like sponge beneath our feet. We were in the Elders.

The low bass hum of the Falls came from below us and to our right. So did stray pops of laughter and shouts, muffled now by the heavy slope of trees. Within a jagged black frame straight above us the sky had a Maxfield Parrish glow, a blue satin. The air was soft and heavy, a fabric woven from a whisper of spray from the Falls.

"Whew," said Angela. "Whew! Well, it was worth it!"

Steve had crossed to the far side of the circle, the edge where you could see the Lewis River rush away towards the Coast. He looked down for a moment and started humming a soulful old tune, *Mr. Blue*, I think, loud enough to overcome the sound of the Falls. Holly crossed over to him.

I took off my windbreaker and sat down on it, leaving more than half for Angela. "This is so pretty, Jack," she said as she sat. We both looked across to where Holly and Steve were standing with their backs to us, her arm in his. After a minute they took a few steps away from the circle and sank below our line of sight.

Angela turned to me and looked intently into each of my eyes, one at a time. I moved my face closer and she met me halfway. She was always a little frantic at first. Her mouth opened like a hungry baby bird's, faster and wider than I liked. Our tongues banged against each other, then spun tight wraps around one another like twiddling thumbs. She relaxed then, as if the effort of taking a plunge into cool water was over. After half a minute she was a terrific kisser.

With our mouths together we slowly sank until we were lying down. I set a leg over her hip and nudged her towards me with it. She squirmed closer to me. Her willingness made me hard and I could feel her warmth through both of our jeans. I held on to her while rolling flat on my back, and she was on top of me. I tried to put a hand in each of her rear pockets, but there was no room. Her buns were tight as hot sausages in a denim skin as I kneaded them. She rocked side to side as I did, pushing her weight down toward my center with little mewling noises from the back of her throat. We breathed hard through our noses with our mouths vacuum-sealed. They stayed fixed as I rolled over and set her beneath me.

I arched my back enough to make some working room between us. She had on a light cardigan that I peeled back to her shoulders, with a cotton blouse underneath. As I fingered the top button it felt like my heart stopped until I could find out if she would flinch or jerk away. She didn't. My thumb felt like a dead stick trying to push the button through its hole, deader each second that it wouldn't yield. If I had to break the kiss to tend to the button she might change her mind. Then a sudden gift of grace: the button fell open and my fingertips grazed the soft warmth of her chest. The second button was easier. I felt the tiny bow where her bra came together in front. I don't remember the other buttons, but an instant later her blouse was peeled back like her sweater. The tight plumpness of her bra cups through my t-shirt made me harder.

A rush inside of me pulled my mouth from hers down to the swell of her breasts. They radiated the warmth from inside her body. They were smooth as dry cream and pushed back against my lips with a soft firmness that is like nothing else. "Oohh, Jack," she gasped, raising herself up to me. I slipped a bra strap off her shoulder and pushed her cup down slowly until her small stiff nipple popped into the open. She moaned as I closed my lips around it, rolling my head around and sucking more and more of her breast into my mouth. I rocked back and forth faster and faster. I sucked, she rubbed my groin with the inside of her leg and arched her breasts towards my face, I filled my whole mouth with one breast and squeezed and kneaded the other. Still bucking against me Angela bit her hand to mute the noise she was making. I felt her thigh stroke my groin and a mass of something warm filling the center of my body so full it could burst, and she rubbed me once more and it did. A hot stream squirted from me once, then again, and one last time as I clenched myself, and Angela below me, with all my strength.

I lay there with my face over her shoulder in the dirt and got my breath back. Slowly I pushed myself back up and helped Angela up to a sitting position. She smiled at me and then looked down. I pulled her towards me and hugged her for a long minute, patting her shoulder like a reassuring friend. Then I got up and walked a few steps away to let her put things back together.

I sat back down and put my arm around her to wait for Steve and

Holly to come back. We talked about whatever we thought of. She asked me if I'd been up there before. The idea that she thought I was new to the Elders got me started on a serious story about the place, but I didn't get far before realizing all her attention was aimed at picking bits of forest debris off her sweater and fluffing shape back in her hair with headshakes and combing fingers. I stopped talking in the middle of a sentence to see if she'd notice. "I wonder where they went to," she said. "Do you suppose they could have gotten lost?"

"They're not lost." I lay back down with my fingers laced behind my head, watching the stars while we waited. Angela talked about how happy she was that we were two people who really respected each other. I knew, didn't I, that that wasn't true with all boys? After a few minutes Steve and Holly's dark forms rose into view. They walked across the circle towards us holding hands. They didn't let go all the way back up to town.

Angela and I walked behind them. "What do you think the ranger would do if he found us here?" she asked when we were off the hill and onto the gravel road. As I thought about that she started telling me about her cousin who lost his job collecting pine cones for the Forest Service because he didn't follow some totally stupid rule that she couldn't quite remember. I tried to build a sound wall between us so I could listen to what Holly and Steve were saying up front. With their heads facing away from me and the background noises of our shoes on the gravel and Angela's constant voice, it was just a mumble. When they turned their heads to look at each other a couple of phrases floated back to me. They were wondering who would notice if they cut school one Friday to get a three-day weekend at a cottage on the coast that Steve's father had the keys to. Something Holly said about one of our teachers knocked Steve's head back with laughter. He pulled her sideways towards him and kissed her head.

Back up in town Angela and I said goodnight to them and walked back over to her house. On her front porch she gave my tongue another beating and asked if I wanted to come in for some pie. No, it was pretty late. She smiled and squeezed both my hands in hers. "That was so pretty down there, Jack," she said. She kissed me again. She really was a nice girl.

WE STARTED OUR SENIOR YEAR TWO MONTHS LATER. IT WAS A BIG ONE for Steve. He was all-conference in three sports and all-state in two, football and baseball. I don't know if he played in a game all year that didn't have a college scout in the stands checking him out.

Holly was all-everything, too. LFHS didn't have enough clubs and activities for her, so a teacher drove her down to Grants Pass twice a week for Debate. She won a wall full of plaques. She edited the *Ax*, our yearbook, and graduated first in the class. When that gets mentioned she always says there were only 27 of us in the whole class. She doesn't add that her grades were so far above whoever was number two that you could have fit another hundred kids between them.

Some people in town can still tell you about the valedictory speech she gave at the graduation ceremony out on the Square. National Guardsmen had shot four Kent State students to death the month before, and that's what she took for her text. She talked about all four by name, the towns they'd come from and when they'd graduated high school, and the hopeful happy speeches that they'd probably heard then, "the kind of speech you would like me to give today."

Then she paused. It was scorching hot, and the audience facing us in folding chairs was completely silent. She jutted her chin over them and tilted her head to one side so that the mortarboard tassel hung in her face. "That is not a speech I can give today," she said very slowly. "For which one among us," her voice rising, "can believe and say to all the world that a country that *murders its young* is truly GREAT?" In the second to last row, Mom and Dad didn't move. Mel Raines, on the end seat of the first row, was massaging his temples with his eyes squeezed shut like he was trying to make it all go away.

14

Eight of the 27 of us headed straight for college. Three went to South Coast Community College (SCCC), two to Pacific Northwest Bible College and two to Oregon State for forestry programs, including Steve on a full-ride football scholarship. Holly went farthest from home, to Stanford University. A picture of her waving goodbye at the Grants Pass Airport was in every paper in Southern Oregon.

I thought hard about SCCC. After three seasons I still hadn't figured out if I had forest blood or not, which in itself told me I probably didn't. So I wanted some choices. But it wasn't my time for college.

Dad had fallen sick by then. He'd quit the woods permanently the year before and now he couldn't walk around for more than an hour without needing to rest. He still had a paycheck because Ben arranged some work for him at the scaling station outside town. It was hard on him. Late one night I heard a single sentence rise in a shout from a muffled conversation between him and Mom. It was in between a snarl and a sob: "I'm not their pet bum!"

They needed my help. But Dad didn't need anyone extra around to witness his slide, so I started looking for my own place nearby. Sam helped us by offering me his raggediest tourist cabin. It was perfect for both of us: I got my own place two blocks from Mom and Dad for next to nothing and Sam got to pull a few bucks from the place without having to spend time or money to make it habitable. Then after about a year I got tired of the mushroom ridges pushing up the baseboard in the front room and the rusty paste oozing from the faucets.

It was time to live like a grown up. When I heard that Bob Henderson was retiring from the Forest Service and moving himself and Flora to Arizona, I called the Company housing office in Port Douglas to see if anyone was in line to pick up their lease. Nobody was. For $100 a month I landed one big bedroom, a bath with predictable hot and cold water and a real kitchen. It was about six blocks away from Mom and Dad, ten minutes walk to supper three times a week and two minutes by car if I needed to get there quick.

I loved having that place. Doing what I wanted when I wanted to was still new enough to be exciting, and unlike Sam's cabin this was a place where I could have actual people over. People who notice things like fungus indoors. Women.

I'm not going to exaggerate this. Hugh Hefner didn't have to worry. I bought an old green sofa with tiny tweedy balls from Goodwill and set it facing a Franklin woodstove with glass doors. That turned out to be enough to accomplish what couldn't get done in family rooms with parents half-sleeping upstairs, or in my truck. In the two years that I lived there, there were two LFHS girls, one from my class and one a year older, a waitress from the Rasty Mariner in Port Douglas, a Forest Service intern taking six months off from Vasser to heal the Earth by planting trees, and a modern dancer from Eugene who'd come up to fish with a father she hadn't seen in fifteen years. Instead of a fishing trip she'd ended up marooned while he drank all night at the Spot and slept all day in one of Sam's cabins.

Every one of them was nice. They were sexy or beautiful and in a couple of cases both. And those nights were fun. Crosby, Stills and Nash or the Stones on the turntable, maybe Bob Dylan when a deep brooding vibe was needed. Berry wines in big economy bottles or a little weed strong enough to make Dylan coherent. Everything floating in a soft orange light from the fireplace and from candles on the end tables I had made from two wooden spools that once held power transmission cable.

Except for those rare times I got really loaded I wouldn't talk very much. I wasn't Gary Cooper, I'd let them know I was in the room. But since I didn't look or move like Steve I figured I had to be interesting. If I could get her thinking that what I was holding inside was wiser and more beautiful than what I was willing to say out loud, I'd be interesting. You pull that off by not saying very much. Lots of short humming sounds and careful head movements, a deep frown at the right moment. Always probing questions. It was very sensitive, very caring to ask probing questions.

And the instant of approach, the suspense of it, was great. You never knew for sure if she had come to play. The odds were good — she probably wasn't there in your candleglow drinking your wine and smoking your dope for sociological survey purposes. But like Yogi said, or maybe it was Casey, it ain't over till it's over. God, it was fun getting there. But then it really was over. She'd usually stay overnight and hold me close to her in the morning, which was when my mind would start spinning into this whole pile of crap about what promises I'd be making if I held her back.

I made guys snort the couple times I tried to describe it. I would have snorted listening to someone else say what I said, but there it was. With any of these gals (except for the dancer from Eugene, who had me going for a while) it didn't take long for the feeling to move from fun and exciting to just exciting to complicated. There were simpler things I could do. Help Mom and Dad with the chores that Dad did before he got sick. Fish Whisky Creek. Head up the coast from Port Douglas with my tent and some paperbacks. Anything I did was simpler.

Mostly I just put my head down and worked at getting as good as I could with a saw. By the end of my first full year after high school I was one of the lead buckers, the guy who's responsible for laying out the lengths on the downed logs so they're cut exactly right for hauling. It was trickier than it sounds, because you wanted to cut out as many side whorls and defects as you could and still get the maximum number of standard lengths out of a tree, and you had to decide fast. I made the most critical cuts myself. It combined a big-muscle dexterity with a wordless geometric thinking. You could do the work dumb and hard or smart and easy.

I liked it. I got good at it. I got cocky enough to let my crew talk me into competing one year. In 1972 I went up to Bounty for the 60th Annual Southern Oregon Timber Carnival and Jamboree, which pulls in logger athletes from everywhere west of the Rockies and a thousand or more spectators. Ray Figuera and I entered the two-man misery whip competition, where each of us took a handle of an eight-foot long straight-blade with massive teeth and jitter-bugged it back and forth as fast as we could through a two-foot log. We came in fifth place, which felt fine. The four pairs ahead of us were guys who looked like members of tribes that might discover fire at any time. I realized the general caliber of competition we were dealing with when I saw Steve lose an event. He scaled to the top of a skinned 75-foot pole, grabbed a flag and slid to the bottom almost three seconds slower than a guy from Alaska, who'd only held the world championship for the event four years running.

What I really came for was the speed bucking event. Two three-foot thick logs, smoothed to uniform size on a plywood lathe, were laid on waist-high sawhorses. Four of us would cut at once, one on each end of each log. The first to drop a disk of wood to the ground won and moved on to the next round. Winning four rounds would get you to the finals. I showed up with five sharp chains and my saw tuned up to screaming perfection.

By the time the first round started I was wound so tight I thought I'd snap. At the sound of the starting pistol, all that juice flowed from my chest to my arms and into my saw, dropping it through the log before the rushing in my head could settle into thoughts. I'd won round one. Round two went just the same way, and I was walking around the edge of the crowd, breathing deeply and clearing my head for the third round, when I saw her. Thirty feet away Holly Burgess was buying a tub of popcorn and a cold drink at one of the food booths.

I'd last seen Holly the summer before on one of her rare visits from Stanford. She didn't like to come home. I rarely went a full week without seeing someone or something that reminded me of her. She still starred in a lot of dreams. She was my yardstick. I couldn't ponder for long what was happening with a particular gal I was seeing, or what I wanted to happen, without thinking of Holly. But it didn't have the weight of yearning; she was a big part of my childhood, like especially fun birthdays or first kisses, that I missed sometimes but knew I couldn't have again.

She didn't see me at first. She handed the drink to a man at her side. His back was towards me, topped by a huge sphere of frizzy blond hair, like a gigantic walking dandelion. He wore a lavender tee-shirt with a tie-dyed design that looked like an exploding star, old jeans cut off at the knees with legs sticking out like two white sticks and Mexican *huaraches*.

Holly smiled at him and then turned her head to look around. She saw me. "Jack!," she said, "I can't believe it! What are you doing here?"

"Well, I live here, sort of. What are *you* doing here?"

"Jack, this is Lyle," she said. He had a thin angular face, smooth and pink except for stubbly patches where a beard and goatee would be. His glasses had gold rims and light blue lenses the size and shape of miniature band-aids. He smiled at me and bobbed his head once, eyes closed like he was realizing how this meeting, as all things, was exactly as it should be.

"We're on our way up to Vancouver Island to visit his brother who does these amazing sculptures, these life-size figures of people interacting with nature," Holly said. "They're so amazing. Lyle does sketches for him. When I told him about Lewis Falls he said we had to stop up here for him to see for himself. For inspiration."

"And are you getting any?" I asked him, lifting my hands to both sides to take in the whole Festival.

"Oh, man," Lyle said. His hair rippled like wind-blown wheat when he shook his head. "It's all here. It's so amazing."

We started walking slowly, Holly in the middle. "So Jack, really, what *are* you doing here?" She laughed when I told her. "No kidding? How amazing! I mean, I knew you could do all this but somehow I didn't think you were *this* into it. Do you have to get going, you know, back to where you have to be?"

"Soon," I said. "I have about fifteen minutes." Then it hit me she might come and watch. She asked more questions. My folks? I told her Mom was the same and Dad wasn't great. That made her want to stop and see him, but she didn't much want to stop in Lewis Falls again on their way out; Lyle and her Dad had eaten breakfast together that morning and she wasn't sure they were ready for more sharing.

As she talked I tried to figure out whether or not I wanted her to watch me in the competition. It would be fine if I won, even if the whole idea of these games was peculiar to her. But to try hard at something she thought was ridiculous in the first place, and then lose.... I didn't need that. When we were on the farthest side of the arena from the bucking platform, with two other competitions taking place between us and where I'd be cutting, I told them I had to go. "Good meeting you, Lyle," I said, reaching out my hand.

He looked at it like a precious gift and then closed both of his hands around it. "Where is it you'll be, Jack?" Holly asked. "We want to watch."

Five minutes later I could feel them behind me as I stepped to the log for my third round. The pistol sounded and immediately I knew it was different this time. What poured through me wasn't concentrated and directed anymore. A little bit of it held back in my head, watching what I looked like as if I were standing behind me. As I moved through the middle of the log, the line of my cut drifted a few degrees to the right. An inch before I finished the lanky older guy cutting the other end of my log stood up straight and lifted his saw in triumph. My adventure was done.

Holly was clapping as I stepped off the platform. "Wow, that was great!" she said. "You were flying through that thing!" Not like before, I wanted to say. Lyle had drifted off. We saw him a few minutes later, mouth open, watching Bill More carve a bear cub out of a four-foot stump with his chain saw. So she and I walked some more.

"If you want to know what I think," I said after she'd told me how well I'd done a couple more times. "I think if you're leaving soon we don't have to talk about cutting logs. I want to know what's up with you." And Lyle.

"Oh, Jack, it's so amazing." She swept a sheath of amber hair with her thumb and hooked it behind her ear. "I have one year left at Stanford, but I don't know if I'll finish or not. There's so much work to do."

"What work?"

All kinds of things, she said. Anything and everything to smash the imperialist war machine that was committing genocide in Southeast Asia. "When the media calls it the 'Vietnam War,' that's Pentagon propaganda. They want us to think we're just fighting this one little evil country, but we're fighting all kinds of people struggling for their freedom, Laos, Cambodia, probably Thailand, too. We'd rather incinerate them all than admit we're wrong."

I looked around as I listened, still walking. In a little pond in the lowest part of the arena, Ray Figuera was losing a log-rolling contest to a leathery little guy in a cowboy hat. With a last yelp and his arms thrashing for balance, Ray hit the water. "Sometimes it's too much to think about," Holly was saying, her eyes on the ground in front of us. "This is our government doing this. The leaders of *my country* are dropping more explosive force in a week on Southeast Asia, on these *peasant* villages of people trying to feed their families, than we dropped on Hiroshima and Nagasaki combined. Richard Nixon and Henry Kissinger are doing it for *us*." She whispered the last word, staring in my eyes. "Does it ever hit you?"

That there was a screwed-up war going on? Maybe she saw Lewis Falls as a peasant village of people trying to feed their families, mindless of the world outside the Range. Six kids we'd graduated with had gone over there; two, Louie Brooks and later Troy Baker, came home in boxes. Did she even know that? "I think about it, sure," I said. "But this is how it always goes, right? Nixon doesn't do anything for us, Holly. Nixon does it for Richard Nixon."

"No! We gave him the planes and the bombs, when he starts dropping them we can't just suck our thumbs! That's the whole thing, Jack. As long as he's president of this quote, *democracy*, unquote, we're responsible. That's what we have to make people see!"

Another round of log-rolling was going on behind her. My eyes wandered towards it for a split second and I wondered if she noticed. She must have. "Well, we get to vote," I said. "That's what the election's for, right?"

"Yes, but it's so frustrating! When you talk to people you think they're *finally* starting to see the truth because you can't fool people forever. Then you hear everyone saying Nixon's going to stomp George McGovern like none of this ever happened! Four more years of this, Jack! Can you even imagine?"

"But Nixon has a secret plan to end the War."

Holly looked at me like I'd just traded our last cow for a handful of magic beans. "Jack? Do you believe Nixon has a secret plan to end the War?"

"No, Holly. I was using a little folk custom that we have up here. We call it humor."

She nodded. "I'm sorry, Jack, but I guess this subject isn't really funny to me."

We started walking again, up towards the chainsaw sculptor and Lyle. "I don't mean to be a complete smartass, Holly," I said when we'd almost reached them. "Just from where I sit it doesn't look like we can do much about it."

She stopped and turned to me. "If I send you some stuff about what's going on now, will you read it?"

"Yes."

"Promise? You'll actually read everything I send you, not just open it up and look at the cover and put it down somewhere?"

"If you send it, I'll read it. I will."

I did. Three weeks later an envelope thick with clippings from *Ramparts* and *The Nation* was in my box and I read every one. They shook me up. It was clearer to me why Holly was bursting to change things. It wasn't clearer how she, or I, could. But I wasn't going to say that when I wrote back. I wouldn't do anything that might damage this new contact.

On my next trip to Port Douglas I found a greeting card with a stylized peace sign in black and silver on the front. I wrote four drafts of a message on scratch paper before I was ready to write on the card. The first two were cute commentaries about the peace sign. It was painful. First I tried humility, something about how me sending a card with that symbol was probably the last thing she'd ever imagined. Not clever enough. The next version went for irony. When I read it over I didn't see how anyone, with the possible exception of me, would have the faintest idea of what it was I was trying to say.

I decided to sleep on which one to send. In the dark of the next morning, my brain still clogged with sleep, I reached for my notepad on the headboard and read them again. OK, I'm Holly. This card comes in the mail from Jack with either of these messages— what do I think? I think he's a sarcastic asshole. I got up and threw both drafts away. Then I left for work almost skipping with relief that I hadn't sent either one off. As I worked that morning, part of my brain was composing, honing in on the right message.

By lunch time I was pretty sure I had what I wanted. I found a flat carpenter's pencil in the glove compartment of the crummy, sharpened it with my pen knife, and captured the words on the paper towel in my lunch box. As soon as I got home that afternoon I popped open a beer and looked at what I'd written. The first sentence was something about how much meaning this simple symbol, an ordinary circle with a few ordinary lines inside, was starting to have in my life. Please. I wrapped the paper towel around a peach pit from lunch and tossed it in the garbage.

In the end I kept it short. I didn't say anything about the symbol. She'd make of it whatever she made of it. I don't remember what I wrote, but I was straight and simple about being glad to see her and hoping it wouldn't be so long until the next time.

She wrote me once more after that, three pages about a march she was in at Golden Gate Park that turned violent. She said it both scared her to death and made her feel they were having an impact. "Just the fact the pigs would do something as amazingly stupid as beat up middle-class white protestors on the streets of San Francisco is a sign that we're really getting somewhere." I'm almost sure I wrote back after that, but I don't know what I said. That's when Dad nosedived.

His emphysema had stabilized. If anything, he started getting around a little better. He didn't have the energy to go back into the woods, but he was putting in about four hours a day at the scaling station and even puttering around the house on little projects for Mom. Then the headaches started. He didn't talk about them. He was constantly grim and grouchy, but it wasn't different enough from normal to worry us. In the evening he'd sit in his old Lazy-boy in the living room in the dark and roar at Mom or me if we were careless enough to turn on a light going through.

I was just beginning to know that we were coming to that moment of reversal when you have to parent your parents no matter what they say about it, when Dad made it easier. We were eating Sunday dinner, a leg of venison I'd brought for Mom to roast, when he dropped his fork and shrieked. The back of his chair hit the carpet with a thump as he pushed it back and staggered from the table, pressing the heels of his hands into both temples with all his might. Mom leaped up, moaning with fright and making two little circles with her hands flat in front of her. I grabbed Dad and held him for the minute it took his screams to soften to groans. "Dad, are you all right?" I asked stupidly.

He nodded, hands still frozen to his skull, elbows pointed out. In a flurry I grabbed a blanket from the sofa to wrap around him and half-carried him to the door. I yelled behind me from the front porch for Mom to call Doc Ford to meet us at the Emergency Room in Grants Pass, squeezed Dad's bulk into the cab of my truck and tore down the hill as fast as I possibly could without losing it on the curves.

Doc Ford was standing by the triple glass doors of the ER when we screeched to the curb. He raised his hand, the doors slid open and two orderlies moved a gurney to the curb. They loaded Dad on it and disappeared inside. "He just about keeled over at the table," I said to Ford. "It's his head and he can't take it. You know him, Doc, he never even complains."

Ford nodded. "Go park," he said, and slipped inside the hospital.

15

DAD HAD A BRAIN TUMOR. IT WAS THE SIZE OF A ROBIN'S EGG, LOCKED tightly in the lobe beneath his right temple. I think Doc Ford had it figured out before the X-rays and the tests. He admitted Dad to the hospital and sedated him enough to sleep. Early the next morning, as Mom and I had just arrived and were shuffling around to find a position around the bed that felt right, Doc Ford strode in, angular and tall. He was the only doctor my family had ever been to. When he nodded at Mom she backed up and gripped the rail at the foot of the bed.

Doc Ford put his hands on the sides of Dad's head with a slight rubbing motion. "Talk." That's the first thing he's said every time I've ever seen him. Not "where does it hurt?" or "how have you been feeling?" Just "talk," and you'd start talking. If you were wandering he'd steer the conversation with a couple of three-word questions until he'd grunt and nod with a force that said he didn't need anymore.

After we took Dad home for the final weeks, Doc Ford came up the hill to see him almost every other day. We had set Dad up in the same extra bedroom I live in now. In the corner where I'm writing we had a set of bullet-shaped oxygen cylinders. One was always next to his bed, fixed to a plastic hose that coiled around and ran up his nostrils. He hated it. Every few minutes Dad swiped at his nose with the heel of his hand and let out a little grunt that by the last days was more of a gurgle.

Late one afternoon Doc Ford came in to check him over. He was putting his stethoscope away when Dad twitched and pawed at the hose. Mom was there as always to take his hands and lower them gently to the blanket, patting them still. I saw Dad unclench a little and let his head drop to one side. "Telling ya, Doc invented 'sdamn thing just to torture me," he said, looking straight at the Doc with blank eyes. "Doc?" It almost sounded like teasing. Dad never teased. I guess dealing with the end takes you all kinds of places you haven't been before. Then Doc Ford did something I doubt *he'd* ever done before. He smiled at Dad. Not a lot, no teeth, but a smile.

The day before the end was a Thursday in August. We sat in the hot early evening watching their little rabbit-eared TV, which Mom had perched on a stack of her cookbooks on Dad's dresser. Richard Nixon's face and stiff torso filled the little screen. His forehead glistened and his jowls vibrated with the slow force of his words.

> "...there is no longer a need for the process to be prolonged. Therefore, I shall resign the presidency effective at noon tomorrow. By taking this action, I hope that I will have hastened the start of that process of healing which is so desperately needed in America. I regret deeply any injuries that may have been done in the course of events that led to this decision. I would say only that if some of my judgments were wrong — and some were wrong — they were made in what I believed at the time to be in the best interest of the nation."

Dad rustled and I turned towards him. "That's a bad man," he said softly. It was the only political opinion I ever heard from him.

Late that night little crags of Dad's cough woke me up in the Lazyboy. Mom had gone off to bed. Dad was looking at me, eyes wide and glassy. I reached out a hand and covered his on the blanket. "Time to tell you," he said, a gravelly whisper. "The Beavers." He swallowed. "They didn't...I didn't..." His face rolled up towards the ceiling as he worked for a breath.

"When you tried out with the Beavers, Pop?"

"Unhhh." He let his head turn back to me. "They didn't want me."

"Oh, Pop, you were a player. No one else from around here even..."

"Mmp-mm." Stronger now, shaking his head to stop me. "Know why?" This would happen his way. "Why, Pop?"

"Didn't hang in." He swallowed and took a breath without moving his gaze. "Put me in the box, threw a good curve. At's all. Watching t'see would I hang in." He shook his head, a bare inch of movement. His eyes were frozen on me, more fiercely than they ever had. "Didn't. I...didn't." He closed his eyes and coughed, fighting to keep his head steady. Then he pulled hard for a breath and opened them again. I lifted his head and helped him sip from a cup of water.

His eyes slipped closed. Mom came in at dawn, handed me a mug of coffee and sat to rock in her chair. An hour later we heard a tap on the screen door, then the soft screech of hinges opening and closing, footsteps across the living room, then a tap on the bedroom door. "Okay," I said. Doc Ford walked in and pulled a stethoscope out of his bag before setting it on the floor. He stepped over to the bed, pulled Dad's sheet back and touched the plastic disc to his chest. He moved it around to three or four spots. He straightened up to check the gauge on the tank and adjusted the valve.

Mom watched every slight move. He knew it. He turned and let his face soften towards her. "Trouble you for a cup of coffee, ma'am?"

"Oh," Mom bounded from her chair. "Yes, I, no trouble, of course!" Her voice trailed back as she started across the living room. "Cream? Sugar? I have a cinnamon roll from yesterday morning, it's not fresh, but I could heat it."

We heard her moving away quickly across the living room. Instead of answering her he spoke to me. "It'll be today."

It was. The three of us sat around Dad through the morning. We had the TV on to Nixon's farewell speech to the White House staff. The volume was too low to hear what he said. All three of us watched him mount the steps of the helicopter on the White House lawn, turn around sharply at the top and fling his arms up in that last desperate defiant salute.

As the hatch closed I looked down at Dad. Doc Ford reached over to him with his stethoscope. I held Dad's hand and searched his face to lock in a memory. It was whiskery, the color of skim milk. Doc Ford straightened up and stepped between Mom and Dad to turn off the oxygen valve. As he backed away he paused at her shoulder, cradling her head for just a moment with his large hand.

16

I PUT MY ENERGY INTO FIGURING WAYS MOM WOULDN'T HAVE TO WORRY about the future. With how little it took to worry her, that was a challenge.

She got total hell scared out of her about a month after Dad died, when these titanic bills started coming in the mail from doctors and labs and the hospital for Dad's care. They amounted to more money than she ever thought about having. I called the Company office and found out their insurance only covered half of Dad's expenses; they took on the full load only when the ailment was caused directly by the job.

I wandered around for most of a week wondering what to do next. It was all I could think about. That Thursday after work I met Steve at the Spot for a pitcher. He was taking off a weekend from OSU football camp and he had a proposal for me on how to spend it. He knew these two stewardesses (that's what they called them then) who shared an apartment in Eugene and didn't have flights until Monday. He'd already told them about me, his rugged chainsaw-packing friend. They'd like to meet me. He watched me try the idea on for a moment, then turned on his bar stool to face Fife Burgess, who sat in his custom niche a few feet away. "Or *you* could go up with me, Fife," he said with the smile. "You could teach all three of us a few tricks, I bet." Fife winked and smiled back.

Steve turned back to me. I said I wasn't in the mood and told him about our bad money surprise. He listened.

The next day when I got home to Mom's after work she was beaming. Mel Raines had called her an hour before to say a mistake had been made, that the Company was picking up the whole tab and she wouldn't have to pay a thing. Then he asked her if there was anything else she needed. I could think of plenty that she needed, but of course she couldn't. The next couple times I saw Mel around town I expected him to find a way to mention what he'd done. I figured if he had any way to make me or anyone else feel indebted he'd use it. He never said a word.

But I was determined that Mom wouldn't be scared like that again. I needed a nest egg that would take care of both of us. The best-paying job in the show is timber-falling, and the next time a faller position opened up I put in the papers for it. The following Monday morning when I got out of my truck the crew boss came over to me to tell me I was a timber faller.

This was it. This was what you shot for from the time you start in the woods, the elite corps, the place for a Few Good Men. There's not much margin for error anywhere in a logging show, but the fallers were the ones who wreaked the bloodiest havoc if they weren't paying attention. When they made you a faller the Company was saying you could handle it. Everyone else in the woods, and pretty soon folks in town, started thinking of you in a different way.

I was ready. There was the money, sure, and the status, but there was another thing, too, something you could say then easier than you can today: cutting down big trees is a gas. I don't know if I can get across what the rush of bringing down those huge honkers is like. There was some blood lust to it, the humming animal sense you get when you're shocked or thrilled. And part of it was about your place in time. I remember moments when I'd be at the edge of the final instant, my bar three-fourths through the tree so that I knew that the weight was about to shift onto the hinge, the wedge-shaped void that I'd already cut out of the other side. I'd pause for a second, the saw still running, knowing that I was about to slice through a toothpick's width of woody fiber that would tip the balance. This tree that had started up from the ground before my great-great-ten-greats-up grandfather was born would be, seconds after I broke that fiber, flat on the ground. I would push the saw forward lightly, watching for the trunk to move.

At first it moves so slowly you think you're imagining it. Then you know you're not, you can definitely see the thin black path that the bar has traveled start to widen as the trunk starts to tip, slowly, then picking up speed until it opens up like a gigantic golden clam with the crackle of breaking fiber, then twisting and ripping itself off the stump and down, hitting ground with a *KrrrrwWWHUMP* that travels all the way through you. Then slowly the rain of debris settles down and the branches on adjoining trees bounce back into place and the quiet is deeper than it was before.

Macho, all right, but there it is. Another part, maybe even bigger for me, was the aiming. This is probably a guy thing. In fact I know it is. If you go out to a playground or a beach, anyplace you can find a little boy and a few stones, he's going to be throwing them. Arm flapping awkwardly as a broken wing, a dead-serious frown on his face, he's throwing stones for the single purpose of seeing what he can hit. If he's any good at it he goes into sports that use balls. For me it was baseball. The fielding was fun and against mellow pitchers so was the hitting, but what really did it was the throwing. Aiming right at a base to throw a runner out, or hitting the cut-off man in the middle of his chest if you were playing the outfield. The most fun of all was pitching, but growing up on the same teams as Steve you didn't get to do much of that.

After balls it was back to stones for me. Most lunch breaks I ever took in the woods ended with a toss. There were variations, but usually two or three of us would scrape around the dirt for little rocks or clods and then stand side by side behind an imaginary line. We'd pick a tree about as big around as your leg and a few truck- lengths away and each throw ten stones at it. Usually three or four out of ten was good enough to collect a pitcher of beer from each of the others. I drank a lot more of other guys' beer than they did mine. If you think it's a game grown men would eventually grow tired of you're wrong.

The same thing goes with hunting, the premier guy thing. Especially bow hunting. I started about twenty years ago when Steve decided he was going to change from rifle to bow hunting. He and Ray Figuera started taking off to Eastern Oregon with Ray's camping trailer to hunt big deer and elk and they invited me along. We'd be out for a week at a time. These were serious guy weeks.

The last time I went was one fall in the late '70s. Ray and Steve and I went after elk up in the Wallowas, the northeast corner of the state. On the third morning this massive bull with a rack like you see over big lodge fireplaces came strolling up a creekbed sniffing for puddles, straight towards where I was crouching behind a boulder. I breathed deeply to slow down my heart, pulled an arrow back carefully, held it, let out my breath and let it fly. I heard a soft whistle in the air, then a mushy *pliff*, then a startled grunt, then the clatter of his hooves on rock as he clambered up through the brush towards the top of the drainage. He carried my arrow in the side of his neck.

I tracked him the rest of the day, led by a string of red dots across miles of rocky hillsides. Just as it was getting dark enough that I was doubting my eyes I found him high up on the ridge, laying in a little cradle of boulders from an old rockslide. His eyes were already getting smoky.

When I finished gutting him it was completely dark. I made dinner from some jerky, a Hershey bar and an orange, cleared an area next to the carcass as well as I could and wrapped myself in the parka and space blanket I was packing. I kept pressed against his side all night long to draw from the last of his warmth.

In the middle of the night it started snowing. I curled into a ball for a couple more hours of half-sleep. As soon as it was light enough to see I stood up and brushed off an inch of snow and tried to rub life back into my arms and legs. I had another Hersheys for breakfast and went to work cutting him into quarters. By mid morning I had three massive chunks of elk bundled as tightly as I could with the plastic and rope I'd been packing, and a fourth wrapped in my space blanket, ready to haul out. I spent another hour digging a shallow pit beneath a pine tree distinct enough to find again. I laid the three meat bundles in the bottom and covered them with dirt and gravel and finally a cairn of small boulders.

It started snowing again as I was digging, and by the time I'd strapped the fourth quarter to the backpack frame and started the trip back to camp it was really coming down. I had a good enough idea of where I was. I had to cross three feeder drainages, down a sidehill each time and up another, before I could drop down to the main stem of the creek. Then I could follow the creek downstream about two miles to the trailhead and our camp.

It was slow going. I'd been lifting some weights and running a few days a week to prepare for the trip, but it wasn't enough. I can't describe how heavy an elk hindquarter gets when you're carrying it up a rocky sideslope, ducking tree limbs, winding around boulders and trying to keep your bearings in a snow storm. At first I had to rest every fifteen minutes, then every ten, always at a waist-high rock that would support the weight of the pack as I stood next to it.

Two hours into the hike I knew it wasn't going to work. I eased myself out of the backpack and took a minute to shake feeling back into my shoulders. I unwrapped the meat and cut off the upper leg up to the haunch and part of the side, maybe one-half of the mass. Then I packed back up and continued on, leaving the two red chunks behind. So when I stumbled back into camp as the steely gray sky was turning dark, I was packing 10 percent, maybe 15 percent, of the elk I'd killed the day before.

That was all the meat we brought home that trip, so we split it three ways. Over that winter a picture of that cache of meat tucked up into the rocks came into my mind a dozen times, usually when I was trying to go to sleep. It was almost June before the Wallowas shed enough snow to get up there. Ray and his cousin and I made the ten-hour drive up together — Steve had something else he said he had to do — with carrying frames and special gear. It took two days to find the cache, and there was no chance we had the wrong place. Patches of dirty plastic and chunks of gristly bone were scattered up and down the slope for a hundred feet. At least we didn't have to dig.

The drive home was quiet. My little aiming fetish had turned nine-tenths of the most magnificent animal I'd ever seen into rotting coyote food. I didn't need to hunt anymore. I remember thinking maybe I'd take up golf some day for my aiming kicks.

There were lots of things I was going to take up someday.

17

IN THE FIRST WEEK OF 1973 BEN TYLER DIED. HE'D BEEN CLEAR THAT HE didn't want a fuss made about it, one of the few times he didn't get his way. Along with just about everybody else in Lewis Falls, I stood on the rolling lawn below his ranch house in a cool February drizzle while the Church choir sang "Amazing Grace" from the porch. Then his widow Betty, who steered so clear of people during Ben's life you forgot he was married, sprinkled a coarse gray powder, supposedly Ben, at the base of a cluster of cedars that separated the house from the corral area. We went inside for vanilla cake and coffee, and it was done.

Ben's duties were sorted out to different people. Some Grants Pass guy we'd never seen became CEO and he hired his banker to run the finance side. All operations, both in the woods and in the Port Douglas and Grants Pass mills, were put in the hands of Mel Raines.

The guy was everywhere at once. At any given time during the season, Lewsco had six to ten logging shows going on at once all over the South Range. Every other day or so Mel would roll right into the center of our show to see for himself how we were doing. He'd hop out of his truck, a Chevy that had all but two feet chopped off its bed and tires so big they raised the running board up to his waist, and strut around like some field commander trying to impress General Patton. He'd pull a steel tape off his belt and run it down a bucked log to check the length. He'd look to see that the big side limbs were cut flush to the trunk, so there wouldn't be any knobs to keep the logs from nestling tight on the truck. He'd tell us to move piles of slash from here to over there. Sometimes he'd take a hand-axe and blaze a little patch on a tree that hadn't been marked for cutting, telling us to take that one, too. He never slowed down to discuss anything and he almost never asked questions. It was like he thought he was personally doing all the logging himself and we were just his fingers.

The guys didn't like it. Some of them had grown up in the woods with Mel and had a little trouble with how he wore his new rank. After one of his visits they gave him a new nickname. He'd just finished raking Marv Howard over the coals about God knows what and then roared off through the trees towards the highway and some other un-suspecting crew. "That guy," Marv said after the turbo-charged roar of the stumpy truck faded in the distance, "has a stick so far up his ass he's choking on it." For a long time after that nobody called him Mel except to his face. He was the Popsicle.

The first time Mel showed a flicker of knowledge I existed was in the Spot one night. It was exactly a week after a Saturday night when I'd gone a pitcher, maybe two, over my usual and started leaking at the mouth. I got onto my rotting Wallowa elk story, which I confess I told a few times back then. I guess a story about swearing off of hunting hit the level of maverick thinking I was trying to style, distinctive but not too wild. I liked to spice the story with some word-pictures I can skip here, images of what must have happened to that meat as it waited for me to return, the maggots and spring thaw turning it to an oozing pudding, that kind of thing.

At some point I must have made a little leap to the subject of trees. The link was probably natural moisture. I was starting to have this thing out in the woods about the moisture in the green trees I was cutting. As you're cutting down a green healthy tree you sometimes feel a light spray come out of it, a mist where your forearms come out of your gloves that seems especially cool in the little pocket of hot air that the saw creates. If you take off a glove and run your hand across the fresh cut of a log just after it hits the ground it can feel as wet as a damp towel. Sometimes you'll actually see tiny beads glistening with the slivers of sun that make it through the overhead branches.

Whatever it was I said that night, it bounced back on me a week later when I walked into the Spot after dinner and saw Mel and Steve sitting at a table near Fife's nook in the bar. That was rare. Steve would some-times come in for a couple of beers, and so would Mel occasionally, usually with a silver hip flask he'd set next to his pitcher, but you al-most never saw them together. Ray Swerdlow (not to be confused with Ray Figuera; for some reason Lewis Falls is lousy with Rays) was sitting one table over, trying to get Mel interested in a conversation. When I walked in, Ray turned and squinted at me, taking a few seconds to dial in who I was.

"WELLL, look who's here," Ray said, glancing at Mel for attention. "It's Ballet Boy!" I sat down next to Fife as Ray cackled and pulled a thought together. "Yeah, the tree of life boy," he said. "Hey, Double-B, tell Mel about the tree of life like you did us the other night."

With my back to him I lifted an index finger to Sam to get a Pabst. "Come on," said Ray, "you know. How you sometimes think you're cutting the tree of life and sucking out its life force, shit like that? How you can feel, like, its *soul* spray out all over you?" A couple snickers came up, Ray's loudest.

"Junior?" It was Mel's voice, thicker than in the woods. He'd had a few, too. "Is that what you said?"

I swivelled around on my stool to face him. "No," I said. Except for Willie Nelson soft on the jukebox, it was quiet. I knew some of the guys around us must have been there the week before for my little sermon. They wanted to hear what I'd say now. "I didn't say they had souls spraying out all over the place," and I was sure I hadn't. Otherwise Ray would have been jumping up and down to argue, and he was just sitting there listening. Everybody was listening. "What I said was there are times when you're cutting a green tree in the spring when it's juicy when it feels a little strange."

Mel looked at me. He had a little water glass with an inch of whisky in it. He lifted it and swallowed, put it down and lifted a mug of beer. "Why?" he asked.

"Why does it feel strange?"

"Yeah. Why does it feel strange, Junior?"

I looked to my left for a moment to think. Fife Burgess was staring at me with watery eyes and the concentration of Moses' best disciple on the Red Sea beach. I turned back to Mel. "Because it's not their time."

"Because they're green," Mel said calmly.

"Right," I said. "You look at the outer rings on some of those guys when they're down, they can have a half-inch of mass, and you know their best years would've been ahead of them if we left 'em alone."

Mel carefully poured another inch from his flask into the little glass and refilled his beer mug from the pitcher before he answered. "So if we left all them big bursting juicy trees alone," he really was drunk, "they'd just stay there all juicy and green until they died of old age. Maybe they'd just go to sleep one night and not wake up the next morning?" Ray laughed, one loud guffaw that broke off when he realized everyone else was quiet. "What do you think happens to those trees in a big fire, Junior?"

"Some die. Some get scorched and heal over and make it."

"Exactly," Mel said. "Some die. Just like some die when we go in with a show. What nature does, we're doing, just with different tools is all. Result's the same, except when we do it folks like you and me and our old pal Ray get to make a living. And somewhere somebody we never see gets a house to live in." He took a sip of whisky. "Junior," his voice a little tighter and higher now, "what happens after you cut that tree?" I wondered what he wanted to hear. "Tell him, Champ," he said, turning to Steve, who'd been quietly rocking his chair back and forth, massaging his beer mug with both thumbs. "What do we do after we cut?"

"We plant," Steve said, looking at Mel for a second, then back to his mug.

"When you cut a tree, Junior, we plant three to take its place," Mel said, like I'd never heard of Lewsco before. "Sometimes five. Then we come back in a few years and see which ones are doing best and cull out the competition. And you know what we're planting?" Of course I did. I'd planted plenty of them myself. But he wasn't really asking. "We're planting the strongest, fastest-growing, bug-resistingest fir trees that ever got root in the Earth. Ever. They're super-trees. While you and me're beating our meat we got guys smarter than we'll ever be mixing the best part of one seed with the best part of the other to make seedlings that'll grow twice as fast as anything you cut down." That was a stretch towards nonsense and everyone in the room knew it. I even felt a little rustle from Fife at my elbow. But no one stopped Mel when he was rolling.... "You want to come down to the nursery one day, I'll show you yourself. The smart guys, they know dogshit about anything but trees, but about trees you wouldn't believe it. Junior, how much did you cut yesterday?"

"Well, we've been at Rocky Top this week. It's a little skinny." I didn't know what kind of numbers Mel expected.

"I know where you were. What'd you cut?"

I thought about it. "He cut some big farts," Ray snickered.

"Oh, maybe ten fir, some cedar, a little scatter of pine," I said.

"Big ones?" Mel asked.

"The fir were, and a couple of the cedar."

Mel swallowed from one glass and gulped from the other. "Well, I'm telling you this: if you live a good long healthy life, stay out from under dropping wood and take care of yourself, you go up to Rocky Top the day before you die and you'll see trees as big as the ones you cut down yesterday. Or damn near. And they'll all be fir, too, none of them sorry weeds getting in the way."

He picked up his flask and added half an inch to the water glass. I felt Fife's hand on my sleeve and looked at him. "Jackie?" he said.

I gave a little nod to Sam, who was listening close by. He brought Fife a Blitz and a V-8 and as he set them down he hopped into the conversation. "All fir, Mel? You want it all in fir? Like a big cornfield, nice neat rows any direction you look, but fir trees instead?"

"Damn right," Mel said. "That's where the growth is and where the growth is, that's where the money is. We don't have business growing anything but fir on our lands."

"Mmm," said Sam, from behind my shoulder. "Kind of like you know how to do it better than God? You and the smart boys down at the nursery?"

As quiet as it was before it got quieter. Mel snorted and looked around dramatically. "Damn," he said. "I thought I was coming into the Spot for a beer. I must have missed a turn and ended up at church instead. Listen, Reverend," he was shaking an index finger at Sam now, his elbow fixed to the table, "You want the junk species, there's plenty of places for that. That's what national forests are for. God's not in the timber business. We are."

"Fuckin' ay," said Ray.

"And I'll tell you something else," Mel said. "You talk to guys who know, they'll tell you, you really want to see trees come back then you don't dick around like we been doing, taking a few here, a few there and be sure you don't step on the grass while you do it. You *do the cut*. You get in, you cut, you get out, and then you plant the sonofabitch. You put in the kind of seedlings we been raising, you get a good cage on 'em for the first couple years, they don't make 'em compete with weed-trees for food and water, and you can *find* the damn things to tend to 'em, which is more than you can say when you scatter 'em all over the woods, the way we been doing. We're the only ones in the state who still cut our lands like we do, like we're afraid we'll break something."

Sam had made a little distance between him and Mel, fussing with the taps down towards the end of the bar. His voice still sounded clear. "I've seen the way the others cut, Mel, and I didn't see anything to brag about. You drive across the range from the valley to the coast anywhere north of here and most of it looks like World War III, especially near the Coast."

"That's *today*!" Mel slapped the table and Steve leaned forward as if he were getting ready to catch something. "That's what it looks like today. There's your problem! People only thinking about what it looks like today! Well, let me tell you something: the way we cut now, blade in a road, take a few trees, leave it alone for ten years then come back and cut in another road, you think that's better for trees than clearcutting? That's bullshit." Steve pulled in a little closer, gripping the edge of the table with both hands. "You know what that gets you in fifty years? A bunch of stunted crap that gets beat up with every show till it won't grow anymore. Now, you cut a place *right*, you clear it good and plant it right and give it what it needs, then you leave it alone for fifty years, then you know what you get? You get as many big trees as you started with, more, and 99 percent of the people if they walk through it'll say it's a 'virgin forest'." He made fun of the term with a prissy nasal voice.

"And then you can cut them all down again," I said.

Mel squinted at me as if I'd just snuck into the place "That's the point of the exercise, Junior. Cutting trees." He turned his flask upside down over the glass and shook out the last trickle. He swayed a little, but the drip hit the center of the glass. Then he looked back at me, squinting with one eyebrow high. "They tell me you're pretty smart, Junior. 'At you know what you're doing out there. Seems to me there's a couple things you don't know. Like business. Like how it works so you get a paycheck. Like silviculture and tree genetics, like fucking science. I'm talking about *science*, Junior, what're you talking about? Black magic? Voodoo? Tree spirits that spit on you when you cut 'em?"

"I don't think Jack's talking about that, Dad." Steve said softly. "I think maybe we..."

"Yeah, well, some of 'em do. I heard 'em talk about how trees start screaming when you cut 'em. 'AAOOOOEEEE!!!'" He sounded like a tortured wolf. Ray laughed, this time not alone, and Mel went on. "See 'em on TV, about they're offended by clear-cuts. Shit. They're *offended*. Like we're supposed t'get their permission. Like they know their ass from fat meat. If they did, so what, it ain't their forest, it's ours. They want to bow down and kiss trees, let 'em get their own. We only been cutting these woods a hundred fifty years and we're supposed to say 'Mother May I' before we take a crap?"

"Fuckin ay!" said Ray.

Mel either went blank or realized how sloppy he was getting because he stopped there. He finished his beer and let Steve help him to his feet. Steve made it look like he was barely helping at all. As the door closed behind them I wondered if Mel was collapsing in Steve's arms on the other side.

"AAAOOOOOEEEEE!" Ray screamed, and laughed again.

18

THAT'S THE ONLY TIME I EVER SAW MEL GO OFF LIKE THAT. HE KEPT HIS private habits private, and it wasn't long before he was a big wheel in Southern Oregon.

If the timber industry had set out to pick a spokesman they would have picked somebody more polished than Mel, probably somebody predictable like the hacks that the big nationals like Mississippi Pacific hired. Mel often said more than he should, so he's who the press would call for a quote. If they didn't call him for a while, Mel would call them, or send a guest opinion column to the papers. They always printed him. When everybody started getting fired up about some companies (not Lewsco) exporting raw logs to Japan while millworkers here were losing jobs, Mel was good for a column in the other direction:

> Start telling American companies that they can only accept certain customers for what they raise themselves on their own lands and you start down the very same road that such countries as Russia, China and Cuba have now traveled down to a destination of tyranny and death.

The good news was he didn't come see us in the woods as much.

By 1980 enough people were worrying about the forests to worry politicians. A state senator from Portland introduced an Oregon Forest Standards Bill that aimed to limit the kind of logging you could do on steep slopes and near rivers and creeks. Mel went up to Salem and met with every legislator who'd see him. There was a picture of him on the front page of the Port Douglas paper testifying in front of some big committee. His mouth is wide open and his arms are stretched dramatically to both sides. Whatever he was saying worked. The committee killed the bill right there.

Mel knew that wasn't the end of it. As soon as the bill died, he was back in the woods. More trees than ever before were marked for cutting. I'd been falling for seven seasons by then and the change wasn't hard to see. I needed a way out, and I had an idea what it was.

It started when I dropped by Mom's one morning while she and Holly's mom Isabel were having coffee. Mom asked if I'd be willing to take Isabel down the hill to Flaming Eddie's in my truck so she could shop his Red Hot Washer-Drier Sale, because her old drier had quit for good the day before. Flaming Eddie was never not having a Red Hot sale, but I just asked her if I could come over and look at her old machine first.

I hadn't been in Holly's old place for a long time. Back in the service porch I popped a couple of screws and took a footplate off the front of the drier. A black hard-rubber belt with frayed edges was lying tangled in plain slight. I took about a minute to figure out that it was supposed to fit on the little electric motor and turn the big drum that held the clothes. That afternoon I drove down to Port Douglas and bought a new belt for $3.95, and that night Mrs. Burgess was drying clothes again. I went home with about three pounds of chocolate chip cookies.

She'd been within a whisker of forking $200 over to Flaming Eddie for a new machine. It got me wondering how many other people were buying appliances they couldn't afford when they all they needed was the right $4 part. Those big white boxes had so much material and parts and labor in them, and every time they had a hiccup we were as likely as not to throw them into a hole in the ground. It was stupid.

That fall I went to college for the first time, driving down the hill after work to SCCC to take classes in small engine repair and mechanics. It was a killer for about ten weeks, getting back home about 11 p.m., studying until about 1 a.m. when my eyes would no longer stay open, getting up at 5, working a full day and then heading down the hill again. But when the woods in November it was great. I added a class in architectural drafting without knowing why, and it got to where I enjoyed driving down every day.

This was 1982. Port Douglas wasn't the same town I first saw in the '50s when Mom would take me to the beach a couple times each summer. Back then it really had been a mill and fishing village, rustic and simple the way it pretends to be for tourists today. The nets and glass floats that you see today draped along the inside of the windows in the spendy dockside restaurants were out in the water catching fish back then.

The change came in the '60s. The magazines and newspaper articles were full of Haight-Ashbury and flower power back then. What they didn't mention was the offshoot of hippies trying to get away from drugs stronger than marijuana and back to basics. They fanned out from San Francisco, mostly to the north. Northern California absorbed most of them, but some crossed into Oregon to settle logged-off hillsides and a few pristine pieces in the little folds and creases of the South Range. They picked up their mail and did what little business they had to do in Port Douglas.

They weren't welcome. We used to hear all kinds of stories. One that actually happened came to be known as the Great PD Chainsaw Massacre. It took place in a bar just south of town where Highway 101 splits into two one-way streets. The simplest surviving version of the story says that four longhairs, three men and a woman who'd been picking up food and building supplies, decided to make a last stop there before heading home. Just as they pulled into the parking lot in an old panel truck with lumber strapped on top, so did a Ford crummy with a crew that had been cutting up on the California line. They'd already polished off three six-packs on the way down the hill.

Everyone went in and sat down, and within five minutes the loggers were on the longhairs' case. Without looking up the longhairs started hurrying their beers to make a quick exit. A couple of the loggers walked over to see if they could get a rise. They couldn't, the story goes, until one of the loggers started handling the woman. Then things went nuts. Sitting next to the woman was her old man, a massive red-bearded guy who turned out to be a retired Hell's Angel. Apparently he'd pent up some energy, because he started cracking heads like some kind of comic book super-hero. The loggers scattered and a minute later walked back in with three chainsaws.

From that point on you can use your imagination. I had dreams about it for years. In the end the ex-Angel and one of his friends died, another lost an arm, the woman was seriously messed up, and their commune closed down and disappeared. Three loggers and a bystander went to the hospital, and four of the guys did jail time, two of them for a serious stretch. The bar closed down until it was bulldozed a few years later. A Wendy's stands on the spot today.

That fight cleared the air. Port Douglas didn't start throwing parades with high school marching bands for the incoming longhairs, but space was slowly made for them. The first definite sign they were here to stay was the opening of PDEC — "PEA-deck," is how people say it — the Port Douglas Earth Cooperative.

People from one of the South Coast's first communes opened PDEC in 1969 as an outlet for the vegetables from their huge garden. It started in a tiny abandoned gas station across the highway from where the chainsaw massacre took place. As people gave more thought to what they were eating, PDEC grew across the pavement, over the islands where the old pumps had been and almost out to the sidewalk. A new annex popped up every few years with no thought given to the sum of the parts. By the mid-'80s the whole thing looked like a cluster of blocks laid down by a disturbed baby giant.

Its main business was still selling food, organic produce and bulk grains, powders, cereals, nuts, herbs, oils, seeds, extracts, dried fruits, teas, potions and spices, natural yogurts, cheeses, ice creams and all kinds of good-health imitations of bad-health foods. The expansions over the years made room for shelves and shelves of vitamins and natural remedies, and later natural-metal kitchenware and natural-fibre clothes.

There was some flack about PDEC when it started. The sheriff's deputy made it part of his town patrol, and for a while a couple of funny-looking guys (one, and this is true, wearing bell-bottom pants and a Nehru jacket) came in regularly to have a look at the bulk herbs and spices. That all went away. For one reason or another, people who'd lived their whole lives on the South Coast started coming into shop until PDEC melted into what Port Douglas is.

It never got exactly mainstream. The bulletin board that spreads across half a wall was covered with flyers on Kundalini Yoga classes, notices for lectures on logging's decimation of the ozone layer, and cards offering up the fifth bedroom of a Victorian house one block from the beach, dogs ok but power trips not. None of which drew a glance from the wives of Lewsco millworkers who were there to grind their own fresh peanut butter and dip into the barrel of whole-grain pancake and waffle mix. PDEC was the South Coast's New Age cultural center, but over the years the hang-ups and dividing lines blurred so that no one thought that much about it. People just went there to shop. And on the way out they usually stopped to touch Beauregard.

Beauregard was a bronze pelican, perfectly real in size, shape and feathered detail. He came to the South Coast with a notorious Sausalito artist who gave it all up and bought a nearly sheer cliff over the beach north of Port Douglas. She dynamited a cabin-sized notch out of the rock and closed it in with bronze and glass to look at 180 degrees of water. The only places people saw her were the bank, the post office and PDEC. Nobody at PDEC recalls talking to her, but early one spring morning when the crew arrived to open up, Beauregard was waiting for them. After trying him out here and there around the store they eventually bolted him to a wooden platform just inside the main entrance, the first thing you see when you enter and the last when you leave. I don't know how it started, but the custom was to rub Beauregard's beak as you leave for good luck out in the world. There was enough room on his platform for people with two bags of groceries to set one down so they can do that. Most did.

About the time I started at SCCC, a little juice and sandwich bar opened up in a corner of PDEC. It had three wooden booths alongside a bank of windows and some small round tables on a covered porch just outside. As soon as the woods closed that first year and I had some time, I got in the habit of going down the hill around noon and hanging out at the juice bar until classes started. I'd have a bowl of soup or a brown muffin thick with chunks of fruit and nuts, and a mug of the heaviest, most coffee-like tea they could brew, and camp out with my homework. If I finished it I'd pull a book from the shelves that lined the top half of one wall, a collection of stuff that people just brought in and left because they thought people should read it. That's where I read all of Baba Ram Dass. I remember you had to turn *Be Here Now* upside down or sideways to read some of the hemp-brown pages, how the reading of them turned things upside down and sideways:

> The Buddhists say: cut out all this middle stuff! They say: don't get hung up on all these different desire trips. Just go beyond it all.
>
> Buddha's 4 Noble Truths are very straightforward and very simple. The first one concerns the fact that life always has in it the element of unfulfillment: call it suffering**birth**old age**sickness**not getting what you want**getting what you don't want**even getting what you want in this physical world is going to be suffering because:
> YOU'RE GOING TO LOSE IT!
> IT'S ALWAYS IN TIME!
> Anything that is in time is going to pass away.
> LAY NOT UP YOUR TREASURES WHERE MOTH AND RUST DOTH CORRUPT. That's the trap of time *** As long as you want anything in time it's going to pass because TIME PASSES.

Sometimes I'd look up from my book and muffin, out the window into a usually gray Port Douglas afternoon. Out there, I'd think, people are fishing, fixing cars, making plywood, installing carpets, drilling people's teeth, paving roads. They're pushing the world forward. In here I'm reading about the pursuit of nothingness. Can that be right? The question never went away completely, but after a while it didn't seem very interesting.

19

I WAS RIGHT ABOUT MEL. HE WASN'T ABOUT TO GET SMUG ABOUT A ONE-time victory up at the Legislature. As more and more Californians without ties to the timber industry moved into the state, the pressure to tighten up on logging was building.

I saw where this was heading early in the 1982 season when I was assigned to a show on Scotch Creek, a tributary of Whiskey about three miles above where Whiskey flows into the Lewis. A fresh road had been cut for us along the side hill about 100 yards above the creek. Scotch isn't an especially rugged canyon. The slope from the creek up to the new road was about half as steep as an average flight of stairs. It hadn't been cut since the '30s some time, so it was beautifully covered in Doug fir and cedar. About four trees out of five had a blue blaze of paint on them, which meant that our job was to all but mow the place clean, the whole damn slope, all the way down to the creek bed. It would be a heavier cut than I could remember us doing on *flat* ground, sites that were nowhere near live streams.

While the rest of the crew was still unpacking gear I drove back to town. I went to the Company maintenance yard out behind the high school, where an old converted warehouse had been cut up into Lewsco office space. Steve was in charge of the place as the Lewis Falls field manager, same as Mel had been years before. I walked past his secretary and straight to his desk and told him what I'd seen. Steve frowned. "That doesn't sound right," he said.

"No shit," I said. I'm not sure we meant the same thing.

"Let me call Dad." He reached for the phone. By this time Mel had drifted up into some vague place in the corporate hierarchy. We never saw him out in the woods and he didn't turn up in Lewis Falls more than once a week or so. I don't know exactly how much juice he had in the Company — the whole picture of who called the shots got hazy after Ben died — but it was a lot. Once I asked Steve exactly what Mel's job was and he said he wasn't sure.

I waited as Steve dialed three different numbers without finding Mel. "Tell you what," he finally said. "You don't want to be wasting time around here when you could be out there making twice the money you deserve." He opened a loose-leaf notebook with operations logs in it and found another show for me to work a mile off the highway towards Grants Pass. He also said he'd get back to me as soon as he found out what the story was on Scotch Creek.

I let three days go by and finally called him on Friday; he was sorry, things had gotten crazy at the office, he was going to call me for sure on Monday. And no, there was no mistake on Scotch Creek. The plan for the summer was "intensive management" up there and on the other headwater creeks of the Lewis.

"Nice *phrase*, Steve," I said. "Have you been up there yourself to check it out?"

"Yeah, I drove up there yesterday," he said.

"Yeah, so was it 'intense' enough for you?"

I heard him shuffling papers on his desk. "Well, I know what you mean. It's a serious cut to take out in one shot, no question about it."

"A 'serious cut'? Steve, you're whacking the holy shit out of that creek. *Scotch* Creek, Steve, for crying out loud, and Whiskey. How many times have we fished in there, you suppose? There were summers we slept more nights up there than we did in our beds. What do you think it'll be like up there after it's clearcut and pounded by a winter of rain?"

"Nobody's clearcutting it, Jack."

"Oh, man, give me a break. Did you just say you went up there?"

"I already said it was a heavy cut, right? But we'll leave some breeders and as soon as it's done we'll be in there planting. Dad said to plant double on creekside slopes to make sure it takes."

"Oh, yeah, I forgot, the Super Seedlings. Ta-te-te-DAAH! With their super little root structures that can hold up whole hillsides in place like magic. This time next year, Steve, those sprouts'll be lining the beach in Port Douglas, and those hillsides will be gone. You know those slopes'll go after that kind of cut, Steve, you *know* it, and you know what it'll do to the fish, I don't care how many trees you put in the ground."

"I don't know that, Jack, and neither do you. We've never done this before."

"That's right! Of course we haven't! That's because it's stupid! We don't have to do it, and if we do we can kiss off that drainage for fish *and* for more wood, probably for keeps. At least for as long as you and I are around." I took a breath and lowered my voice. "Steve, I can't believe I'm hearing what I'm hearing you tell me."

The pause was long enough for me to start wondering if he was still there. "I'm not gonna bullshit you, Jack," he finally said. "Things are changing. It used to be we controlled things out there. We cut where we wanted to cut, how we wanted to cut. I wish it were still like that, but it's not. Hey, can you hang on a minute? Thanks." He was back after a short pause. "Hey, man, somebody just came in I have to talk to. I'll get back to you soon on this, okay? I will, Jack." With a click he was gone.

He didn't call back. Two days later, though, I thought of what he said, how we don't control things anymore, as I read an interview in the *Oregonian*. It was with a University of Oregon biologist who was likely to chair the Senate Water and Natural Resources Committee in the next legislature. He said the evidence that streamside logging was hammering coastal salmon runs was too solid to ignore, and that his number one priority would be to pass an Oregon Forest Standards Act to protect riparian zones around the state. Yes, he realized that an OFSA proposal had gone down in flames the session before, but he was sure public opinion had turned the corner since then. He said the days of logging the edges of salmon- and steelhead-bearing streams in Oregon were over.

Not quite they weren't. I borrowed a friend's military jeep and spent the weekend driving up little drainages all around Lewis Falls. Most of them had fresh roads cut right to the edge, and sometimes across, small creeks that you could only reach on foot the year before. And wherever you looked, far more trees had blue paint blazes than didn't. Mel was going to win this argument one way or another. If Lewsco ever stood for something that the other companies didn't, that day was gone.

I called the Lewsco office to tell them not to expect me at work for the rest of the week. I headed to the Coast and turned north, making camp in little coves between the state parks, notches in the bluffs that tourists hadn't found. Watching the waves break during the day and the stars at night, I missed Holly more fiercely than I had in years. I thought about calling her every day. At a little general store on the highway out of Coos Bay I actually got into the phone booth to call her mom (the phone number I had for Holly was way out of date), but I stopped before dropping the coins. I didn't need for my first words to Holly in seven years to sound like a whine.

I turned around and headed back south. I hit Port Douglas early on a gorgeous wind-scoured Saturday afternoon and went to PDEC for lunch. Waiting for my sandwich I pulled Ram Dass off the shelf and looked for a passage I dimly remembered.

> I am a doctor...a student...a drop-out...ALL THE SAME GAME. Don't let that offend you, but the external world is all the same. It's all the EXTERNAL WORLD! People often say to me "I would really like to do Sadhana but...I'm a teacher now. If only I could finish being a teacher, I could do Sadhana." **BALONEY!** You're either doing Sadhana or you're not. Sadhana is a full time thing that you do because there is nothing else to do. You do it whether you're teaching, or sitting in a monastery, whether you're lying in bed, going to the toilet, making love, eating, EVERYTHING is part of waking up. Everything is done without attachment. Another way of saying it is: it's all done as consecrated action.
> It's all sacred.

I rolled back into Lewis Falls late that night. On Monday morning I went to the Company office and handed the receptionist a note that said

> Due to personal reasons, I will no longer be able to work as an employee of the Lewis Corporation. This change will take place immediately.
> I want to express my thanks to the Company for the opportunities and kindnesses it has extended to my family.
> Sincerely,
> John Adams Gilliam, Junior

On Wednesday morning I moved out of Mom's house. She protested less than I expected her to. I got the place I still technically rent today, the last house on the left as you leave town on the way to Bounty. When I was growing up Dougy Ferrin's family lived in it. His Dad was lead mechanic for years and the company built a big metal garage in the backyard so he could work on heavy vehicles at night. Dougy didn't want the place when his Mom died and his Dad moved down the hill, so I put in to take over the lease because the garage was perfect for my shop. I could fit almost fifty appliances in there at a time, and after they were beyond hope I could store them to the side under a lean-to roof where they'd be handy to cannibalize parts.

I liked the house, too. It was kind of small but neat as a pin after thirty years of Mrs. Ferrin's fussy care. There were even raised garden beds off the kitchen side of the house that I did a halfway decent job of keeping up. I'd like to move back there but I don't know how likely that is. The doors would all have to be ripped out and widened, and it'd need a whole new kitchen and bathroom. Maybe the Company would do it all on their dime if I asked. Right. Just as likely somebody over there is wondering where my rent check is this month.

20

IF YOU ASKED ME THEN IF I'D EVER GO BACK TO LOGGING I WOULD HAVE said no. Within three months word-of-mouth from pleased appliance customers kept me as busy as I wanted to be. I didn't make quite as much money working a full year as I used to make in seven months in the woods. But I didn't feel like recycled dog meat at the end of the day, and I had direct contact with customers who were tickled as they could be with what I did.

It also gave me the luxury of watching the changes overtaking Lewsco from a distance. Most of the '80s were a roller coaster of rumors in Lewis Falls. Unlike the four generations before them, Lewsco workers didn't know what to expect when they started a new season. The plunder of the creekside lands turned out to be a one-year spike on Lewsco's chart to beat the logging restrictions that the Legislature did indeed lay down in the 1983 Oregon Forest Standards Act. After that the Company slipped back to a cutting regime that was both heavier than anything Dad ever saw and timid compared to the nationals like Mississippi Pacific.

But the days were gone that Lewsco could be just a nice little operation in the lower lefthand corner of Oregon. Ronald Reagan was busily unshackling Big Business from regulation and most of its taxes so that all kinds of great stuff would trickle down on the rest of us. Except what they did was search the landscape like hyenas looking for weaker companies to dismember, ripping out valuable organs and leaving the rest for buzzards.

The first signs of the carnage ahead for us showed up on the FUNNIES. Sam started pinning up *Wall Street Journal* clippings about how the big money guys were salivating at the prospect of getting their hands on certain "underdeveloped' natural resource companies. Sam circled the Company's name in red on a 1986 *Journal* article:

> Another object of investor speculation is the Lewis Corporation, owner of more than 250,000 acres of prime timberland in Southwestern Oregon and three sawmills that produce plywood and dimensional lumber. It was maintained in continuous family ownership by direct descendants of fabled explorer Meriwether Lewis until 1966, when limited blocks of shares were made available to company employees. Ownership has since diffused to an extent that could prove problematic to corporate suitors.
>
> "Whoever wants to land this company has their work cut out for them," says Reed-McDonald analyst Jeffrey Foote. "But the game's probably worth the candle. Lewsco's raw asset inventory exceeds book value as much or more than anyone's."

At the time this was new to me but it seemed pretty simple. These guys were talking about titanic versions of the Get Rich in Real Estate With No Money Down game that had seminars in a Grants Pass motel every few months. It was about collateral and cash. The collateral they could offer — the market value of the standing timber that would be theirs the minute the deal closed — was worth at least twice the cash they needed, which was the price of a Lewsco share times the number of shares that Ben created over the past twenty years, plus a big enough premium to get normally Company-loyal people in a selling mood. Or at least enough of them to account for 51 percent of the shares. It was kind of like borrowing $50,000 to buy a house that was wall-papered with 100,000 one dollar bills.

The second article Sam pinned up had a name in it: James Nielsen. Nielsen had climbed to the top rungs of Shell Oil when he decided to go out on his own about the time Ronald Reagan was running for President. He pulled together three little companies around his hometown of Tulsa to start Oklahoma Oil. After that he went on an acquisitions tear that no modern Justice Department before Reagan would have tolerated. By the end of Reagan's first term, the name Oklahoma Oil, OO, didn't begin to describe what the company really did. OO's logo was on golf resorts, passenger jetliners, movie credits, food labels (in tiny form —I guess you don't market canned beans and peaches with images of Oklahoma crude), vacuum cleaners, outboard motors, denim pants and flannel shirts and, still, the signs above 3000 gas stations west of the Mississippi.

Soon all the suspicions and fear that Lewis Falls had about the future had a name: James Nielsen. James Nielsen was going to buy the whole mountain for his empire, kick us out of our homes or triple the rent, fill the Falls with concrete and build an airstrip on it, make us all wear uniforms with OO stamped on them. You wondered if in the privacy of their homes exasperated parents were telling their children that James Nielsen would get them if they didn't behave.

The man kept himself out of the limelight. The only picture of him I ever saw was in a framed clipping that Steve showed me on the wall of his office at the maintenance yard, a *Washington Post* photo of Ronald Reagan sitting at a table on the White House lawn. The caption says he's signing the Energy Security Act, a package of nice tax breaks that were supposed to get the oil companies eager to fatten reserves that government could tap in case of emergencies. Standing over Reagan's right shoulder, looking straight down at the growing signature with his hands folded over his crotch, is James Nielsen. Six onlookers to Nielsen's left, standing where he's almost sliced by the edge of the photo, is the reason it's hanging where it does: Mel Raines. There are fifteen people in the picture, and Mel's the only one looking straight into the camera. He's smiling.

IT TOOK A LONG TIME FOR THE RUMORS TO TURN INTO SOMETHING. THE FUNNIES had a new clipping every few weeks, and once in a while the Grants Pass TV station ran a news story that wasn't much more than Mel or some other Company bigshot flying off to a meeting somewhere. Nothing actually changed, but now when conversation died of its own weight at the Spot, we had a ready topic to fall back on.

Scholarly opinion at the Spot ran along two lines. The leading one said no fat cat from the East, meaning the region that starts on the other side of the Idaho line, is going to stroll in here and have his way with our town. Sam's summary of this position was fuck him if he can't take a joke. People who saw it that way split into two sub-camps on strategy. One said we needed heavier cuts to get more logs out of the woods, more lumber out of the mills and more cash in our pockets so Lewsco wouldn't look so ripe for the picking (we were all starting to get the drift of this thing; it got to where when someone used the term "LBO," right there at the bar of Sam's Spot tavern in downtown Lewis Falls, Oregon, nobody asked what it meant). To others that sounded panicky. Sam pins up some bogus stories from these half-assed experts, and you're ready to cut everything in sight to keep somebody else from doing it? Peter Thomas compared it one night to the Vietnam tactic of destroying a village in order to save it, which immediately yanked the conversation into a whole different spat. The point, though, was to have a little faith in your friends and neighbors to do the right thing; no matter what kind of genius James Nielsen is, he still has to talk people owning 51 percent of the shares into selling to him, people who grew up on and around this range, and that won't happen.

Then there was the whole other point of view, which also relied on trusting Lewsco shareholders. Trusting them to keep an open mind and do what's smart. If James Nielsen thinks the Company's worth a lot more than we've been paying for it, let's see what he means by a lot. Nobody's saying we have to sell $17 shares for $18, but what if he offers $25? Is it written somewhere that while Nielsen and his pals get richer and richer, we have to be idiots about money all our lives?

The number, when it finally came, was in between. This past spring, with a Company share going for about $17, this showed up on the FUNNIES:

NOTICE TO ALL LEWSCO EMPLOYEES

This is to announce that the monthly option to purchase shares of the Lewis Corporation will be postponed for a period of six months from the date listed below. This postponement is intended to provide current shareholders with an opportunity to consider a tendered offer from the Oklahoma Oil Corporation to purchase outstanding shares of the Lewis Corporation from any and all interested shareholders for the price of $22.00 (twenty-two dollars) per share.

All shareholders will receive formal notification of this offer along with the necessary details within the next two weeks. Please read all material that you receive carefully in order to exercise your individual judgement regarding this offer. The Lewis Corporation and its officers will be make no recommendations to shareholders in this matter.

George Olsen, Comptroller
The Lewis Corporation
March 6, 1994

It was a month later that Mrs. Burgess called me. She was organizing a surprise get-together to welcome Holly home and she didn't see how it would be complete if I wasn't there.

It had been at least five years since Holly had been home and I'd last seen her. At that point she'd been working almost ten years for Friends of Wild Rivers, trying to stop dam projects that farmers and developers wanted to build on half a dozen California Rivers. I kept loose tabs on what she was up to by listening to Mom and Mrs. Burgess talk. I never asked questions because there was no point. "A week from Friday night?" I said. "That'd be great, ma'am. Is she staying through the weekend?"

"Actually, she'll be around all next week. She's driving up Pacific Coast Highway Monday so she can be in Port Douglas Tuesday morning for the meeting. Where they're deciding this business about the Company? It was in yesterday's mail."

Not in mine. I wasn't a shareholder. I remembered the modest formula that Holly's dad worked out to slowly pile up a stake in the Company. A flicker of memory of my Dad flushed through me like sour adrenaline. "I don't have that here, ma'am. Could you read it to me?"

She did. All parties interested in the proposed acquisition of the Lewis Corporation by the Oklahoma Oil Corporation are invited to informational meetings at the Cove Inn in Port Douglas, Oregon on Tuesday, April 28 at 1:00 pm and in the main ballroom of the Portland Hilton on Wednesday, April 29 at 9:00 a.m. The ballot enclosed with this notice will be explained at those meetings and can be filled out and turned in at that time, or ballots postmarked by May 1 will be accepted by mail.

I sifted her words for the kernal. A meeting in Port Douglas, location of the main mill and the main business town for most Lewsco folks who worked the woods. Nobody could say they're trying to get it done behind closed doors. But was it more than a side show? People who worked around here didn't have the juice to decide this deal. The serious Company shares had settled over time in the pockets of upper level guys whose paychecks were big enough to deduct a healthy chunk every month. Some of them had retired to little gentleman-farms on the Rogue River outside Grants Pass that they'd picked up back before prices were obscene. They weren't going to give up a day of golf Tuesday to drive over the mountain to Port Douglas. Even more shares lay with the distant family members Ben gifted in his will, probably scattered all over the country and thinking God knew what about this whole deal.

"That's all it says, Johnny," Mrs. Burgess said. "Except for this ballot they have here. Should I read it to you?"

"No, that's okay, ma'am. Look, would you like to go down to PD on Tuesday? I'd be happy to take you."

'Oh, Johnny, thank you, dear. You know, the salty air down there isn't very kind to my bursitis. I always feel it for days afterwards. I think

I'll just send my form in the mail. They even have an envelope here where you don't have to put a stamp on it to send it back in."

"That might be easier," I said. "You know, I was wondering something, and this isn't really any of my business and you shouldn't tell me unless you want to, but I was just wondering if you think you'll be voting to sell." I heard her sigh. "I mean it, now, I don't have to know."

"Oh, no, it's not a secret, Johnny," she said. "It's just I don't know what to do. I know that Holly thinks it's a terrible thing, that it will change everything. I know what she means. But maybe change isn't all bad — Holly says that too, sometimes. I want to do what Holly wants, but I also wonder what George would want if he was here. I've thought a lot about it. I think George would want me to be sure that I have the things I need from now on. I think he'd say 'you have to take care of yourself and not be scared all the time about how you'll end up.' And I'll tell you the truth, Johnny, sometimes I am a little scared. I'm doing fine now, there's enough if I'm careful every month, but I feel my bursitis and I wonder. I don't even tell your Mama this. I just wonder."

"Well, that's just natural," I said. "I think anybody would have to be a little scared, anybody who pays attention to things."

"I think George would tell me to sell, Johnny," Mrs. Burgess said. I waited for more but that was all.

"Well. Listen, what can I bring for the party? Some drinks? Or how about dessert? I've gotten to where I put out a mean berry pie, nothing like yours, nobody's are like yours, but not too bad. What if I bring a pie?"

"No, Johnny, you don't bring anything. I mean it now. Just yourself."

"Okay, you don't believe me about the pie. I'll show you one of these days. So I'll see you...a week from Friday, right? And if you change your mind and want to go to that Company meeting next Tuesday to see Holly down there, you'll give me a call, right? Will you promise?"

"Yes, Johnny, I promise," she said. "I'll see you Friday, dear."

21

SO THERE WAS NO SPECIAL REASON TO GO DOWN THE HILL ON TUESDAY. I didn't have shares to vote and it wasn't a spectator sport. The smart thing was to mind my own business, of which I had plenty. Four or five machines were disassembled in the shop and my bench was half covered with motors in every kind of disarray. I needed to apply nose to grindstone, to head into the shop and lock the doors and plug away for a solid week to catch up.

That's what I tried to do Tuesday morning. By 11:00 I'd dinked around with three machines and accomplished nothing. I swept the shop floor, went into the house and washed a sinkload of dishes, put on cleaner clothes and headed down the hill to Port Douglas.

The Cove Inn banquet room, really four smaller rooms joined together when the folding walls were pushed back, looked through plate glass over the bay and the same rock formation that drew Benson Lewis to shore 160 years ago. I came in a side door and looked over hundreds of chairs without seeing an empty one. Lots of people had come down from Lewis Falls. In the middle of the first row I saw Steve's profile. His father stood behind a podium at the front of the room, and next to Mel was a table that had on it a TV-sized plywood box with a slot cut on top and a padlock that sealed the lid. It looked like someone's pure concept of a secret ballot box.

As I walked in Gina Arnstead was speaking. Gina was Chair of the Lewis County Board of Commissioners. Five years before she'd been a homemaker with four kids and a husband who graded lumber at the

Lewsco mill. When new computers started doing some of his work, she took a half-time job filing and typing at the Company headquarters. A year later she started Families For Forests, which she called 3F, a group of timber wives, parents and children, to lobby Congress and the legislature to loosen up on logging. The whipping post 3F liked best was the Endangered Species Act, which Gina called the law that puts owls, fish, insects and snails in front of people.

She was tireless. She shepherded 3F into the national spotlight, passed the day-to-day operations to others, and by a huge margin became the first women elected to the Lewis County Commission. After almost a full term she announced that she wanted to be the first woman ever sent to Congress from Southern Oregon. She was a sure bet to win the Republican nomination in the primary election that was three weeks away.

"Let me tell you something," she was saying as I found a slot of unoccupied wall to lean on. "I've talked to Mr. Nielsen myself. I just called him straight on the phone. Before I let him hang up I got his personal word of honor that Oklahoma Oil was committed to Southern Oregon for the long haul. That means Port Douglas, Grants Pass, Lewis Falls and all points in between. I asked him specifically, 'Mr. Nielsen, are you ready to tell me that you will treat my county exactly the same as you would if you lived here personally, if you were born and raised here and planned to spend your whole life here?' And he said 'Yes, Commissioner Arnstead, that's exactly what I'm telling you.'

"Now, you folks know me. You know you don't fool me easily. And I want to tell you right now that I know for a fact that Mr. Nielsen is a man of his word. This is a man we can trust. It's a relief to be able to say that, because he's also a man with a record of great business success. I don't think anyone can contradict me on that?" She looked around the room, daring. "I know many of you here. I know for many of you the Company stock you own is the difference between a comfortable life and a life none of us wants. And to be completely honest with you, I think you *deserve* a comfortable life. I think you've earned it. And I think you deserve to have the best business mind around watching out after that investment. You deserve it," she said, pointing to someone close by and then turning, "and so do you and you. And so do you. And that's the opportunity you're being offered right now. Who knows when it will come again? Who knows *if* it will come again? Thank you very much for listening, and good luck to all of you with this important decision."

There was applause as she sat down. Mel clapped from behind the podium, and when it was quiet pointed for someone else to speak. As she rose I saw it was Holly. Her hair was cut in a fancy kind of shag and she looked thinner than I'd ever seen. She cleared her throat and then started talking fast, with a tremor you'd notice only if you knew her.

"My name is Holly Burgess, and I'm the forest resource coordinator for the Western Resources Defense Council, which has its main office in San Francisco and it's so wonderful to see so many old friends here today." There was no sound at all when she paused.

"First of all I'd like to say I'm very pleased that Commissioner Arnstead has been able to talk to James Nielsen, which is more than almost anyone else can say. I've never talked to him, but do you know what? I agree that he probably is a man of his word. I think he's somebody who does what he says he'll do. So let's see what he says he'll do." Holly reached down to her seat to pick a magazine out of a stack of papers. "This is the January 1994 issue of *Commodities Business Journal*, about three months ago, and it has an article on what Mr. Nielsen says he'll do. He says here, and I'll just read one sentence, that 'I was initially attracted to Lewsco by the quality of its underrealized primary assets, which can be converted into capital for debt service and repayment with little or no difficulty.'"

She looked up from the magazine and scanned the room. "'That's what Mr. Nielsen says he's going to do. Now what does it mean? 'Underrealized primary assets.' The word we use around here for what he's talking about is 'forest.' He's talking about the woods that cover this range from Port Douglas to Grants Pass and from the State line up to past Bounty. The woods that have been part of Lewsco since the 1830s and will be Oklahoma Oil's if you approve this deal. So then" — she held up the article — "what does 'converted into capital for debt service' mean? That means cut down and sold, maybe as lumber and maybe as raw logs to the highest bidder, and it means cutting them down right *now*, because if he waits he'll have to pay a lot more to everybody who bought the junk bonds that gives him the cash money to give you all $22 for a share of the Company that's only worth $16 or $17. Do you think he's giving you that extra five dollars because he's a nice man? Maybe he is a nice man, I haven't gotten to know him like Commissioner Arnstead has, but I think it's pretty clear that Mr. Nielsen can pay $22, or $25 or $30 for that matter, because he can borrow it from people who know there are more than enough logs out there to pay them back. It's like funny money to them, and for Mr. Nielsen the only question is whether he gets to put one billion or two or three billion dollars in his pocket."

Holly paused and looked from one end of the room to the other, including my direction. I don't think she saw me. "So I guess I'm kind of agreeing with the Commissioner that Mr. Nielsen probably is an honest man, because here," raising the magazine over her head, "he's telling us exactly what he plans to do. My question to all of you is, is this what you want? Are you ready for the woods you grew up in and that your parents and their parents worked in, always making sure there'd be plenty for us," looking down to read again, "to be 'converted into capital for debt service and repayment with little or no difficulty?' So that when you're driving from here to Grants Pass with your grand-kids someday and they ask you where all the stumps came from, you can tell them all the money you made on this deal?"

The energy of her early jitters had iced up into a demanding plea. She must have heard it herself; she took a breath and lowered her voice. "You know, I grew up here. I know a lot of you. And those of you I know, and I'll bet everyone else here, too, don't want that to happen. And it doesn't have to happen. You can bring a stop to it right here, today. You can say to James Nielsen and his friends 'Thanks but no thanks, we may not be rich but we know what's important, and we're keeping it.' You can say that today. Thank you very much." She sat down to the sound of a dozen clapping hands that quickly quieted.

The attention in the room turned back to Mel behind the podium. He'd been making restless clenched movements with his closed mouth and cheeks as Holly finished up. Now he ran an open hand across his lower face and down his neck. "Well, thank *you* very much, Miss Burgess. That's all very interesting. Maybe you could..." he paused, rubbed his face once more and saw a raised hand near the front row. "Ben, you have something?"

It was Ben Allen, the swing-shift floor foreman of the Port Douglas mill who had twenty years and probably a nice pile of Lewsco shares . He was standing now, hoisting the waist of his pants as if they'd been slipping. He turned to face Holly. "I just want to say it sure is nice of you to come all the way up here — all the way from San Francisco? — to tell us what we all should do. To take the time even to find a maga-zine to read to us. I brought something to read, too. I was so pleased when I heard you might be coming up that I decided to go back to a little file that we keep at the mill, just so I could remember all the smart advice you people give us."

Ben unfolded a sheet of paper from his shirt pocket. It was a photo-copy of a *Chronicle* business article from a few weeks before. It quoted staff from the Sierra Club and the Wilderness Society, then briefly mentioned Holly and then Stanton Freed, executive director of the Western Resources Defense Council. Ben looked up from his read-ing there, straight at Holly. "That"d be your boss, then, I guess?" I hadn't heard the name before either. "Well, here's what the boss of Miss Burgess here has to say about us. He says, 'By accelerating the cut and exporting raw logs, Lewsco may be able to stave off the take-over, but at some point one starts to wonder if the medicine will kill the patient.'"

Ben snorted as he folded the paper to slip back into his pocket. "'One wonders,' does one? So it comes down about to this: if we sit around and let James Nielsen buy us out, we're just terrible, and if we do something so he won't be able to buy us out we're terrible. Fact is, we just can't get it right no matter what." He turned back to Holly. "Pretty hard, was it, looking out the window from the 60-something floor of that pyramid building, or wherever the hell in Frisco your office is, looking down at the Golden Gate bridge and telling the news-paper what idiots we all are? Then driving up here in that little German coupe of yours," he said, tossing a thumb towards the front parking area, "to give us the message in person? Because we probably can't read, right? That's a real beautiful car, Holly. They only come with California plates? That's the only ones we see them with up here."

Ben paused. No one spoke, not even a side whisper that I could hear, but the soft creaks and rustles of people shifting in their seats made enough sound. "Well, I just want to thank you for sacrificing your precious time to come up here and straighten us out again. I just don't know how we've gotten by all the years you've been gone. But for me, I'd be willing to take the risk that we can do it again."

Ben sat down. Everyone was watching Holly. She was looking straight ahead of her at no one. Her chin was high and her lips pressed tightly together. She wasn't going to be saying anything else.

Without any plan or warning my body pushed away from the wall and took a couple of steps towards the middle of the room. My hand went up and Mel saw it and nodded towards me before I completely realized that I was about to speak. I watched people's heads move al-most together away from Holly towards Mel for direction, then my way when they saw he was looking at me. The seconds that passed pushed up the stakes. Whatever I said had to deserve the drama of a long pause. I started talking and hoped.

"We can do this, if we want," I said. "Sure we can. We can start trash-ing each other about what's right and what isn't and who cares and who doesn't. But so what?" It wasn't a great start, but it's what came out and I had to make it work. I scanned the crowd and saw Holly watching me like everyone else. "So what? Does that help us figure this thing out?" I picked Ben Allen's face out of the crowd. His eyes were narrow and sharp. "You know, I grew up my whole life here, too, but that doesn't make me so smart I can't learn anything from people who are watching this thing from the outside. Maybe they made that old saying about not being able to see the forest for the trees just for us and our situation, for today," which I probably meant to be a little joke to lighten up the air. Not extremely successful.

A few hundred faces were frozen on me as if I were a little green man who'd walked to the bottom of my flying saucer ramp to deliver the master plan for the Earth's future. "I don't think this is about who lives where. I think this is about trying to find a decision we can all live with, whether or not we own Company stock or whether we live here all the time or just come back home to visit sometimes. I think it's about listening to what each other has to say and trying to understand what it all looks like from their point of view, and then using our own brains to figure out what makes the most sense for the most people. That's what we have to do, instead of shutting out what some people have to say because they're different from us, they don't care about what's best for us, they're just our *enemies*. Because I think that pretty soon after you start seeing enemies, you see them everywhere you look. And whatever else happens, that's the thing that I'm afraid will come out of all this. No amount of money can be worth that. And I guess that's about all I have to say." My glance touched Holly as I backed up to my spot on the wall. She was looking down at her hands.

A couple of other people rose and spoke, but I don't know what they said. I was vibrating, the valves inside me wide open to release the charged fluids that had dammed up as I spoke. I replayed my words inside, counting all the ways I could have been clearer and more compelling. Much more compelling. When I looked back at Holly she was slipping out of the seats as delicately as she could to head for the back exit.

I caught up with her in the parking lot just as she reached her coupe. I said the first words to her I had in years: "You okay?"

She set a briefcase down and unlocked her door as if I weren't there. "Holly, don't let these cretins get to you," I said.

She pushed her seat forward and put her briefcase in back before answering. Then she put both arms on top of the car and looked straight at me, squinting in the fresh April sunshine. "It's not the cretins, I know who the cretins are. What gets me is *you*. Jesus, Jack, don't you believe in anything?"

"Believe in anything?" The afternoon's second dose of cold fluid washed through me. "Yeah, as a matter of fact, I do. I think I just finished talking about a couple of things I believe in."

"Oh, yeah, that little sermon just now?" she said, her head tilting with the question. "That wasn't exactly what I meant. What I was talking about was having some clarity and some *cojones* when things are obviously right and wrong."

"Okay," I said, leaning now over the passenger side, "number one, let's slow down a little on this right and wrong stuff, unless maybe you forgot to show me the stone tablets God carved just for you. You have them in the trunk?"

"Come on, Jack, you've got eyes. You've got a brain. Still." Wisps of her hair pinwheeled madly about her face in the ocean breeze as she squinted hard at me. I'd expected this to be different.

"Okay," I said, "let's say you're right. Let's say every word you said in there was 100 percent right. Now. What do you do about it? How do you move things the way they should go? By coming up here and making everyone feel like an moron? I hope that does something for you, or wins you points with your Board or whatever, because I can tell you it doesn't do shit to make anything better up here. Are you in this to make a point or to be effective?"

Holly's mouth opened and her eyes rolled. She caught her blown hair on her forehead and pushed it back. "Oh, please. What are you, writing bumper stickers these days? Let's talk about 'effective.' What have you been doing, Jack? Oh, I forget, you don't cut down trees anymore, do you?. That's great, that's been real effective. Everybody all at once said, 'Oh, Jack's given up cutting, I guess we all will, too.' Jesus F. Christ. What, do they hold services at the Spot every night to thank you for showing them the way?" I was boiling up to answer but she gave no room. "And when you *do* have a chance, like in there," a thumb flicked back towards the building, "what do you do?" She shook her head. "Jesus himself comes down the mountain to the unwashed masses. 'Oh, my children, there is no enemy, the enemy is within us, you must all live as the lilies of the field...'" She closed her eyes and let out a raspy sigh. Then she slipped down into her car.

I crouched and tapped on the passenger window. I had a moment to think as she lowered it from her side. "This isn't how to end this conversation," I said. "When do you want to talk again?"

She started her engine and released the parking brake. She looked at me calmly. "Jack, you have to decide. This 'I'm the far-sighted reasonable guy who can see everybody's point' shit is really getting old." She moved the lever into first gear. "I'll see you around."

I watched her car all the way out the lot to the entrance of the highway. As I walked back towards the hall I tried to remember all she'd said. Actually, all she'd said was *you have to decide.*

22

WHEN I CAME BACK INTO THE BANQUET ROOM MEL WAS TELLING PEOPLE they were welcome to drop their ballots into the padlocked plywood box. People stayed around hoping that they'd count them and announce the results right on the spot, but Mel said no. He claimed he didn't even have the key. Not that counting would have told us much. For all the noise there weren't a lot of shares collected in that box. The mail deadline, May 1, would have to pass before we'd know.

For some reason or another it ended up taking a month more than that. Summer had almost come when I stopped at the Spot on my way home from a delivery to see a couple of guys crowded around a new clipping on the FUNNIES. It was the lead business story of that morning's *Oregonian* with a headline that said DOING IT TO THEMSELVES?

The big news was in the first paragraph. James Nielsen had won. Like NBS-TV, Pantages Studios, Crestview Foods and Rawhide Men's Wear, the Lewis Corporation would be a subsidiary of Oklahoma Oil. After a quote from an OO flack about how much they were looking forward to this new gateway to the Pacific Rim, the article laid out the numbers:

> Stockholders voted in late April at separate meetings in Portland and the coastal town of Port Douglas, site of Lewsco's primary mill and shipping facilities. About three-fourths of the company's shares were tallied at the Portland meeting, including proxies collected by mail. Sixty-two percent of those

136

votes favored the offering. In Port Douglas the returns were closer, with the offer rejected by a margin of 55 to 45 percent.

The announcement prompted immediate reaction from environmental groups monitoring the buy-out. Western Resources Defense Council Executive Director Stanton Freed predicted that the upper elevations of the Southern Oregon coastal forest would soon be "liquidated" to pay for the acquisition. In a press release issued yesterday Freed called the relatively close vote by the segment of shareholders that still work for Lewsco a "sad irony." He speculated that with more complete information they would have voted in a block to prevent the buy-out.

"The day will come, probably soon," Freed said, "when those unfortunate people will look at the barren mountainsides all around and want more than anything to turn the clock back to the days when they still had their forest. And the worst part about it will be the knowledge that they did it to themselves."

As I finished reading Steve walked up from behind and looked over our shoulders. "Well, thanks, Sam," he said when he saw the clipping. "Saves me the trouble of telling everyone myself."

Standing next to me, Dave Willard pressed his finger to the article beneath Stanton Freed's picture. "Lookee there, man," he said. "Your babe's boss says we're doing it to ourselves. Isn't that special. Asshole ought to go ahead and do it to himself while he's at it. Like he's probably already doing to Holly, think so, Steve?"

"Oh, man, you had to say that, didn't you?" Steve said. "That is so cold. You know I just lay awake and worry all night long about who Saint Holly's screwing these days. I'm really hurt you'd bring this up, Dave." Steve moved through the Spot's front door to the bar, churning an invisible wake that pulled us in behind. "Hey, Sam, cold ones for me and my so-called friends, okay?"

"Pabst here," I said. I walked over to Fife's nook and put a hand on his shoulder. "Hey, partner," I said. "What's new with you?"

Fife blinked and brought me into focus. "Jackie! Hello, Mr. Jack!" He smiled and took my wrist in both hands. "You know what they did, Jackie? They went and sold the damn company. That's what they did. Went and sold the damn company."

"Yeah, I heard that, Fife. What do you think?"

"Just sold it like it was a cull log," he said, shaking his head. "I'm glad your daddy ain't 'round to see it."

"I know what you mean. So you're okay, Fife?"

He tried another smile. "Never better, Mr. Jack. Though who knows, now they went and sold the damn company."

"That'll be okay, Fife," I said. "You don't have to worry about that, okay? Promise." I picked my Pabst off the bar and touched it to Fife's glass. "Okay?" He stared at me with glass eyes.

Someone shushed the talk and we all focused on the TV back above the mirror behind Sam's bar. The early dinnertime news show from Grants Pass was on with the slick-haired anchor who always looks like he's borrowed his dad's suit. In a box over his left shoulder was the stylized OO logo superimposed over an aerial photo of forested hills. "...so we followed the campaign trail to hear what Southern Oregon's congressional candidates think," he was saying. The picture changed to videotape of a lanky guy in his forties with a smoothly-trimmed beard, standing in the back of a pick-up in some kind of parking lot with people clapping behind him. The anchor's voice and the clapping stopped at the same moment, and the picture changed to a close-up shot of the speaker.

"We have to make it clear to James Nielsen," he shouted, "that as of today he's just taken on obligations that go a whole lot farther than the stockholders of Oklahoma Oil." The words

ARTHUR LANE
Dem Cong Candidate

appeared on his chest. "If he's taking over these timberlands he has to promise to continue the kind of stewardship that has kept the forests of Southwestern Oregon healthy and productive for generations. Instead of big profits today, he has to think about the workers and families who live here, not just for today, but for the long haul. We have to be 100 percent clear with James Nielsen about that."

Then Gina Arnstead came on the screen shaking her head. "Well, I'm not running for the job of telling private businesses that are operating fully within the law what they should and shouldn't be doing. That is the job of the people who own the company, not liberal politicians or Members of Congress. We have a name for how we do things in this country. We call it the free enterprise system, and if Mr. Lane has any questions about it, I'd be happy to explain how it works to him."

"Ooooooh...she *nails* the dude!" Dave Willard said from a couple of stools down.

"You got a problem here, don't you, Dave?" said Sam, drawing a beer from the tap. "This time you have to vote for either a jerk or a woman."

23 🌲

THINGS DIDN'T CHANGE ALL AT ONCE. AS SPRING TURNED TO SUMMER Lewsco hired additional crews, and you started seeing old RVs and big cabover campers filling up the vacant lots around town. But that happened almost every year. What was different this year was that it didn't stop with the fire season's curtailment of heavy cutting. Lewsco just kept hiring, mostly surveyors and timber cruisers and road builders, until you got the feeling that every square foot of the forest was domesticated and plotted onto a master grid somewhere.

The serious wood started coming out a little before Labor Day. A week of rain ended the fire season early, so cutting was permitted all day long. Soon a loaded log truck was rolling through the center of town, right between Sam's and the Square, every three or four minutes. Most were headed for Port Douglas while a smaller share, the one- and two-log loads of monster firs, went the other way, towards the plywood mill in Grants Pass.

It was the week after Labor Day when Steve walked into my shop. I was repainting a Maytag washer that looked like it had been scrubbed with kerosene and gravel when I heard him. "Hey, man!" he yelped cheerfully over the whop-whop-whop of the air compressor. I turned it off. "Can I get a hit off those fumes, or are you keeping it all for yourself?"

"Uuunnnh?" I grunted like a brain-fried zombie would. Extremely clever. I went to the workbench to wipe my hands. "What's up, Doc?"

"Same-old, same-old," Steve said. "Just passing by and hadn't seen you around much, thought I'd see what you're up to."

"Same-old, same-old." I took two cans of Pabst from a knee-high refrigerator in the corner and gave him one. He took it and hoisted himself up backwards to sit on the workbench. I sat on a chest-type freezer across from him. We cracked the beers in the same second and took sips. "Cutting a few trees these days, are you?"

Steve puffed up his cheeks with air and let it out with a soft pop. "Yep," he said, "you could say we're cutting some trees."

"Man's gotta do what a man's gotta do," I said.

Steve looked tired. "Jack," he said, "I think I know the answer to this before I start, but I need to ask you anyway."

"Just as long as you're in the neighborhood, right?"

"I want you to work for me," he said. "Don't say anything for a minute, okay, just let me talk. We are taking a lot of trees, okay. Maybe too many, you and I could fight about that if we wanted. Maybe I wouldn't fight too hard. But it's what's happening for now, okay? It won't last forever. They're maybe figuring out they didn't know everything there is to know about timber when they started this thing out. They need a lot of sticks right now to get on top of their financing, but after that they want to drop the cut to where it was before."

"How do you know that?"

Steve drank from the can and raised his eyebrows high at the same time, a cute look. "I have friends in high places."

"Oh. Right."

Steve slid off the bench and leaned against it. "You may not be crazy about my old man, but you can't say he doesn't know what he's talking about."

That was true. "What does this have to do with me?"

Steve took a slow sip. "The fact remains, right now we have some serious cuts to get out. It's not like they're not sending me enough guys to get it done — every time I go back to the office there are three more sitting there, filling out the papers. But they're kids, bright-eyed and bushy-tailed, they're like we were..."

"Frightening thought."

"...smart enough to get trees on the ground and that's about it. Or they've been around and burned out someplace else and can't resist the sign-up bonus we advertised, bad as I told them that idea was." He hopped back onto the workbench. "What I don't have enough of," he said, "are guys who know how to lay it out. We got a bunch of grab-asses out there dreaming about the brand-new rigs or ski boats they'll be able to buy who could give a fuck about what they're leaving behind. It's pitiful out there."

"Oh, Steve, stop, you're breaking my heart. What the hell are you *talking* about? You guys are annihilating this mountain. Now you're all worried they're not showing the right finesse, or what? Are they using rough language out there?"

"Jack…"

"Why don't you have 'em take their boots off when they go in so nothing gets trampled? I don't, I don't…what are you talking about?"

Steve was nodding. "I already told you, I don't like it much better than you do. But you know what, Jack? It's happening anyway. What I'd like to see is that there's still something growing when it's over."

"Talk to your Dad about that."

"Fuck you, too, Gilliam. You know what I'm talking about. You can go in there like Hiroshima, which is the method of choice at the moment because I have to use kids who don't know any better for crew bosses, or you can leave some healthy understory. Cut roads on top of the older roadbeds. Do your falling right, skid the right way. What, *I'm* telling *you* this?" He shook his head. "Nobody fell more carefully than you did. Six months after one of your shows it was hard to see the cutting."

"Oh, bullshit," I said. Though I had been pretty good. Steve was smiling at me. "I was careful back then because they gave us time to be careful. James Nielsen doesn't seem big on patience."

Steve put his beer down and brought his hands together, excited now. It was the same coiled energy as twenty years before when he'd drop a fly on top of a big steelhead in Whiskey Creek. "If you boss a crew for me the rest of this season and the first part of next year, I'll get you enough time to do it right."

"Yeah, like 'Mr. Nielsen, I hired an old friend for one of your crews who's kind of an ar*tiste,* so we need to give him lots of creative license, but there's so much *quality* to his work, you'll be glad we did, I promise.' Right."

Steve just smiled. "You boss a crew for me. I get you the time."

How had we gotten down to bargaining on the fine points? I slipped off the freezer, dropped the can in a recycling bag, opened the little refrigerator, closed it again. I straightened up to look at Steve. "This is a strange conversation to have."

"I can appreciate that." He nodded. "Well, you know, you don't have to tell me now. Think about it and I'll call you in a couple days. That too much to ask?" He held his beer can upside down for the dregs and tossed it towards the bag, banking it in off the wall. "And you know as well as I do," he said with a smile, "I'd never ruin a highly-principled discussion like this with something as crass as money, which means I won't mention I have a $2000 bonus to give any crew boss I want to sign, plus $400 a day, at least for the rest of this season."

"You are shitting me."

Steve unloaded a big shrug as he slid off the table. "No, I'm not," he said. "But I'm not going to mention it. It wouldn't be right."

Then Steve smoothed off the visit with a little small talk. As we gradually moved towards the door he started scorching his recent ex-wife Lynn, a favorite topic, and the alimony games she was playing. I wasn't listening. Four hundred bucks a day was twice what the appliance work brought in. Not that I needed very much. Rent was cheap, I ate simply, my flatbed and pickup were reliable and they were mine, when I went away it was to sleep outside on the ground somewhere, and you couldn't spend much at the Spot unless you worked really hard at it.

Only Mom kept my mind on money. She was getting by, too, with the small pension and Social Security, but without anything left over. She never said anything but I knew she was worried about what was coming sooner or later. It would be later, judging from how healthy and strong she still was, but that made me think about money, too. She'd never been outside a box bordered by the Coast, Northern California, North Dakota and the Canadian border, and half of that travel had been following Dad's great summer of baseball.

I knew from what she read and watched on TV that her imagination went further than that. She had a thing for England, especially the Royal Family, all the way to an elegant china and silver tea service decorated with some old coat-of-arms that she kept behind glass. Dad had brought it home from some auction down the mountain when I was little, and I don't think she actually used it three times since. But she loved it. What would it be like for her to sip some tea in the fancy drawing room of a London restaurant for a couple of days, somewhere near Buckingham Palace so she could walk to see the changing of the Guard afterwards? I'd have to battle her like crazy at first to pull it off, but if I kept at it I'd win.

Saintly purposes, that's the only reason I ever thought about making more money. Sure. I never even noticed the new 4x4 trucks and sports utility vehicles guys like Steve tooled around in, or the big-ticket fishing trips in Alaska and New Zealand I read about. No way. Never gave any of that shallow stuff a moment's thought. My only interest in money was to do something wonderful for Mom while she still could enjoy it. Yeah, that's the ticket.

"...you've met Sherri, right?" Steve was saying now, stepping up into his oversized pickup. We'd strolled slowly out the door of the shop, across the yard and through my front gate. "But you haven't met the friend she works with at the bank. You want to, though, Jack. Trust me. You got anything going next weekend?"

"Probably," I said. "My social calendar's always jammed, you know that."

"Yeah. Well, let's talk. I'll call you in a couple of days." He started the truck. "This doesn't have to be complicated, Jack. You can give it a try, and if it doesn't work, nobody loses. But I'm pretty sure we can make it work for you."

"What are we talking about now, Sherri's friend?"

Steve laughed. "Well, yeah, that, too. We could start getting in all kinds of trouble again, like the glory days." His smile looked real. The truck started moving. "I'll call you."

24

I NEVER DID MEET SHERRI'S FRIEND. STEVE LEFT A COUPLE OF MESSAGES
that I didn't return.

A week went by and the log traffic seemed more intense every day,
until you could see two loaded log trucks stopped at the flashing red
light next to Sam's at the same time. One afternoon I saw three. Then a
second wave of newcomers showed up. Like the loggers who'd rolled in
for the boom of work of the last few months, a lot of these people camped
in their rigs. They were older rigs, though, and odder. Old Volkswagen
and Ford and Dodge vans painted colors they never thought of in Ger-
many or Detroit. A few old pickups with rough miniature A-frames cab-
ins densely built on the back and an assortment of tiny station wagons
and hatchbacks on their third and fourth odometer cycles. Lots of
bumper stickers showing these weren't loggers or scenery tourists. They
didn't stop in town, other than for food staples at Sam's store. They
congregated at the campgrounds out by Whiskey Creek.

We were mulling it over at the Spot one evening when Sam stretched
to turn up the volume on the TV. The news was showing video of a
demonstration at Lewsco's Grants Pass headquarters that afternoon,
twenty-five or thirty scruffy pickets walking the sidewalk in an elongat-
ed circle with hand-painted signs. The anchorman's voice sounded
over the pictures, talking about threats of civil disobedience planned
for the Lewis Falls area. Then they switched to a reporter on the scene,
holding a microphone under the chin of a dapper blond man in a
blue workshirt and a gold paisley tie. The picketers were doing their

thing in the background as the reporter asked how the guy would respond to the argument that people who live far away have no business meddling in how Oregon forests are managed.

The man smiled. He had a sharp blond goatee and mustache like a Dutch Master and small bright teeth. "This 'far away' business is interesting," he said as letters appeared over his chest.

STANTON FREED
Western Resources
Defense Council

"Hey, that's the guy!" someone down the bar said. "'They're doing it to themselves.' That's him!"

"...might say that San Francisco is not a significant distance away," he was saying to the reporter as the camera zoomed in on him, "unless you're talking about the different evolutionary stages of human development, but that's another subject. What is important is that on the most basic level none of us 'own' these forests. My belief is that the Native Americans addressed this very situation when they observed that the Earth is not something we inherit from past generations. We borrow it from future generations."

"That's what I've always said," said Sam.

"That's beautiful, Sam," said someone down the bar. "So very, very beautiful."

Holly wasn't in the news story, but I had a feeling. I went home by way of Mom's house to say hi and look for a car parked at the Burgesses'. There wasn't one, but when I walked into Sam's store the next morning, there she was, reading the label on a puffy-looking loaf of brown bread. "Hi there," I said.

She looked up calmly. "Hello, Jack. How've you been?'

"Why aren't I shocked to see you?"

Holly shook her head and put the bread down. "Not a lot of big surprises in this one, Jack. It's like a slow-motion trainwreck you can see coming for a long time." As if on cue a truck carrying a single huge log rumbled past the front window. We watched it and Holly let out a soft snort, shaking her head again. "Nice conveyor belt you have going up here," she said. "It's unreal, Jack."

I couldn't think of anything to say. That 300-year-old log, heading down the mountain on its way towards Grants Pass and then sixty years' service as plywood beneath the kitchen linoleum of somebody's split-level ranch-house in some mushrooming west coast suburb, stirred up the same kind of feelings in me as it did her. Maybe not as strong. But I wasn't going to wring my hands about it with her now, not while living my quiet get-along Lewis Falls existence. Not with her last wind-blown sneer in the Cove Inn parking lot fresh in my memory.

She was looking at me. "How long are you up for?" I asked.

"I'm not sure," she said. "Three or four days, a week, maybe. It depends on how things go."

"What things?"

She inspected something on Sam's shelves and put it back down. She turned directly towards me. "It''s crunch time, Jack. We have to go into the woods now. There's no other way to get enough attention. Believe me, we've tried."

"You need a lot of attention?"

"*This* does, yeah," she said, waving a hand towards where the truck had passed. "It needs as much attention as it takes until people understand what's happening."

"Who doesn't understand what's happening?"

"The whole world, Jack. Anyone who doesn't live in Lewis County or doesn't make a point of keeping track. There's too much going on for people to pay attention. We have to find a way somehow to grab them and just *shake* them."

"And what would that be?" I asked.

"Tomorrow," she said, her voice lower, "we're having our first action up here. It'll be at the top of the Falls road. There are maybe ten loads a day coming out from near the Falls, you know." I didn't, exactly. "We're going to see about slowing it down."

It didn't seem real. Protest demonstrations had been going on in the Northwest woods for years, but those were fights over cutting public lands. There had been a big one a few drainages north of here in the southern part of the Pioneer National Forest. But never here. Not in Lewis Falls. "You know what you're doing, Holly? I've seen some of your eco-troopers coming through town and they're not exactly Green Berets."

She shook her head. "No, it'll be mellow. We just have to make the point so it gets heard. We've already told the state police everything we plan to do. Almost. Like I said, this isn't about surprises. At least we don't have any." She leaned slightly toward me. "What about you, Jack? Do you have any surprises up your sleeve?"

"What did you have in mind?"

"Well, that's up to you. I could think of plenty you could do that would surprise me. Starting tomorrow, if you want to come." She was watching me with an odd intent look, her arms folded and her head tilted a little to one side.

Looking at her I thought of Stanton Freed's cheery smugness on the tube the night before. It must be nice to have the corner on all the right answers. "How very kind of you to ask me," I said. We heard another loaded truck shifting up from the stop light and followed it with our eyes from one edge of Sam's windows to the other.

"Suit yourself, Jack." Holly shrugged and moved towards the far end of the aisle. "For a minute I thought all this mattered to you. Then I remember," she said, turning the corner out of sight, "you only live here."

25

OF COURSE I WENT.

There was so much traffic coming into town as I cleaned up my breakfast the next morning that I walked the four blocks to the top of the Falls road. Its intersection with the highway was flanked by two State Police and two Lewis County Sheriff squad cars. Their bubble machines were turning, flashing blue and red.

The Falls road met the Highway in a gravel clearing, a space the size of two basketball courts before you got to the Forest Service gate, which was closed. That kept the crowd of two hundred or so from moving any farther down the road. A cordon of helmeted state troopers and sheriff's deputies stood along the gate elbow to elbow, facing the crowd. They didn't look especially tense. Nobody did. An old Jefferson Airplane song played over the jumbled murmur, loud and distorted. It did look like an event without surprises.

It looked well planned all-around, actually. The shoulder of the highway by the Square was lined with vans from commercial TV stations as far away as San Francisco and Portland. I saw three video cameras work their way into the crowd, and then I saw what they were shooting. On the edge of the clearing two people were holding up poles, the ends of a banner made from two halves of a bed sheet sewn end-to-end. In foot-high red letters it said

ENVIRONMENTALISTS MAY BE A PAIN IN THE ASS TO LIVE WITH BUT WE MAKE GREAT ANCESTORS.

Then almost with one movement the video cowboys turned to shoot somebody stepping out from another spot in the crowd. It was Zenith. He took three big strides towards the center of activity and planted himself with his feet spread wide and his hands around the middle of a six-foot spike. Actually it wasn't a real spike. It was a six-foot log about four inches thick, honed until it was almost as smooth and symmetric as a spike and painted gun-metal blue. One end had a round plate shaped to look like the spike's head and the other had been tapered to a blunt point. There was even a long white parallelogram painted on the side of the shaft to make it look like it was gleaming in the light, an effect that worked from more than thirty feet away. All in all it was an artful lifesize-times-ten replica of what Earth First! supposedly drives into trees to scare loggers away.

I have to explain about Zenith. He's what you might call a bold color in the Lewis Falls palette. What he was wearing that day was what he wore everyday: painter's overalls that were probably once white over a green fatigue shirt. The shirt had sergeant's bars and a name patch that just showed above the bib of the overalls: MACPHERSON. But the only name anyone called him was Zenith. His body was long and sharply angled and a huge hook nose took up most of his face. Wispy brown hair fell from the edges of a tortilla-sized bald spot straight over his shoulders and down his back. He had straight inch-wide burns dropping from the side of each ear and bending around his jawline, and a nickel-size thatch of hair in the middle of his chin.

Zenith came to Lewis Falls in 1975. I've heard it was his first stop after Vietnam. He came to bring a small package of personal things to Tom and Noreen Baker. Their son Troy, who was in my class at LFHS, was one of the last marines killed over there. Zenith was his squad leader.

But the Bakers were gone when Zenith arrived. They had left after getting the news about Troy and never came back. Zenith didn't leave. It was as if he wasn't allowed to with his mission incomplete. He wandered around town with the package dangling from his belt for a few days until Sam put him up in one of his cabins. Then Zenith found an ancient school bus somewhere and drove it a few final miles up the skid trail behind the Stagestop Store, which sits on the Highway five miles towards Port Douglas from town. He drove it right a stump that high-sided its front end. He found a jack to raise up the back end to something close to level and from that day on it was his home. And in the nineteen years since, nobody has heard him say a single word.

He was making some noise, though, at this demonstration, a steady bear-like growl that burst into sharp grunts as he pretended to lunge, his jumbo spike pointed like a spear, at each of the video cameras surrounding him. They kept their tape rolling non-stop until he slowed down. Out of breath, he jabbed the spike in the ground like a staff and pushed his hair up out of his face. That's when he saw me and suddenly froze. I can't think of a word for what was on his face at that moment other than hatred.

It really surprised me. Though I've seen him a lot over the years, I barely know Zenith. The only time I ever tried to talk to him was back in 1980 or '81, when I was up near the top of Possum Butte, near the landing area of a big cut we were finishing. I was by myself because it was Sunday morning, one of the few I ever worked. I was planning to take Monday and Tuesday off to go fishing up on the central coast, but before I could I had to mark a few dozen logs so my bucking crew would know where to cut them. Strictly speaking I didn't have to do it. They were grown men who knew how to use a steel tape. But if they screwed up even one log in twenty, civilization as we know it would be gravely threatened, if you bought the hysterics we got from the guys at the mill. It was easier to just do the measuring myself, even if it took a slice out of my weekend.

The truth was I liked being out there alone. All the noise and thunder it had taken to get the wood on the ground was so different from all this quiet, as I stepped among the logs with my tape and a can of red spray paint. The birds that we silenced with our saws early each weekday ignored me and sang to each other. A weak autumn sun dropped thin shafts through the high branches — back then we left high branches — onto the sizzling reds of maple and the yellows of ash trees. All just for me.

I took a break when I was about two-thirds done to eat the sandwich and slab of Mom's cobbler I'd brought. I decided to hike a couple hundred yards to the top of the butte, a natural meadow that gave about 200 degrees of view, from a sliver of blue ocean off Port Douglas on the west to the edge of the Trinity Alps on the south to the stretch of Cascades that walled off Eastern Oregon. Like the Elders, Possum Butte had probably been a Medicine Circle, a place so close to center of the sky that tribes from the coast and inner valley met there for sharing thanks.

Near the top of the butte is a little outcropping of boulders that forms a bowl-shaped shelter, and as I passed it my eye caught on a dark shape inside. With a little rush I realized it was a person. Settled among the rocks, staring down motionless towards where I'd been working, was Zenith. I could tell he had been there a while, watching me measure the logs down below.

"Well, hey," I said, trying to get calm. "How are you doing?" Zenith kept staring past me down the hill for a moment. Then he slowly turned his head towards me. Only his neck had moved; nothing on his face other than the aim of his gaze showed awareness that I was there. "Zenith, right? I'm Jack." I stepped forward so he could reach my outstretched hand without leaning forward. He looked at it like he had never seen one before. When I pulled it back after a couple of stiff seconds, he kept staring at where it had been.

I kept trying. "What a place, huh? Especially when it's quiet."

At that he shot me a look so fierce it sliced through any doubt that he was all there. He could not have been more there. With that glare searing me I couldn't think of anything else to say. I just stared back as long as I could, probably three seconds, then shifted and looked back over my shoulder down the hill. In one swift movement Zenith was up and out of the rock enclosure, taking long sure strides across the top of the butte and down the other side. I watched him until his head disappeared behind the tiny horizon.

That was so long ago, it couldn't really be the reason Zenith was staring daggers at me now. But I couldn't think of any other. As I stared back at him a screech of feedback on a portable PA system filled the air, and he turned and slipped into the crowd. "Hello?" an amplified voice said and the awful sound faded. "Hello? Testing. Okay... " Then on the edge of the clearing, rising above crowd level as he stepped onto an old stump, I saw Stanton Freed. He was still in his denim shirt and fancy yellow tie. Next to him was a cardboard sign that said YOU CAN'T "HARVEST" WHAT YOU DON'T PLANT.

Stanton lifted a wallet-sized microphone on the end of a black curly cord to his mouth and shouted "Good morning!" into it. The crowd shouted back. A last chirp of feedback cut through the air and was gone. "It is wonderful to see all you troublemakers and misfits out here today!" The crowd roared back louder.

Stanton started into a well-honed summary of the OO buy-out and all it did to Lewis Falls and to us and to the volume of forest cut. "You notice I didn't say 'harvest?'" he added, looking down to the sign holder next to him. The crowd cheered and the placard bounced up and down.

"You know," he continued, "I keep reading the timber barons talking about how we environmental ex*trem*ists are hell-bent to put their workers out of a job, and what great friends *they* are to their workers. Well, allow me to ask a question or two. If James Nielsen loves his workers so much—"

He stopped there. The rumble of big trucks had filtered into the clearing, quickly getting louder. The cops stretched a rope along one edge of the crowd to herd it towards Stanton's stump so that over half the road was clear. As people scrambled I saw Holly for the first time, walking backwards until she was next to Stanton. Then a truck appeared around the bend from the direction of the Falls pulling a single log almost six feet thick. Right behind that was a second truck hauling two smaller logs that weren't small.

A woman in Forest Service green opened a padlock on the gate and swung it open. The clattering diesel sound of the idling engines mixed with ugly jeers into a brutally loud noise. Stanton's amplified shouting barely carried over the top of it. "Here we are! Here we are!" The first truck crept slowly past the gate towards the edge of the highway as the news cameras rolled.

"Now you see," Stanton shouted on, "you and I thought those logs were just fine as trees! We don't have any vision! They had to come down for some really important reasons. See this first one?" He pointed to the back of the first truck as it angled to turn onto the highway. "James Nielsen's Lear Jet needs its one thousand-hour overhaul, and that'll just about cover the bill! And those other two?" He waited until the second load was towering right over the crowd and the ranger was locking the gate back closed. "Those will keep his polo ponies in premium oats for the rest of the season!" Holly looked straight up at him and smiled. He was good, it's true. She looked out over the crowd and saw me. Our eyes caught for a second but I couldn't read her.

She looked back up at Stanton as he was shaking his head. "So selfish of us, isn't it? We ought to learn how to share! Here Nielsen has let those trees stay whole for centuries now, hasn't he, so we should at least let him have a turn with them, isn't that right?" The crowd kept booing. Stanton saw that it was starting to drift apart as the second truck moved onto the highway. "It's up to us, people!" he yelled. "If not us, who? If not now, when?"

The truck curved out of sight towards Port Douglas and the state troopers got into their cars to leave. Four sheriff's deputies walked over to form a sparse line behind the gate. When I looked back towards Stanton he was down off the stump in front of two TV cameras, his face glowing with concern. Holly stood a few feet away from him, saying something to Zenith. She had a hand on his forearm and a soft look on her face. Without thinking about it I slowly angled towards them. Zenith strode off quickly the second he saw me. Holly watched him with a little frown before turning to me. "You want to meet Stanton?" she said.

"I don't think so." Just then the news camera clicked off and Stanton stepped towards me with the beginnings of a smile.

"You wouldn't be Jack." It sounded like an order.

"Jack, Stanton," said Holly. "Stanton, Jack."

"Hello, Jack." The smile filled out as he extended his hand. When I took it he squeezed my fingers together hard.

"How you doing," I said.

"I've had better days," Stanton said, tipping his head in the direction of the highway and the departed log trucks. He watched the TV guys move out to work the thinning crowd, then turned back to me with a spark of friendliness. "I think. I had something a little more adventurous than this in mind. But I've learned that unspectacular days sometimes turn out better than you think. I've heard a lot about you." Holly was at our elbows, but we didn't look at her.

"Yeah. Well, of course you would," I said. "I'm incredibly famous." An odd noise pulled our attention towards the edge of the Highway, where the video guys had circled Zenith. He was brandishing the huge spike over his head and making peeved bear noises again. "Just like him," I said to Stanton. "I can't begin to guess what pictures they'll use on the tube tonight, can you?"

"They won't just use it, Jack. They'll lead with it. All through prime time tonight, in between 'Cosby' and 'Dynasty' and what have you, they'll show that picture and say that it's coming up at 11:00, so stay tuned. And most people will."

A sharp breath went out my nose. "So that's all this is about? 'Film at 11?'"

Stanton tilted his head and tugged on his ear. "Do you know what, Jack? This will probably shock you to death, but they don't ever ask me what they should put on the news. If they did, maybe we'd carry signs saying 'These enormous conifers have stood here for centuries, stabilizing the hilltop terrain, purifying rainwater on its way to the river, providing shade and clean water for critical salmon runs and generous oxygen supplies for all of us, contributing fibrous matter that decays to replenish the forest floor, providing habitat for hundreds of species of fauna and flora. Ripping them out to fatten the wallet of Wall Street investors and add ten minutes of work for deluded workers who are doomed anyway exemplifies Reagan-inspired raging capitalism at its very best.' Would that work for you, Jack?"

"Don't worry about me," I said. "I go to bed before 11:00."

He looked at me intently. "What's your point, Jack?"

"My point is that's bullshit." I said, nodding towards Zenith. "Who are spikes meant for? James Nielsen? Oklahoma Oil? You're hurting them? Sure. They probably never set *foot* in Oregon. The first guy who runs into one of your spikes with a saw will be some bozo who lives right here, or maybe a sawyer down in PD who James Nielsen's already screwed anyway. That's who the spikes are for."

Stanton tugged his ear again and smiled. "Holly claims that you're smart, Jack." She was a short distance away now, talking to a reporter. "And Holly's usually right. So see if you can stay with me, would that be okay? Number one: nobody's going to run into a spike with a saw, because spikes don't go into trees. They go into the news. We talked about that, remember?"

"You don't think any trees have been spiked?"

"Do you? Do you yourself know of actual spikes going into actual trees, not rumors, not Film at 11, but actual spiking? Tell me about spiking you can swear really happened."

I tried to think fast. There were plenty of stories. There was the big one down in the Redwoods near Eureka, but I think that might have turned out to be a hoax. Stanton would know if it was, so I wasn't going to bring up that one. But there was no way, with all the stories, the warnings and threats when logging protests got really hot, that *none* of them were real. Was there?

"Right," Stanton said. "I'll tell you what: when you think of some, be sure to drop me a post card. Number two. Yes, they are in fact for our friend Mr. Nielsen. They're a little visual aid to help with his education about what he's taken on here. See, Jack, Nielsen goes days at a time without thinking once about trees or Oregon or Lewsco. Maybe weeks. He's a busy fellow with a lot on his mind. He has an airline to worry about. He has a network and movie studios, he has resorts scattered from here to Bora-Bora, he has factories all over the place, he has industrial farms and canneries and bottling plants and clothing sweatshops in Malaysia and I don't know what else. Hemorrhoids, probably. But then," his face warmed up into a smile, "he sees something. He sees a stick, just a long piece of wood painted to look like a nail, and he suddenly remembers us. And perhaps he starts wondering if this might turn out to be less fun than movies and airplanes, and if perhaps he could live without being a timber baron after all."

I wanted to ask if he really thought Nielsen would see any of this but Stanton was on a roll. "Number three. You know what we want. Cutting has to stop on this whole range, from California to Washington. It's been thrashed almost to death already, and anybody who's honest knows it. We don't want one more tree to come out of here, not old growth, not peeler cores, not one punky snag. Period. To some of the upstanding citizens watching "Cosby" tonight that might sound a little radical. But then they tune in at 11 and see him," he tipped his head towards Zenith, "then maybe they read a couple of letters to the editor next week that we write with our best manners, full of Oregonians' birthright to their glorious forest home and what this asshole Nielsen is doing to trash it, and the wonder of our free and open society where everyone has the right to express their own opinion as long as they do so *peace-*

fully, and do you know what happens? All of a sudden we're not so radical after all. All of a sudden what we have to say might be worth hearing.

"And number four? Spike-man there isn't ours. It's called free assembly. It's one of the quaint customs we supposedly have in this glorious land of ours. It means we're not responsible for every idiot that shows up."

Holly walked up, looking at me then at Stanton. "I'm dying to know what you two are talking about."

"Well, Jack was just giving me some constructive feedback. Very valuable, getting the local perspective." He smiled brightly. "Thank you, Jack."

"Mmm," said Holly. "He does know everybody's opinion, don't you, Jack?" Then she looked at her watch. "What time do you have to be at the newspaper? One o'clock?"

Stanton shrugged. "Don't you know?"

"One o'clock, I'm pretty sure. Come on, we have to get down there." She turned to me. "So see you around."

"Probably will," I said.

As they turned from me Stanton frowned. "You put together those harvest numbers for 1980 and 1990, didn't you?" he asked Holly as they walked towards the highway. I couldn't hear her answer. I saw Stanton nod and wrap his arm around her shoulder. Holly started to lift her arm towards his hip and then dropped it. I saw her face in profile as she turned it to him, still talking. I saw Stanton tip his head back and laugh. As they reached the edge of the blacktop I saw her lift her hand again and weave it around his waist.

26

"STEVE? HEY, IT'S JACK." STEVE'S ANSWERING MACHINE HAD JUST BEEPED at me. "Listen, we were going to talk again and never did. Can you give me a ring when you get this? I have to go somewhere about noon, but I'll be in the shop solid until then." It was almost 9:00 in the morning after the demonstration. She'd been right — I did have to decide. "So...talk to you when I do." I felt a jittery relief hanging up.

I pulled the motor out of a Frigidaire compressor and cracked the case open. Steve would call when he called, not sooner or later. I went to the corner to turn on the stereo system I'd happily taken in trade for an apartment-sized Kenmore refrigerator the year before and flipped the tuner to the AM side.

"...with half my brain tied behind my back just to be fair." Perfect for bludgeoning a jumpy mind into dullness. Just as Rush was starting to roll on an insightful analysis of the pivotal public issue of our times — the lines Clinton might have used as he was hitting on Paula Jones — the phone rang.

"Jack! Hey, man," Steve said. "What's up?"

"Well, I was thinking about our talk when you came over, about how it can make a difference who's on the ground supervising as you guys rape and pillage out there, and I decided you might not be 100 percent completely full of shit."

"An apology? Thanks, Jack. Accepted."

"So I wondered if you're still looking for a crew boss."

"Yeah, I am. You know one, Jack?"

"You need me to fall on my knees and kiss your ring? Do you have a spot or don't you?"

"I just said I did, son. You want it?"

I was looking at a blizzard of dust motes, tiny silk whiskers floating in a slice of sunlit air next to my work bench. The image is in my mind, whole and perfect, right now. "Yes," I said.

"Perfect, Jack," Steve said. "Perfect decision. You'll see as soon as you get out there, I promise. Let's see — tomorrow?"

Tomorrow. Tomorrow was sudden. The best way to do it. "Well, I have a couple of ends to tie up. Tomorrow's Wednesday? How about Thursday?"

"That works," Steve said. "Listen, I'm doing some mixing and matching this week and I don't have your own crew for you right now. I'm going to put you on Dusty's crew for a week or so, which is good anyway because he's got the drill down cold, and it's changed some since you were working."

"Indeed," I said.

"Don't let's get started, okay, Jack? You're either in or you're out, and you just told me you're in, right? Tell me once more so I know it, Jack. Are you in?"

"I'm in, Steve. Do I come down now and we prick our fingers and mix our blood together?"

"I love it when you talk like that," Steve said. "Christ, I can't believe I'm doing this. You're the biggest pain in the ass to ever work for this company. I must be fucking crazy." He was loose and happy like he used to be after winning a big game. "So, Thursday. I guess you might want to know where to meet Dusty."

"No, that's okay, Steve, I'll just start at the Square and keep cutting until I find him."

"Very funny. Let's see." I heard snapping pages as he flipped through a notebook. "Oh. Dusty's working down near the Falls. Look, if you want to, I could also put you out on Strawberry Saddle. Ray Oates is working out there, and he could line you out almost as good as Dusty can."

"I can go with Dusty."

"Down towards the Falls."

"Right. I heard you."

"They're cutting on the west slope below the Elders."

"Right. Well, you're not paying extra for travel time to Strawberry, are you?"

"At four hundred bucks a day? At four hundred we're thinking about *charging* guys for travel time."

"Fine. I'll stay around here and cut for Dusty."

"You got it, son. So you need to be here at the yards at six on Thursday morning to meet up with Dusty's crew."

"I'll just meet him down at the Falls at 6:30."

"Uh-uh," Steve said. "Everybody goes down there together in one crummy."

"How come?" I said. "If we're just going down below the Elders why not meet down there?"

"Because we don't know if Holly and her pals are planning another hissy-fit at the top end of the road. State Police wants as little traffic going through them as possible until they chill out." When I didn't say anything he gave a little snort. "Man. What a piece of work. They're hugging trees up and down five states and Saint Holly has to do hers here? How does she think she's making us look?"

"Why don't you ask her?"

"Right," Steve said. "Then I'll tell her to stop, since she always did exactly what I told her to. Shit. Do we even have to talk about Holly Burgess?"

"No," I said.

27

I MET UP WITH DUSTY AND HIS FIVE-MAN CREW EARLY THURSDAY MORN-ing at the maintenance yards. I knew two of them, Dave and Bob Willard. The others were part of the wave of workers that the OO takeover had brought to the mountain.

They barely took notice that I was there, which made me wonder what Steve had told Dusty beforehand. As I climbed into the back of the crummy, a middle-aged Dodge with a full back seat between the driver and the bed, Dusty nodded from the front seat. "Glad to have you back, Jack."

Lewis Falls was already humming in the dawn light with the gravelly drone of diesel engines. In the six blocks between the Lewsco yards and the top of the Falls Road we passed four empty log trucks, their rear trailers piggy-backed onto their front trailers for highway travel, headed back into the woods. When we got to the top of the Falls road Dusty got out to unlock the gate. There were four or five people on the edge of the clearing, bleary-eyed longhairs wrapped against the early chill in rough blankets that gringos buy in Mexico. The debris from a larger group, placards, tarps and duffle bags, were scattered around them. I saw Zenith's jumbo spike leaning against a tree, but no Zenith. They glared at us silently. Dusty locked the gate behind us.

"Faggots," said Dave Willard from the far end of the back seat. I was back in the woods.

We coasted slowly down towards the Falls. No one was in a hurry to get there. The sun wasn't quite in the canyon yet, but it had spread an amber coat of color across the east-facing slope to our left. The sky straight above was a blue so perfect anyone would notice it, and the gravel on the road had a sheen from the last moments of frost. The sour nutty smell of coffee in plastic Thermos caps was the same as I remembered. Some smoke from Dusty's cigarette drifted into the back, even though he was holding it next to the inch of outside air he'd opened up above the passenger-side window, a courtesy I didn't remember. Some bouncy electric tune from the Port Douglas country station came softly from the radio. As we came around a steep downhill turn two deer, a doe and her fawn, trotted across the road into the trees. Nobody commented. Only Dave spoke, rambling on with a whiny story about an in-law who wouldn't stop trying to borrow money.

I watched the trees pass outside my window. I'd only had half a cup of coffee and my stomach was clenching like a fist. In the '80s I'd done a rafting trip on the Tuolumne in California, a river with a flesh-eating reputation, and the long bus ride down into that steep river canyon towards something big and unknown had the same feel this ride did. In a way it was helpful, this swirly tumbling in your gut. It took your focus away from thinking.

We came to the parking area next to the Falls. A couple of dozen logs lay in stacks along the edge. Right beside them an empty log truck and a big yellow loader, its arm bent sharply so that its pincers rested on the ground, waited for their operators to show up. We were the first ones down this morning. Instead of parking, our truck turned to the left and started down a raw-looking spur road I'd never seen before.

I touched the driver's shoulder in front of me. "Let me out here," I said.

Talk in the truck stopped as the driver pulled over and looked at Dusty. "The show's still a little ways up, Jack," Dusty said. "We're cutting around on the back slope." He was pointing to the steep hill on our right, the hill topped by the Elders.

"I'll get there." I opened the door and stepped down from the running board. I walked around the back of the truck and leaned into the bed to pull out my saw and backpack.

Dusty rolled his window down and twisted around to look at me. "Hey, Jack," he said. "You afraid you won't get enough exercise today, or what?"

"Ah, you know. First day of school. Have to get the kinks out."

"Yeah. Jack, there's lots to get done today."

"I'll be there, Dusty," I said, fitting my arms into the pack's straps. "I'll be right there. Where do you want me to start?"

"There's a little landing another quarter mile up this spur. That's where we park. Anything that's blazed between the crest of the hill," he nodded up towards the Elders, "and the truck, have at 'er." He looked at me again. I think he was looking for a way to say something else. But he pulled his head inside the cab and the truck rolled away.

I walked across the gravel clearing, past the empty log truck and loader. Things looked surprisingly normal. I must have had some image drifting through my brain of World War III down here, the landscape mowed down and smoldering, nothing but stumps and slash piles with huge root-balls tipped over and pointing towards the sky like the legs of upended potato bugs. What I saw was pretty much what was always here, a hard open clearing surrounded by the hill of the Elders on one side, forest sloping up more gently like the sides of a shallow bowl on two others, and in the direction I was walking, across the river and Falls that I couldn't yet see, a nearly vertical wall of granite and more trees.

On the ride down I'd watched for new cuts, and there were some. The corridor of trees along the road was noticeably thinner, and further back I'd seen fresh stumps studding the higher ground. As I reached the rim of the parking area overlooking our beach and the Falls, I could feel my breath deepen and slow down. But it was okay down here.

I walked onto the beach and sat on an old barkless log. It was a fixture there, one-third buried in the muddy sand, the backrest we'd leaned against to sip beer and tell silly and serious stories thirty years before. *Thirty years* before. I set my saw down on the sand where we had sat and slipped my pack off to fish out a plastic pint of orange juice. I watched the Falls as I drank it, the startlingly regular wall of water reaching almost all the way across the river, swelling up like a broad shoulder flexing against the fall, then surrendering and breaking into a glistening fabric of white tatters and beads that pounded the water below with a thousand hits. The mist that bounced back up softly blurred the crisp lines of falling water; that's where the rainbows would shimmer on summer afternoons when sunlight reached the bottom of the canyon. Not now. The sun wouldn't find this deep nestled spot again until next May.

Lots of memories as I sat there, more than I'd had in years. Summer memories. Sprawled half-sleeping on my back in the brazen sun, eyes closed, nothing but the Falls in my ears. Drinking beer with Steve and Ray on hot afternoons until I was stupid, flopping into the water to clear it out. Sidling across the wall of rock to crawl into the eerily lit ledge behind the Falls to smoke a joint, then bursting through to the world outside full of girls wondering when we'd appear. Standing under the Falls, a head barely above the water to take the longest possible pounding while the girls kept time with slim wristwatches. Coming back to the beach to hear them say how crazy we were. Watching them, glistening with lotion, float out on air mattresses to the quiet part of the pool, the edge farthest from the Falls. Seeing Holly floating out there — now I was looking at the same tiny eddy that used to hold her — on her stomach, both hands holding a paperback book in front of her, until Steve surfaced like a seal next to the raft to make her squeal and giggle at the same time. Watching as he took hold of the mattress, smiling, to bring her face close to his.

I finished the juice and tucked the bottle into the pack, slipped it on and picked up my saw. I hiked across the beach to where the path to the Elders started and made my way between the trees. There were no new stumps. The sound of the Falls softened as I climbed. I looked up to the top of the hill and then higher, up the broad brown trunks of three Elders that were coming into sight, three cedars that formed the edge of the ring nearest the Falls.

Twenty more strides to the top. I made ten of them, each one bringing a little more of the crest into my view. Something cold and hard started turning inside me and then, as I took the last few steps, burst into an icy flow rushing up to my head. I stopped between two of the big cedars and faced an open sky. The far side of the Elders, two giant fir and two spruce, was gone.

My breath wouldn't come. I was looking across the flat crest, strewn now with limbs and shards of bark, at four barrel-sized stumps. Their tops were uneven, sloping in three angles from three different approaches of the saw. Two of the fir stumps had tall pointed remainders sticking up out of them like wooden stalactites; they'd been brought down carelessly, in a hurry. They were gone.

Beyond them, down on the west slope of the hill, the sound of saws and a cat coming to life broke through the morning's quiet. I moved slowly to the middle of the clearing, trying to focus. I looked at the saw in my hand and it felt like the seeing part of me drifted out of my body. A logger is holding this saw, I thought, and he's standing in the middle of where the Elders were. I was able to make the logger put down the saw, then pick it up again, then walk the rest of the way over to the stumps. I watched the logger move his hand over the long dagger of wood sticking out of the stump, then press down so the point pushed against the softest part of his palm. It pushed harder, the skin gathering tighter and pink around the point until the sensation jerked me back into the logger's body. I lifted my palm and ran it across the stump's raw damp plane of wood.

I looked down the west slope across a newly opened channel in the forest. It was a mess. The smaller growth was trammeled into lumpy green piles of dirt and brush where the trees had fallen, and where the buckers and choker-setters had moved in to turn them into logs. Layers of slash, limbs and branches that had been growing high above the forest floor were scattered like a drunkard's clothes. The logs themselves were gone. I thought about the girth of the logs that trucked out a few days before as Stanton was ranting and raving to his crowd. They could have been Elders.

It looked as if about half of the stand on the west slope had been taken out. A few hundred yards down there I saw specks of red, the color of the crummy, through the remaining trees. Most of the crew was moving around closer to me, easy to see because of their yellow hardhats. One was limbing a log below me to the left and two were on the cat, scraping clear more room to work. Another, Dave Willard I think, looked like he was setting up to fall a 3-foot thick spruce down and to my right. Dusty was down there someplace. Lots to get done today, he'd said.

I'm not going to lie. I didn't suddenly have a soul-ripping debate about what I was seeing and the part I was about to play in it. I obviously didn't heave my saw into the woods and hike back to town and a quiet life of fixing stoves and refrigerators. Now, weeks later, it's easy to think of things I should have thought of then. Could have would have should have. I don't have any excuses. I remember having a speedy unhinged feeling, a little like what I felt the first minutes after a young navy guy ran a stop sign and slammed into my truck in Port Douglas a few years ago.

But one thought cut through the daze: I can't go backwards. I'm not saying I didn't have any choices, standing there between two fresh Elder stumps with my blood pumping. I've come to think we always have choices. I'm saying that the one thing I wouldn't do was go back to being nowhere.

THE FACT IS IT WAS SURPRISINGLY EASY TO GET BACK IN THE GROOVE. The first tree felt a little strange, especially when I was making the up-cut for the hinge to set the falling direction. I wasn't getting the leverage right, and by the time I was done it was a sorry excuse for a wedge. It didn't matter. The crew was way downhill from me — I started with the first blue-blazed tree I came to, and there were plenty, as I walked down from the crest — and even if they'd been closer they were too busy to note my handiwork. I felt awkward right up to the moment I finished the cut on that first one, watching for the first microscopic sway of the trunk and then seeing it, stepping back as it tipped faster and faster until the whole broad mass of limbs and needles was rushing towards the ground, the shaking burst of thunder as it hit, the slight bounce and gusting cloud of dirt and twigs. What rushed through me then was the same juice that rushed through me ten years before. It may as well have been ten hours before.

The next two went down more easily, but as I crouched to start the hinge on the third tree I felt the old tweaks, thin currents of pain curving across my lower back. They were reminding me yes, it's true, a decade really had gone by. I wasn't going to get away with the slop that I did when I was thirty. Not that I'd exactly been lying by the pool all the years in between. I'd wrestled with I don't know how many refrigerators and washing machines, but I'd learned to do it smart, always with a handtruck or dolly. Out there they don't give you a handtruck. There's just something about the position you bend yourself into to fall a tree that backs hate. One trip to the Spot to watch the older guys shuffle around the room tells the story.

So I adjusted. I went back to the position I fashioned years before, standing straight with my elbows planted on either side of my navel and rotating my hips like a good fastball hitter in slow motion. It gave great leverage and calmed down the tweaks. The only rub, like before, was that I ended up cutting a little higher on the trunk, six or eight inches above where the blaze mark said I should cut. If I hadn't let that worry me back when Mel was stomping around the woods looking for mistakes, I wasn't going to cry about it now. At the rate James Nielsen was scouring this mountain he could leave a couple of extra inches on the stump and still feed his family.

The woods got brighter and warmer as I worked my way down the slope. Late in the morning I came to a big spruce that had to come down in a channel between a boulder and a tree that hadn't been cut yet, a slot that wasn't wider than six feet. That's exactly where it fell, smack in the middle of the safe zone. There was a smoothness to it now, that old calming feeling of all the parts coming together just right, with me as the smallest piece of the whole. For a passing moment I had to wonder: it couldn't be, could it, that I have the Blood after all?

I shut off the saw and listened. Further down the slope the drone of the other saws was rising and falling, a zigzag of mutant insect buzzing. I sat down against the stump I'd made and pulled out half a sandwich, a small brick of two thick sourdough slices separated by peanut butter and lots of honey. I bit off a corner and unscrewed my water bottle for a drink. I felt my shoulders let go. My thoughts skittered quickly across the surface — the texture of the bark on my back, the sweet stickiness of the sandwich, how I should leave the water bottle in the freezer tonight to make it stay colder. With care I pulled apart the remaining half of my sandwich like a clotting bandage from a wound. I should use less honey next time. I looked down at my feet, at a hidden point under the rim of my right boot where I could feel a blister start to form. Do I have anything to put on it? I don't.

I heard a rustling behind me and turned to see a boy in his mid teens coming my way. He carried two red metal cans and on his back was a chopped rucksack with a pegged wooden cross piece that carried several loops of saw chain. He was doing the same job I did more than twenty-five years before. "You want a change?" he asked me.

Way back when, I never let anyone else change out the chain on my saw. "Let me see what you've got," I said. The boy stepped forward, turned his back to me and kneeled so that I could inspect the chains. Half a dozen of them, dull, greasy and flecked with forest particles, hung together on the center peg. They were on their way back to the crummy and then the filer, who'd work through the night at the maintenance yards. On either side of the dull chains were sharp ones, also dark with use but with tiny silver half-moons at the front edge of every tooth that gleamed in the light. I ran one of the slicing edges over the soft part of my finger.

"Nice," I said, lifting the chain off the peg. "Sure, do it." The boy turned around, took the chain and kneeled next to my saw. He was big, softer in the face than the body, with moist skin and oddly round patches of pink on his cheeks. He unclipped a saw wrench from his belt and started unbolting the bar from the saw's housing. A half-inch of tongue stuck out in concentration. "What's your name?"

"Matthew Wright," he said, fitting the wrench over the second retaining nut.

"Norm and Billie Wright?" The Wrights had a little dairy a few miles down the Port Douglas road. I used to buy raw milk there in wide-mouthed gallon jars back when the state allowed it, and when my stomach could handle milk. I remembered little kids running around back then that would be his age now.

"He's my uncle," Matthew said. He pulled the bar free and dropped two nuts and lock washers next to the saw.

"You might want to set those little dudes on top of the housing, right next to the fuel cap," I said. "That way they won't try to escape down into the duff."

"Nnnhh," said Matthew, not moving the little parts and not looking up. He tightened the bolts back onto the saw and topped it off with fuel and oil.

"Got any cold water?" I asked.

He shook his head. "Bring you some next time."

"That's okay," I said as he finished packing his tools. "It's close to lunch time, I'll get some." He stood up to go. "Well, thanks a lot, Matthew. Is Matthew okay, or do they call you Matt?"

"Nnnhh." He headed down the hill towards another faller. I watched and wondered if he'd be sitting against a stump like this one day, watching some other teenager walk down the hill with dull chains swaying behind him.

I pulled a cheap sports watch from my pocket. 10:55. I could probably drop two more before they honked the horn for lunch. Just below me on the slope another spruce stood next to a fir that looked half again as big, probably three feet across at the base. Both had blue blazes. I'd get those two.

I walked towards the fir tree and started the saw. The fresh chain jumped right through the wood and soon I'd sliced out a clean wedge the size of a long watermelon quarter. I stepped around to the uphill side, braced myself straight up, and laid the chain in a hand's width above the paint blaze. I could feel the moment it passed through the softer bark and reached real wood. Tiny blond ribbons of fiber flew out of the growing groove and dusted the hair on my left arm as I pushed on.

What I felt then was just like an electric shock running through my saw and hands and into my belly. The half-second it lasted was enough for a strange shard of thought: there's a *power* line in this tree, and I've hit it. Then there was the noise, a throaty squeal like beebees in a high-speed blender. I think I was starting to back off when a jerking snap moved through me. The corner of my right eye picked up a dark blur of movement just before what felt like a burning I-beam crashed into my back. I remember the ground rushing towards my face, and wanting to push it away. I couldn't.

PART II

28

FIRST IT IS SOLID DARKNESS WITH LITTLE RUSTLES OF SOUND. THEN SOME movement, mine or from others around me, I can't tell. Then hints of color start to streak the blackness like the thin fractures that begin cracking the Arctic ice free at the end of the long winter. Then the streaks gradually come together into bleary shapes that glide through the right edge of my world; straight ahead of me is still blackness. I hear my mother's voice.

"Mom?" Someone calls out. "Mom?" I know that the voice will call out again and I know when. "Mom?"

"I'm here. I'm here, Jack." Her hands are dry and cool, pressing my face.

"Mom?"

Her lips are on my forehead. "I'm here, baby."

Around me it is warm and heavy. Above me is a pink shape laced by the web of blackness, pressing me more heavily now and shuddering slightly. "Mom?"

"Hush, now," my mother says. "Shhh." Wetness passes from her face to mine. The webbing closes into solid blackness.

BLEARS OF COLOR SHOOT THROUGH THE BLACKNESS AGAIN. DOWN AT my side I can feel my hand held tightly by two others. "Mom?" It is more of a croak than a word; my throat is dry and huge.

"Jack. Jack?" Not Mom. One hand leaves mine and touches my face.

It's Holly's hand on my face. I reach up before she can take it away and press it to me. I have dreamed this before. I'm dreaming it now. No. It's not a dream. It's...what?

"Jack, you're going to make it," Holly says. Her voice is husky, not quite in her control. "You really are. Oh, Jack." She shudders. I can see only her outline, not her face.

"Hey, come on," I say. "Holly." I reach for her with my right hand, the one near her. I try to lift my left hand across my body towards her but it is too heavy. She lifts my right hand to her face and kisses the palm. Holly kisses my palm.

Did I ask her then to tell me what had happened? I don't think the words came out. I closed my eyes for what seems like seconds. When I opened them again the dark web was almost gone and Holly was standing with Mom at the foot of my bed. Nearest to me, where Holly had been, was a doctor who looked too young. He had a crewcut and aviator glasses that covered a third of his face. "Welcome back, Jack," he said. "How do you feel?"

Fine, I started to say. Then I looked at the four faces staring down at me — Doc Ford was standing at the corner of the bed, between this boy doctor and Holly — and closed my eyes. More than anything else I felt heavy. My neck, shoulders and arms felt like I'd finished swimming the butterfly stroke to Japan. From my belly down I couldn't feel even exhaustion; it was as if my lower half was a four-foot loaf of solid lead so heavy that the bedsprings strained to hold it up. The lowest I could feel any sensation was a ring around my midsection, from the small of my back around the bottom of my ribcage to my navel. It throbbed a dull clamping pain. "What day is it?"

"Wednesday," the doctor said, watching his watch as he took my pulse. The last day I could remember was a Thursday. He nodded and set my hand by my side like precious pottery. "I'm Dr. Weldon, Jack," he said. "We haven't met before, but I've been talking with Dr. Ford and he tells me you're not somebody who has time for lots of chit-chat. He says you like things straight, and that's what your mother says, too." I looked at Mom, squeezing the rail at the foot of the bed with both hands.

"So let's be straight," Dr. Weldon said. "Jack, the chain of your saw flew off your bar and wrapped halfway around your body. It slashed you right above the belt, and if your friends hadn't done exactly the right things and called in a helicopter you would have bled to death right then and there. It turned out there wasn't that much damage to your side — there was a wound above your right hip we sewed up, but it didn't penetrate to the organs. The full impact concentrated at your lower back, almost like the chain was a bullwhip and all the power gathered down at the tip. That's where the teeth dug in. They sliced through the muscle right by the second lumbar vertebra, just about straight back from where your navel is. The amazing thing is how little bone damage there was, probably because the chain was so sharp. I don't think we'll even need a body cast."

Here he looked away from me, but then rushed on to keep his momentum going. "The problem is the wound caused a swelling underneath that has severed the spinal cord. There's no way with these things to know exactly how someone will heal, but we have a pretty good idea. What I have to tell you is that you won't ever have the use of any part of your body below your waist again."

People have asked me what my first thoughts were at that instant. The very first one was how preposterously big this guy's glasses were. He looked like a disco-nerd. Then it started feeling a little like what happened when I was standing in the half-logged Elders: I was listening to some doctor tell some man he'd never walk again. When he finished I scanned the row of faces around me to see how the story sounded to them.

It was Holly's face that made me understand. There wasn't much in her expression. She looked drained and tense at the same time, pale and flat, reflecting nothing as she looked down at me. A stab of panic hit me, because Holly looked *helpless*. I had never seen her like that before, outside the boundaries of action that make things happen certain ways in the world, just outside the fence with her fingers clutching the chain-link, without resource or idea for changing what was going on in front of her. The only sound as we looked at each other in that bright white room was the rattle of a cart passing in the hallway outside. That was when the mass of fear reached me.

Dr. Weldon had a little more to say but I can't tell you what it was. I asked him something or other, when I could start exercises that would get me walking again or something else that must have made him think I was too drugged up to understand what he'd told me. I wasn't, but something inside like a screaming child was trying mightily to push understanding away, *no, it can't be, no, they got it wrong, maybe it's bad but it's not forever like he said, it's not, no, it's a sick sick mistake, no no NO*, rushing through my brain and chest and veins on gallons of adrenaline, so that I could only watch the doctors' lips move with whatever last soothing words they said, then Doc Ford's big hand on my shoulder. Then they were gone.

Mom came around the bed and burrowed her hands beneath my shoulders to hug me. Her silent heaving surged against my neck. After a moment she lifted her wet bleary face and looked at me. "It'll be all right, baby," she shuddered. She stroked my hair back from my face and tried to say something else. Her mouth tightened inward to a small wrinkled hole. She shook her head, tears flowing free now, pulled her arms free and stepped quickly out the door.

Holly watched her leave and her eyes stayed for a moment on the empty doorway. Then she slid a chair from the wall into the slot where Mom had just been and sat down next to me. As I looked into her green eyes, glistening now as she took in a deep breath, my inside screaming settled down into a perfectly clear thought. It was this: *How about now, Holly? Can* this *make a difference for you and me?*

I swear it's true. Five minutes hadn't passed since finding out I'm crippled for life and I was lying there running the odds that this, finally, would bring her to me. Cutting my legs off wasn't a strategy I would have picked, but then the ones I *had* picked over forty years — macho man, funny man, politically sensitive man — none had worked. None had come close. This one couldn't fail worse than the others.

I listened to her voice and watched her body for clues as she began telling me the rest of the story. What she told me was what anyone who follows the news already knows. My saw hit the bottom inch of a six-inch spike that had been driven downward at a steep angle, buried just enough so that its head passed all the way through the bark and out of sight. The small hole it had made had been plugged with a chip of loose bark, a quick patch job that kept the bright inner wood from showing through. The metal detector Lewsco had used since the buy-out to check marked trees had been useless; the spike was made of ceramic, no thicker than a pencil but much harder than the thin teeth of my chain.

Holly told me the mountain was crawling with lawmen, county deputies, state police, even a few dudes in shiny suits and wingtips that had to be feds, looking for a handle to grab. They were covering every square foot of ground between the Falls and town, talking to people on the street and in the Spot, even in their front yards, trying to find who knows what. "There isn't any focus to it," Holly said. "I don't think they know enough to focus."

That didn't stop other people who weren't anywhere close to the scene from having it all figured out. They were all over the news. After Holly took Mom home for the day the nurse offered to turn on the TV bracketed high up on the wall across from me. It was 7:00 p.m. and CNN was just dropping into its half-hour cycle. A story about police shooting more demonstrators in Haiti, then pictures of O.J. looking bored and disgusted while his team whispered secretly at Judge Ito's bench, and then I was looking at an exterior shot of the hospital I was lying in.

"…and in Grants Pass, Oregon, doctors say the victim of the worst incident of forest sabotage on record is out of danger and resting comfortably. Forty-three year old John Adams Gilliam" and there I was, smiling out from under the bill of a McCullough chain saw cap, a goofy photo somebody took at that timber carnival in Bounty a million years ago, "was paralyzed from the waist down when his saw exploded on contact with a large iron spike believed to have been planted by environmental extremists protesting the logging of virgin trees in the Pacific Northwest." The video showed a huge Ponderosa Pine coming down somewhere in the high desert at least a hundred miles east of here, then a pasty executive-looking type behind a podium covered with microphones in a fancy ballroom.

"If there was any question before, now it can be laid to rest," he read from a paper in front of him. Letters came on the screen:

EDWARD THOMASON
National Assoc of Timber Operators

"The same individuals who would have us believe that their protests are based on respect for the sanctity of all life are apparently willing to maim or kill other human beings who are lawfully engaged in activities they don't agree with. We only regret that it took a human tragedy of this order to expose the true agenda of these individuals for all to see."

The picture cut to an outside scene, a platform with another cluster of microphones in a sunny park somewhere. I almost recognized the man behind the microphones. Then the shot changed to a close up and filling up the screen was the face of Stanton Freed. "No one," he says, "condemns this terrible act of violence more strongly than we do. Unlike some others, we won't recklessly speculate about who's responsible for this hideous crime, but in a larger sense we all know who is guilty: those whose greed has violated the order of things. Is there anyone left who really believes we can upset the entire balance of the Earth and expect nothing to happen?"

Then they went back again to the grinning idiot photo of me. Me. The Human Tragedy, the Hideous Crime that however many million people were mulling over at that second in the glow of their TV sets, was about me.

THE IDENTICAL STORY RAN ON CNN ALL THROUGH THE NEXT DAY AND into Friday. I kept the TV on with the volume too low to hear. I saw Stanton Freed moving his lips half a dozen times. He looks even snootier when you're not distracted by the words he's saying.

On Friday morning when it started playing again, Mom got up from her chair and reached up to turn it off. "Hey, I was watching that!" I said. I punched the red button on the remote control clipped to the bedframe and saw my old photo warble into place on the screen.

Mom shook her head. "It's just the same thing again, Jackie. How many times do you have to watch it?"

"It's CNN, Mom. The only way to know when they update the story is to keep watching."

"Well then, we'll check on it again tonight when your dinner comes and see what they have." She put a hand on my bed rail again to extend her reach to the set. "Because watching the same thing over and over and over again, Jackie, what can that possibly do except get you more upset?" And she turned the set off again.

"God DAMN it, Mother, get your fucking hands off that thing!" I punched the power button again and turned the volume up. "I don't need you deciding what'll upset me and what won't, okay? Just stop trying to turn this into a sweet little story like you always do, because you can't. You *can't*, don't you get it? I'm a fucking cripple, Mom, your little boy's a gimp now and forevermore, so save me this shit about not getting upset! Okay? Can you do me that one favor, please? God, everything's just wonderful, isn't it? Nothing that happens is ever a problem, just so long as we don't get *upset* about it. Give me a fucking break, okay?"

She was quaking, holding the center of her chest with both hands, and I didn't care. I made a big point of looking up to watch Stanton's lips move around the same speech again. Out of the corner of my eye I saw her walk out the door. When the story ended I started channel surfing to keep from thinking anymore.

That was when two guys in dark suits, one with a gray crew-cut and the other an Asian, the first I'd ever seen in Grants Pass, came into the room and asked me how I was feeling. Before I answered they showed me FBI badges and asked if I felt up to answering a couple of questions. Before I could answer that they pulled two chairs up to the left side of the bed and sat down.

The older guy, Don something, sat closer to me and asked the questions. He had me walk through every step of the day I could remember from the time I met up with Dusty's crew at the yards. He interrupted twice, once for more details about the handful of sleepy protestors we saw when we drove through the gate and once to push my memory for everything I noticed when the kid, Matt, came over and put a new chain on my saw. Down towards the foot of the bed the Asian guy was taking notes of what I said in a pocket-sized notebook.

"And this happened on the first day you came back to logging in what, ten years?" Don asked.

"More," I said. "Twelve, I think."

"You stopped logging for twelve years and then all of a sudden decided to go back to it? Can I ask why?"

"I don't know how sudden it was," I said. "It's something that I'd been thinking about a while. The money's good, and I had a few things going on where it seemed to make sense." The words came slowly. I was starting to feel tired.

"Yes, but what I'm asking is why *then?*" Don was leaning forward closer to my face. "Why on this particular day?"

"I think he's already answered that, Don," the Asian guy said, his first words. "There wasn't anything special about the particular day, was there, Jack? No special reason this happened on your first day back?"

"I don't know any," I said. There was a pause. Don was turned away from me, looking at his partner. He cocked his head and seemed to check out my bedsheets before turning back to me.

"So it's all coincidental, then," Don said. I looked past him to his partner, whose eyebrows bounced up and back down, almost like a wink. Don was looking at an index card from his pocket. "Do you know a woman named...Holly Burgess?"

"Yes."

"Other than your mother," Don said, "she's the only one they let in to visit you. Why is that?"

It was getting harder to concentrate on his words. I felt like arching my back, feeling some kind of movement, and I couldn't. "Because I want her to."

"You want her to," Don said. "How long have you known Holly, Jack?"

"Years. A long time."

"How many years?"

I was so tired. "I don't know that we have to know how many," I heard the Asian say. "You were friends way back before the protests started, right, Jack?" I nodded. "What more than that do we need, Don?"

I was asleep before Don answered.

SO EVEN BEFORE THE WEEKEND CALLS CAME I KNEW IT WAS A BIG DEAL. Then early on Saturday morning, a couple of hours before dawn, a doctor I hadn't seen before woke me up and moved the telephone from the nightstand to my bed. He raised the back of the bed and pressed the receiver to my ear until I could manage to hold it.

"Mmhhh?" I said.

"Mr. Gilliam?" It was a woman's voice, very formal.

"Yah."

"Please hold for the president, sir." There was a click. A hard frosty feeling seeped into my chest. A second doctor and three nurses came silently into the room, gliding in a way that made me wonder if I was awake.

The phone clicked again. "Is this John Gilliam?"

"Yes?"

"John, this is Bill Clinton. I sure hope I'm not disturbing you, am I?"

"Uhh...no." It was 4:20 in the morning, I found out later. "I had to get up anyway to answer the phone." Don't ask where that came from.

He laughed, a raspy chuckle. "Yeah, that's right. I like that one too." The only person who had that laugh was Bill Clinton, President of the United States, and I was on the phone with him. "Man, it's a relief to hear you in that kind of spirits with what you been through. Say, John...can I call you John?"

"Uh, yeah. Yes, Mr. President."

"John, I've been meaning to get in touch for a while to tell you how sorry I am for what's happened and to let you know you're in our prayers."

"Thank you, Mr. President."

"You know, I came to Oregon last year just to find a solution to this thing, the Vice President and I came out to Portland and brought everybody to the table — you're out there near Portland, are you?"

"Well, we're..."

"And we've worked real damn hard on it ever since, and we finally have the thing figured out. Not that everybody will like every little thing we have to do, that's not what I'm saying. That's not how these things go. But we've come an awful long ways, and then something like this up and happens. It's damn stupid, John, and it's wrong. It's just wrong. And here's what I want you to know: we just don't plan to put up with it. Whoever did this thing, we'll find him. We can't undo the awful thing that's been done to you, but we can find who did it and bring him to justice. You understand me there, John?"

"Yes, Mr. President."

"And I mean it. I do. Now — hold on a minute, will you, John?"

"Yes, sir." Ten seconds went by. There were a dozen people in my room now, silent as statues. The night nurse was the only one I recognized.

He came back. "John, they're calling me away now. It's a radio morning and I haven't even looked at the damn script. But listen, now, I want you to hang in there, you hear me? And when you get better, I want you to come pay me and Hillary a visit. Will you do that, John? So

you hang in there, partner, and you take care. You're in my prayers."
And he was gone.

Three hours later we were all in my room, Holly, Mom, me and what
seemed like half the hospital staff, looking high on the wall at CNN.
The screen was full of a photograph of Clinton in a red plaid shirt and
earphones, leaning intently into a mike with his mouth open and smil-
ing at the same time, as they played some tape of that morning's talk.
He finished the written part of his speech by challenging Congress
to face its responsibility to do something or other. Then his voiced
shifted almost like he was starting to wing it.

"There's just one more thing I'd like to share with you this morn-
ing," he said. "I've just had the privilege of talking to the most coura-
geous individual I've met in a long time. His name is John Gilliam, he
lives in Lewis Falls, Oregon, and I'm sure you've heard of his situation.
A cowardly act of terrorism in the forests of our Pacific Northwest has
left John Gilliam paralyzed below the waist. I'm very happy to report
that Mr. Gilliam is out of danger and resting comfortably. He told me
all about his experience and his plans for an active productive future.
And what touched me more deeply than anything else was that this
man who's been dealt such an unfair hand, who you would think would
be filled with nothing but sorrow and bitterness, actually took the time
to share a private joke with me, one that I promised to keep between
him and me. I don't have many modern-day heroes, but I believe I
met one today.

"And what I want you to know, John Gilliam, is that this attack on
you is an attack on all of us, on every American dedicated to honest
hard work and the peaceful resolution of our differences. I have di-
rected the Attorney General to place the highest priority on identify-
ing the party or parties responsible for this crime and bringing them
to justice. John Gilliam of Lewis Falls deserves that much. The Ameri-
can people deserve that much."

That's how my first conscious weekend as a cripple started.

29

AND THAT WAS JUST SATURDAY. ON SUNDAY AFTERNOON THE *TODAY* SHOW called to see if they could do a live interview on Monday morning, right there in the hospital room. That set off a sparky little debate among the doctors. I don't think any of them loved the idea, but they didn't rule it out. It could be their beady-eyed world view of proper procedure and malpractice suits had been knocked out of focus by my friend Bill's little testimonial to me. Mom was sitting in the corner when Dr. Weldon came in to say the decision was mine, but she wasn't about to offer up her opinion on this or anything else. I wasn't ready to apologize yet, probably because I knew she was waiting for it.

At 6:00 p.m. the producer from *Today* called back, right when she said she would. She needed an answer right then in order to get a camera crew down from Seattle in time. "I want to be 100 percent clear," she said. "We only want to do this if you do." But she sounded like she already had her answer. "You'll be the first feature in the 8:00 segment, 5:00 a.m. your time. My crew will roll in an hour earlier to set up."

She was so matter-of-fact I almost said no. "You guys don't futz around, do you?"

"Futzing doesn't work very well for us," she said. "So we're on?"

I looked at Mom in the corner of the room before I answered. I didn't know if her glare was disapproval or leftover hurt. I knew two things: the way not to be pitiful was to bounce back as fast and as pumped-up as I could, and this was the one chance in my life I had to meet Katie Couric. "We're on."

TEN HOURS LATER ONE OF THE NIGHT NURSES GENTLY SHOOK ME AWAKE. The other one was busy trying to keep some distance between the bed and a puffy red-bearded guy pushing in behind her. His blue ballcap and leather-sleeved letterman's jacket had the same logo, a stylized peacock over a block-style TODAY. "What, you gonna sleep all day?" he growled in the middle of a skilled pivot around the nurse. "I'm Chas Burton, Jack," he said, cracking a smile the color of Camels, "and you" — he lightly tapped my shoulder with a clipboard — "are almost a star."

Half an hour later the room was a TV studio. Blazing light from two directions met at the head of the bed, where I was raised almost to a sitting position. A third light bounced off a reflective screen above me. My face felt tight from some pasty powder that a woman with green hair tucked under a TODAY cap like Chas' had spread across my face. Through the blaze of light I could hear the whirs and clicks of someone fiddling with a camera at the foot of the bed. Chas was out of the room for most of the preparation but strode back in a little before 5:00 with a Styrofoam cup of coffee in each hand.

"So" — he checked his watch with a swivelling move that kept the coffee upright — "in eleven minutes, Bryant will do his thing and then go to you. Just keep looking at the camera and relax and when he asks a question, you talk to the man. Just a chat, okay? Here," he said, handing me a steaming cup. "Wake-up juice." I didn't need any. Everything was too weird and bright to be sleepy. I sipped two small swallows before he took back the cup and set it on the nightstand.

So much for meeting Katie. "Where do I look to see Bryant?" I asked.

"You don't. You just listen to him through this," he was putting a soft plastic plug in my ear and draping a connecting wire over and behind my ear and shoulder so that it disappeared in the bedding.

"I can't see him but he can see me?"

"Mmm-hmm," Chas said, checking the small microphone they'd pinned to my smock. "Jack hears Bryant but doesn't see him. Bryant sees and hears Jack. So do 17 million other Bozos eating their cornflakes and putting on their pantyhose." Something in my face made Chas smile. "It's called *star*dom."

The minutes passed slowly, time I knew I should use to imagine the questions that were coming and how I'd answer them. But my brain wouldn't do it. We sat there quietly in the thrum of the waking hospital. The crew murmured now and then through their headsets to people far away. What I heard faintly through my ear plug was the *Today* show just as people on the East Coast were hearing it. An ad for an airlines, another for steak sauce, a scene from a TV movie playing tonight about twins trying to kill each other. Then the bum-bump music of the show, a deep male voice telling the date, Katie talking about the shadow of terror falling over the woods of the Great Northwest and how they'll be talking to America's most famous father-daughter fashion designer combo after the news. Then the news in a woman's voice dark with concern, five or six stories with mine in the middle — still no leads in the case, but I was doing much better, as they'll see after the news — then music and an ad for dog food.

"One minute," Chas said. I closed my eyes and drew a deep breath. Seventeen million people.

The fanfare music again. "The Spotted Owl," Bryant said. "Ancient Forests. Clearcuts. Earth First! Eco-sabotage. They've become familiar terms to most of us, the dramatic script of one of the longer-running environmental battles in American life. But ten days ago, on September 29, they became far more than words and slogans for one man in Oregon. That was the morning when John Adams Gilliam Junior was cutting down a virgin pine tree in the mountain forests near the California border, when he struck a spike — a large nail driven into the tree by party or parties unknown for the express purpose of sabotaging the logging operation. The collision of the powerful chainsaw and the giant nail caused an explosion that left John Gilliam paralyzed from his waist down."

"Ready," Chas whispered next to me. I looked through the glare towards the camera.

"John Gilliam is with us now," Bryant said, "recovering in his hospital bed in Grants Pass, Oregon. Mr Gilliam? Welcome. How are you feeling?"

"A little sleepy." A lie right off the bat.

"Well, I'm sure," Bryant said, "but are you doing well? Is there much pain?"

"Pretty well. Actually you don't feel very much."

"Just before the top of the hour, Stanton Freed of the Western Resources Defense Council was telling us there's a good chance the spike was placed not by environmentalists at all, but actually by the timber industry itself. He says that the company you were working for — Lewsco? – even Lewsco could have planted it, just to discredit the environmental movement."

Chas nodded once at me as Bryant stopped talking. "Well, that's...not something anyone can say," I said. "They don't know at this point who did it."

"But would you say that it's likely? That the spike was put in the tree you cut by the timber company?"

I wanted to think. I wanted time they weren't going to give me. The wave of humanity briskly moving towards its day's business around the country couldn't wait. "I...no. I don't think it's likely at all."

"Why not?"

"Well, that's not what they do here. It's hard in the woods, it's a hard thing to get all those logs to the mill, and they want it to happen fast and this thing has just messed it all up for everyone. For them, too. No." Maybe that would be enough.

"So you're sure then that it was environmental extremists who did this to you."

I felt my throat knot. I looked at Chas, who tipped his head towards the camera. "No. When you say 'sure,' nobody knows who did this. No."

"But, gut feeling? If you had to guess, who do you believe spiked that tree?"

Gut feeling? My one chance in life to dance with Bryant Gumbel and I couldn't do it. "You know, I don't know. I'm sorry, but I don't. All I was was where it happened. Other than that I don't know more than you do."

There was a moment's pause. I looked at Chas and then heard Bryant. "We've had a report that authorities in Lewis County are close to making an arrest in the case. What can you tell us about that?"

For an instant I thought of old dreams, the ones with final exams in school on material you never studied or walking to center stage in front of the opening-night audience with no idea what your lines are. I could feel Chas' eyes heavy on me. I made lines up. "They're investigating hard here, that's for sure. I guess they're talking to everybody and anybody they think might know something."

"Of course they would be." All the interest had washed out of Bryant's voice. Somebody backstage in New York was going to have a rough morning when he got off the set. "John Gilliam in Grants Pass, Oregon, victim of sabotage in the Ancient Forest — good luck to you. Heal fast."

"Thank you very much."

"Back in a moment," Bryant's voice faded in my ear plug, "with a much lighter note..."

"Clear," Chas said. He took off his headset and left the room.

30

IN THE BACK OF MY MIND I HALF EXPECTED A CALL, MAYBE AS SOON AS that same day. It didn't come. Instead he showed up.

It was two days later, on Wednesday morning. Mom was with me and so was her friend Betty Sulkin who drove her down the hill. Since our fight Mom seemed to be arranging things so we wouldn't be alone together, but other than that you couldn't tell it had happened. I could. Her eyes wandered a certain way from my face down towards the center of my bed when we talked. Her hurt look, visible only to me, was a low-voltage prod to keep me mindful of what a crappy son I am until I made things right. But that was the point: things weren't going to get right. For her all this amounts to is not getting to have grandchildren. Isn't that just a damn shame. For *me*...never mind. Betty was doing most of the talking that morning, something pointless to fill the hole, when Holly walked through the door with an odd smile. Two steps behind her was Stanton Freed.

Holly didn't sit down. After big hellos to Mom and Betty she asked them if they'd had breakfast. They hadn't. Mom never does. "Well, I'm starved," Holly said. "Would you let me treat you, just this once? People actually survive the cafeteria food here, don't they Lois?" Mom gave me a quick glance for permission — when the outside world poked into the room we were on the same team — and I nodded. Holly led the two of them out.

Stanton pulled Mom's empty chair closer to me and sat down. "Well," he said with a sigh, settling in. "They say you're doing well, Jack. Easy for them to say, isn't it, when they're not the ones lying here?"

"Make yourself at home, Stanton."

He smiled. "Thank you." He looked around the room. "And a lovely home it is." Then he looked me over slowly from my feet to my face. "Shall we get right to the subject at hand? I've been trying to solve a bit of a riddle, Jack, and I am hoping you can help me think it through." He frowned slightly, a display of special effort to lay it out just right. "You're in the woods doing the job they give you to do, and you hit a spike. It does this to you," running his eyes the length of my body. "Now, here's what I want to know: who gets hurt the most by this? Besides you, I mean?"

"Who gets hurt the worst?"

"*We* do." His intensity came as suddenly as an electric shock. "This is killing us out there, no matter what we say. So what environmentalist in his right mind would do this to us?"

"In his right mind? No one."

"Actually, 'his or her' right mind," Stanton said, just as suddenly casual again, smiling. "Let's not forget proper form."

"Yeah, well, 'right mind' has nothing to do with it. There are tree-huggers out there, maybe even some who listen to your brilliant speeches, who maybe don't piece strategy together the same way you do."

"You're absolutely right, Jack. It could have been one of the looneys out there, some fried head case from the Sixties like the ones who drift into every rally. Like our friend Mr. Zenith, perhaps? And if someone like Zenith did it, would you call it a focused, purposeful act or more like a random act?"

"Random."

"Exactly. So would I. Now let's consider the other possibility." He leaned back until the front legs of the chair came off the ground. "Say you were one of the timber dogs, and you were watching the likes of us close down the federal forests, dancing in front of your log trucks and showing up in the *New York Times* every other week looking like David, and you're Goliath, and you have to turn it around. Let's even say you'd poured a few million into ads in the big magazines and on TV, the ones with the long golden shots of an eagle riding an updraft above a virgin rivershed and 101 Strings playing Aaron Copeland and a voice like God's about the umpteen trees you plant for every one you cut down. *Beautiful* shots...that don't work. You're still losing."

The front chair legs clicked down on the floor as Stanton surged towards me. "So now what?" he said. "What do you do to stop this tide, this new attention to the planet that will eventually pull down every-thing you've built? How do you convince America to listen to you instead of the tree-huggers? What can you do to grab them by the throat and make them see?"

He brought his hands together palms-up and slowly spread them to his sides, like a dramatic maitre d' presenting a table: *voila*. "So you're here because one of two things happened, Jack. Either it was an irrational act, a random act by some fruitcake who somehow managed to find a select space-age ceramic and sneak it into a tree in a surveyed stand that was being patrolled pretty much around the clock. Or it was a completely rational act. Something that could work better than anything else the timber dogs can do to turn the tide. Can you see that much, Jack?"

"Is this why you came up here? To tell me the facts of life?"

"Answering a question with another question, Jack? That is so rude." He smiled. "I'm here, my friend, because nothing this important has happened since I started working for forests, and because if we can't play this smart, we are 100 percent fucked. Not just us — you, too. Holly says you care about what happens on that mountain as much as she does. Which is saying something. If they can get John Q. Citizen to write off the movement as a bunch of bloodthirsty scum, you're going to see Lewis Falls turned into the backside of the moon."

I wasn't ready to learn from Stanton Freed. I was listening for flaws, a loose edge I could grab to rip away at the whole. I felt tired. "What do you want from me, Stanton?"

"Not much, Jack. Not too much." His voice was soothing now. "All I ask is that next time they ask you who you think did it — and they will, perhaps not the *Today* Show, but someone else who talks to millions of people and thinks you're the only one with the truth — when they ask, just think for a second about what I've said. Think about what makes sense before you answer. Help those clueless millions understand what makes sense. That we'd slit our own throat from ear to ear?" He scoffed with a tiny shake of his head. "I won't write you a script, Jack. I have far too much respect for you than that." Finally an obvious lie. "Just think about it before they stick another mike in your face. Think about how this 'only God knows' garbage makes you look. Think about the free ride it gives to the corporate propaganda machine. And if none of that matters, think about what that mountain looked like ten years ago," he nodded out the window, where the Coast Range lay in profile through the gray morning, "and what it looks like today and what it will look like ten years from now if we let them control the story."

"Since I care so much about the land?"

He smiled. "Exactly." He stood up and lifted his leather-elbowed coat off the door knob. "I'm just asking you to think about it, Jack." I looked away as he put on his coat. "Do you want me to come back? I'll be up here until Friday."

"How come?"

Stanton stepped around to the foot of the bed. "The truth will out," he said. "You're not the only person I came to visit. Tomorrow I'm going to try to get in to see the Mad Spiker."

"Who?"

"The CRAZED ECO-TERRORIST who did this to you," said Stanton with a bad radio announcer's voice. He finished straightening the cuffs on his coat and noticed my stare. "You don't know, do you? They've picked up Zenith."

"Zenith? Vietnam zombie Zenith? What for?"

"He's not the Vietnam Zombie anymore. He's the Mad Spiker. Holly went to the Courthouse when she heard they arrested somebody, but they wouldn't release the name. It probably took her the better part of a minute to pry it out of some poor deputy down there."

I closed my eyes and saw the feathery brown hair falling to his shoulders, the filthy camouflage jacket under overalls that never changed, the round dollop of hair in the middle of his chin, the beaked nose and watery eyes as stagnant as two blue birthmarks. I had an image of him at the Falls road demonstration, the last time I saw him. "Because of the spike?" I said. "That pole he was waving around over his head?"

Stanton shrugged. "I don't think it escaped their notice."

"*Zenith?* Jesus. I don't believe this. He's..." I couldn't think of a way to say it that I wanted Stanton to hear. "Zenith didn't do this."

"You're right, he didn't. You might want to share that intelligence with your friend Bryant the next time he asks."

"What are you going to do, Stanton? Will you get him released?"

"Right. Some Andy Griffith sheriff down there is going to let the Mad Spiker loose because I say so." He laughed softly, as if just getting the subtler point of a good joke. "Then, too, I'm not sure that Zenith isn't useful where he is. I know that the timber dogs did this, and I think you do, too. But if we can't prove it, maybe Zenith will be the consolation prize. There are worse outcomes to this than having Jimmy Nielsen and his friends thinking that if they won't deal with us they can deal with the Zeniths of the world."

"So why bother to go see him?"

"To give him support." Stanton's tone plainly said this wasn't a smart question. "There still is press hanging around the Courthouse, waiting for something to happen. Any bloody thing. They deserve something new to shoot, don't you think?"

"You're a fucking saint, Stanton." Now when I looked at the news I could look forward to the prospect of seeing him pontificating on the steps of the Lewis County Courthouse.

"My theory is somewhat different from that," he said, stepping towards the door, "but I'm willing to consider yours." At the doorway he put his hand on the jamb and turned half around to face me. "So. Thanks for the hospitality, my friend." He was gone.

I stared through the doorway to the small slice of empty hallway I could see, wondering which part of his visit had scoured me out and left this numb feeling. What if Zenith really did do it? What if he had the skill or luck to find a ceramic spike and plant it in the tree without a trace? Could that be the entire, complete reason I'm a cripple? Could it be that stupid?

31

I SPENT THE REST OF THE WEEK IN THE HOSPITAL. IT WOULD HAVE BEEN longer without Doc Ford's help. He came around every day. Steady as a metronome, right through the succession of earnest-looking docs and nurses that seemed to change daily, he'd walk in early every morning and at dinnertime. Every time he'd poke around, squeeze my feet and calves and above my knees, searching for feeling that the other doctors had stopped looking for. "Talk," he'd tell me, kneading away, but I never had anything to say.

He said there was no point keeping me there. I'd need therapy, but you don't have to be a prisoner to get that. The day of Stanton's visit they started teaching me how to move from the bed to the wheel chair. The movements weren't hard — the therapist says my upper body strength is way beyond average — but the weight of my lower body pulling down on my back, especially moving from the chair back into bed, almost made me scream. The therapist fine-tuned my movement and I got more used to the feeling, so that Monday morning, exactly a week after *Today*, Mom rolled me out of County Hospital into a flat Grants Pass fog. It looked great to me.

The moment was quieter than I thought it would be. As we came out the back entrance where a tall van with ambulance lights was waiting with its side doors open, I saw a videocam and two still photographers. They rushed over for pictures, they asked me how I felt, but they weren't nearly as hyper as you'd expect after waiting for me for eighteen days.

"Where are all your buddies?" I asked the video guy when I was sure his camera was off. "Don't tell me the thrill is already gone already."

"New thrill," he said.

Then he told me about PDEC. Sometime after midnight the night before a monster fire had burned it to the ground, the whole thing, every one of the strung-together buildings. Unbelievable. Unbe*liev*-able. But a big enough deal to pull the whole press herd over the hill to Port Douglas? The pictures had to be better than shooting the outside of a hospital for two weeks, I knew that, but what would the national networks and wire services care about the burning of some podunk food co-op?

The video guy must have read my face. "Thing is, there was a note. About you." Then the van doors closed and we started up the hill. The two ambulance guys in front didn't know anything about it. The driver didn't say a word the whole time and the other kept asking me to tell him the joke I told Clinton. I asked them to turn on the radio but they claimed it didn't work.

The camera guys followed us all the way up the hill. By the time we got to Mom's a string of press vans was parked in the gravel clearing out front. The ambulance driver backed up as close as he could to Mom's porch, which had a new plywood wheelchair ramp off to the side where a set of three steps had been. From the moment they rolled me out the van's back doors to when I crossed Mom's threshold I was the center of a moving mass of cameras, microphones and shouting people. Their questions crashed together in a jabbering pile. It took both of the ambulance guys to get me inside, one clearing a path like an All-Pro lineman and the other pushing my chair and yelling at people to get back. The front door opened just as we reached it and Holly stepped out. She stepped around me and started herding the reporters behind me off the porch, her arms straight out to her side like a moving wall. "Okay, okay, okay," she shouted. "A little room now, okay?"

The noise level dropped in half when the door closed behind us. The ambulance attendant went over to set up something in the midst of the hospital equipment we were renting. Mom had come in from the kitchen and I asked her to turn on the TV while I rolled myself over in front of it.

The Grants Pass station was doing a live feed from PDEC, a reporter in a parka squinting through a heavy drizzle and pressing a plug into his ear to hear the anchorwoman back in the studio. She asked what he knew about the note found at the scene.

"Not much, Brandy. Officials say they have a letter claiming responsibility for the fire and we *think* linking it to the tree-spiking sabotage two weeks ago, but they won't comment on the details."

That was all there was until the next day's *Oregonian*. FOREST WAR

BLAZES ON stretched across the top of the front page above a night-time picture of orange flames and a morning picture of black steaming remains. The story said the whole structure was ablaze within a minute or two after someone first called it in at 2:30 in the morning. There was stuff about the "pungent scorched food and spice smells that clogged the air" and the sounds of exploding glass jars that a few witnesses heard. They quoted an old guy who lived across the alley behind the store saying it reminded him of Normandy.

Another picture took up the top of an inside page. It showed a black and gray jumble of debris with feeble-looking metal pipes twisting up from the floor here and there. In the front corner of the frame was a shapeless object the size of a bath tub. The caption said

> The partially-melted bronze sculpture of a pelican (bottom left) that co-op visitors regarded as a token of good luck was an ironic casualty of Monday morning's fire in Port Douglas.

Beauregard.

The note that gave the story its size was found inside one of those little beige insulated boxes with a twisting handle on the lid, the kind you're supposed to protect mortgage and insurance papers from fire. Inside was a single three-hole piece of lined notebook paper sandwiched between a couple of old asbestos house tiles. It had a ragtag assortment of single words cut out of magazines and newspapers just like ransom notes in the old movies. "Violence is not our way," it said,

> We are happy to be left alone, simple men and women going about our work as our families have since they came to Oregon many many many years ago. But no longer will we sit by while our livelihoods, and now one of our lives, are destroyed.
> — Jack's Avengers

LET ME TELL YOU SOMETHING ABOUT FAME: WHEN YOU DON'T HAVE IT IT looks better than it is. It looked fine to me when there wasn't the ghost of a chance I'd have any. When you're famous you're automatically important. Everyone wants to be important. Famous people are a super-class of beings who walk around like they're backlit with a golden glow, pulling everyone's energy when they pass. More than important, they're "fascinating." Pick up Personality Magazine for the last dozen Decembers when they list America's 25 most "fascinating" people. Lots of Mel Gibson, Christy Whitman, Alan Greenspan, Courtney Cox, John Kennedy. I'm sorry, but these people aren't fascinating. They're famous.

Now I have a lock on being one of the most fascinating 25 people of 1994. The spike by itself might have gotten me there. It was plenty to get the attention of my buddies Bryant and Bill. But whatever idiot burned down PDEC raised me up another big notch. The networks and newspapers must have thought they died and went to heaven, like when Patty Hearst got kidnaped and turned into an armed revolutionary with her little Che Guevara beret. "Jack's Avengers?" It was Marvel Comics come to life.

From that day on Mom's front yard was like a cross between the floor of the agricultural futures market after a spring blizzard and Mardi Gras. It's just a little patch of ground, maybe half a basketball court's worth of hard chalky dirt with little clumps of grass that can't take hold because a tiny grove of cedar trees covers them with shade. Nearly every square foot of it was covered with the press, camera and sound guys (almost all guys) and field producers and reporters whose only aim was to get something from me no one else had. It didn't matter that I had nothing to say to them even if I'd wanted. They were extra revved up because after all those days waiting outside the hospital the PDEC fire made them miss my trip back up the mountain. How happy their bosses must have been about that.

It was quickly obvious that we had more than we could handle at Mom's. I wasn't inside five minutes before they were banging their hands on every door and window. Mom stood in the middle of the living room, pale and shaky, trying to look every direction at once. As they were leaving the ambulance guys radioed the sheriff to get a deputy up here as fast as they could.

Holly stood outside for a minute before rushing in, bolting the door and grabbing the kitchen phone. "Steve?" she yelled into it. "I'm at Lois' with Jack and there's a crowd here trying to push in like you wouldn't believe." She paused. "Yeah, we did already, but we need you." Another pause. "No, now! *Please.*"

Steve and two other Lewsco office guys were there so fast I didn't have time to get scared. First I heard the yelps of some of those hunkered on the front porch, just outside the door. "Hey hey HEYYY!" "What the, who the hell are you pushing?" "Hey, whoah, you don't want to be doing that, Mister!" The muffled clatter of feet on wood and the grunting and shouts sounded like Steve was clearing the porch without discussion.

"Okay, folks, let's get something straight," I heard him yell. "You do *not* have permission to be here."

"Who are you?" some woman yelled back.

"Doesn't matter who I am," Steve said. "What matters is this is private property and you're not welcome on it. Right out there, where the gravel ends, the edge of the blacktop? That's a public road out there, no one's saying you can't be there. But you got exactly one minute to get away from this house and off these people's property."

"Sieg HIEL," somebody yelled.

"What's the big deal?" the first woman shouted. 'Why can't we talk to Jack?"

"Does Jack say we have to leave?"

"Who burned down the food store?"

"Why's Jack afraid to talk?"

"Fifty seconds," Steve yelled.

It took more like five minutes, and they didn't clear off Mom's lot completely. But they backed off to where we didn't feel like they were about to swallow us. Steve pulled two folding chairs out of the back of his truck and set one up on the front porch and the other on the corner of the house that leads to the backyard. A rotation of Lewsco guys sat in them continuously for a solid week to watch the crowd.

IN THAT WEEK THEY LET ONLY THREE OUTSIDERS THROUGH, THE FIRST almost exactly twenty-four hours after I got home. His name was Will Hayama, and I'd seen him once before. He was the quieter FBI agent, the one taking notes, when they interviewed me at the hospital. I liked him right away even while knowing he was half of the good cop/bad cop number they ran on me. He has this vital energy, a steady contained excitement about just being here and drawing breath. In a conversation he concentrates every particle of attention on you. The intensity's heightened by his piercingly beautiful Asian face, dramatic high cheekbones like the guy on the old Star Trek crew.

I was in the rented hospital bed in my old bedroom when he came in. Mom slid a rocking chair over for him and I liked the way he thanked her. He sat down and asked me how I was feeling.

"Pretty hollowed out," I said.

"Then we'll make this brief," he said. "You would have been finished with me by now if it weren't for this fire. I have some questions you might be able to help me with if you're willing, but we don't have to do it today." Will only stayed five minutes. Mostly he wanted to make sure I knew that no one was laying any part of the PDEC fire at my feet, or on my friends, and that he'd like me to start paying attention to any stray thoughts about it that rolled through my brain. Even strange and stupid ones, he said. They might not turn out to be stupid.

"Do you mind if I check back in with you soon?" he said on his way out.

"Not a bit."

"You didn't ask, but let me say something: all those people crowding outside right now are dying to talk to you, and I wouldn't be surprised if they start offering you money. A lot of money, possibly. I don't think you want to take it, or to say anything to them. When things get testy like this we don't find a lot of news coverage to be very helpful."

Without trying he illustrated the point a minute later when he let himself out the front door. A wave of loud voices, half a dozen questions canceling each other out, swelled up and evened out, following him even as his car door slammed and he drove away.

STANTON DIDN'T GET THE BENEFIT OF WILL'S ADVICE. THAT SAME NIGHT he was on the local news (and half an hour later, from a different camera angle but saying the same thing, on Dan Rather), standing in front of the PDEC rubble. He'd pushed off the hood of his parka and was squinting in the rain. "What you see here," he said, his voice breaking slightly, "is not the simple loss of a food store. A piece of the heart of this community died here yesterday. Perhaps — and this could be too optimistic, but per*haps* this will finally make the timber industry realize that they can't make their inflammatory, completely unfounded charges about recent events in the forest without hurting innocent people." He looked very sad.

32

Turning down interviews wasn't effortless. *Today* called me three times, once putting Bryant on the line to beg me to come on. You haven't heard begging until you've been begged by Bryant Gumbel — how badly he needed help here, how I was the only one in this godawful mess who *could* help him. Only the feeling of being so far over my head kept me from saying yes.

My unofficial Lewsco bodyguards let only two more people through, both the day after Will's first visit. The first was Gina Arnstead. Since she was a County Commissioner they must have thought she was the law. They even let her pull a video guy in behind her. "We're just going to turn on this little light for just a minute, okay?" was the first thing she said to me, moving fast into my room. "Just for a second." The video guy snapped on the lamp mounted above his camera lens and a blaze of white space surrounded my bed.

"That is enough," Mom said, moving between Gina and me, "you can't do this." A second guy who'd just slipped in behind Gina moved over to Mom with soothing sounds and tried to steer her back to the kitchen.

"Hey," I yelled at him. "Come back here." He did. "You can wait outside, pal." He looked at Gina, who looked down at me. She nodded and her guy walked out the door. As it slammed we heard a spasm of questions greet him. Meanwhile her cameraman moved around the bed with his hot beam of light to where he could get Gina and me in the same frame. "Turn that thing off," I said.

"I'm sorry?" she said like she hadn't heard.

"Turn the light off."

"The light for the camera?" Gina asked. "But that's how these cameras work, John." She was talking slowly, moving closer to me as the camera guy got on one knee to shoot her at an upward angle. "You're probably used to seeing them outside, where there's plenty of daylight." Her face was solemn and earnest, like she was telling me secrets from the center of her soul. "When they shoot inside like this they have to bring in their own light or the tape won't pick up a clear image."

"Off. I mean it. If you want to talk, kill the light." Gina frowned and then nodded, looking very thoughtful. No hurry here. The videotape rolled on. I raised myself on my elbows as far as I could. "Alright, this is *complete* bullshit..."

"Oh, I know, I know, I know!" she said. "He deserves his privacy, Tom! You can wait outside." The light clicked off and it was too dark to see anything as Tom walked away. Another burst of tangled voices came into the room as he went out the front door. By then I could see Gina again. She'd moved to the corner of the bed, one hand on a rail of the footboard. "I understand," she said. "This must be a terribly hard time for you and your mother." She looked over at Mom, who was peeking through the doorway. "How are you holding up, Mrs. Gilliam? In all this hubbub, that's the thing nobody bothers to think about. How are you, dear?"

Mom looked over to me. "I'll tell you what," I said. "Since you came to talk to me, how about if you talk to me?"

"Fine. I just want you to know you're in all our prayers," she said to Mom, then turning to me, "and so are you. We're praying for your full recovery, Jack. Thousands of us are."

"Right," I said. "And you needed the big lights and camera to pray, right?"

With a sigh she first shook her head, then nodded it up and down. "I know. I understand. But what you have to know is you're not in this alone, Jack. You're the one who has to live every day with this tragedy, I know that. But you have to realize that in another way this is an attack on all of us. And we all have to be strong, as you've been strong, to make sure that it doesn't happen again." She stepped up close to me now. "That's why I've come, Jack. To give you my solemn promise. If I'm elected next month, and I will be, my first bill in Congress will give us the tools to make sure this never happens again. That is my promise to you."

I could feel the first leaden twinge of pain return to my back. It was almost time for pills. "And how will you do that?"

"By dealing with these so-called environmentalists trying to push us out of the woods like the criminals they are. If we had done that when all this started instead of treating them like some kind of romantic heroes like the papers do, you wouldn't be lying here right now. I'm convinced of that." She was as close as she could come to me now. Her legs touched my mattress. "The truth is *I'm* an environmentalist, Jack. Much more than these thugs coming in from who knows where to scream and wave their banners and block machinery. I grew up here, Jack, just like you. My husband and boys have hunted and fished this whole country, and my dad and brothers before them. There is no way we'd sit by and let anyone do real harm to our mountain. Never. Never, never, never. You know that, don't you, Jack?"

"Actually I never met your family. But I'm wondering how it is that you know more about who did this than anybody else does."

"I don't, Jack. Everyone knows what happened, even if they don't want to say so out loud. I just happen to be someone who's not afraid to say what I know. And I know, even if it's not fashionable to say, that we have enemies. These people have a different agenda for Oregon, for the whole Northwest, and it means locking us out of the woods completely. And they won't stop until they do. I don't have to guess about that. They're saying *themselves* that nothing will stop them." She closed her eyes and rubbed the inside corners with thumb and a finger. "You know what I'm talking about, don't you, Jack? You know who did this to you."

"You mean Zenith?"

"Is that his name? The one who's been threatening everyone for months?" She shrugged. "Doesn't it make sense?"

"Do you know if they've found any proof?"

Gina shook her head. "I don't think you understand what I'm trying to say, Jack. We might not have proof that this particular deranged lunatic put this particular spike in this particular tree. What I'm talking about is, who's attacking our way of life. There's plenty of proof about that, wouldn't you agree?"

"But I'm kind of interested in this particular spike in this particular tree, to tell you the truth."

"Of course you are," Gina said earnestly. "Of course. And whoever did it, this Zenith or whoever was behind him, has to be punished. I don't want you to worry about that."

The front door opened and Gina's first guy, the one who tried to steer Mom out of the room before, stuck his head in. "Gina?" he said. "Kiwanis. It's 11:30."

"Yes," she said. He closed the door. She looked down at me for a moment before speaking. "Jack, can I tell you something I discovered in the last few years? As you know, I got involved to get some things done. What I've found out is that there are two things that keep you from getting big things done: fear and doubt, which is really a kind of a fear, too. Now, you can have doubt about the facts. Sometimes you have to, because the facts change. That's how facts are different from the truth. The truth doesn't change." She was slowly gliding away from me. "The problem happens when you let your doubt about facts become doubt about the truth. When that happens you will not get done what you set out to do."

She smiled, quick as a sneeze, and moved to the doorway. "It was nice getting to know you, Jack. Would it be all right with you if I stopped in again when I'm in Lewis Falls? I just love this little town, you know — the people here are so real. I'd live up here in a minute if I could. You take care of yourself, now, don't try to rush it too fast, okay?"

She actually stepped outside the room and then back in. "Oh, and it wouldn't be any problem if I showed some pictures of you and me, would it?"

"Showed them where?" I said.

"Oh, I don't know," she said. "I don't have any plans. I'm just determined to see that nobody forgets about you, Jack, and maybe the video-tape can help. So there'd be no problem with that."

"I don't know," I said. "I would want to know how it was used."

"Only to wake people up, Jack," she said. "To make them aware of what you're up against. You can count on it." Then she turned her head away from me and towards the living room. "Mrs. Gilliam! I was afraid I wouldn't get to say goodbye before I left." She walked out of my sight. "If he starts giving you trouble, you give me a call and I'll come sit on him, okay?" Now I could see them through my doorway, standing by the front door. Gina was handing Mom a business card. "No, really, if you need anything at all, you don't hesitate. Promise?"

She took Mom's hand in both of hers and looked at her intently. As they stood there the door opened behind Mom, and all of a sudden she was standing exactly in between the Republican and Democratic candidates for Oregon's Fourth District Congressional seat. I am not making this up. In the doorway, in a rumpled tweed sport coat and tan Levis, stood Arthur Lane. "Is this a private party," he said, "or is everyone invited?"

33

LUCY MCFADDEN IS GOOD. I DON'T KNOW HER, BUT UNDERNEATH THE two pictures on the front page of the next morning's *Oregonian* a tiny line of print said "photographs by Lucy McFadden." When something interesting finally happened in Mom's front yard, she was ready. She's responsible for a great front page, Thursday, October 20, 1994. I have it pinned up above my desk. Gina Arnstead and Art Lane are looking smack at one another without knowing it.

Gina's facing the center of the page from the photo on the left-hand side. She's on Mom's porch, walking towards the front door to come see me. On the right side of the page, Art's approaching Mom's front door from the other side of the porch, so that it looks like they'll collide head-on in about three steps. The caption that runs beneath both pictures starts out with a single word in bold, BOOKENDS?, then says

> Republican Congressional candidate Gina Arnstead and her Democratic opponent Arthur Lane pay their respects to tree-spiking victim John Gilliam Wednesday. Arnstead called the incident a "criminal tragedy" and Lane promised a full investigation of the incident if elected.

I wish I could have seen the reaction in the two campaign offices when that paper hit their desks. Verily there was much moaning and gnashing of teeth.

On Gina's side, anyway. Wanting less, Art got closer to what he wanted. I won't be saying anything about this before the election, but it turns out Art Lane's not a bad guy. He is probably as real as you can be and still have a good shot at going to Congress, though I don't think he will.

When he showed up with a tight grin at the door, Gina kind of harumphed past him into another messy roar of questions outside. When the door closed Art was inside. "Is this a bad time, ma'am?" he said to Mom. "Maybe you don't need another stranger pushing in on you right now."

"Jackie?" she said, turning my way. "Now the other one's here."

"Let him on in." I was tired and my back was starting to cramp up, but this was almost fun.

"Thanks," he said, crossing the room. He pointed at a chair with a little requesting sound and I told him to sit. "So how are you feeling?"

After going a round with Gina I decided to take it right to him. "How much difference does it make to you how I'm feeling?"

He leaned back in the chair and looked me over. With his forefinger he traced the upper edge of his closely-trimmed beard from his sideburn down to his chin. "Fair question. I'm truly sorry this happened to you, but if you really want to know it wasn't my idea to come here."

"Whose was it?"

"The team." He pulled one ankle onto his other knee. "When you run for Congress, especially an open seat, you get a team, whether you want it or not. They knew Gina would try to get her arms around you while the press was up here, so the question was what to do about it. I didn't see why we had to do anything. People know what kind of cold calculator Gina is. They'd see through it."

Maybe this was his way to make sure *I* knew she's a cold calculator, but I don't think so. "But here you are," I said.

Arthur nodded. "Here I am. We voted on it — I get a vote, too — and I lost 3-1. Whenever I argue that people will figure something out on their own, they look at me with this 'have we taken our medication today, Arthur?' look and plow ahead like I wasn't there."

"'The masses is asses,'" I said.

"No, not quite that," he said, fingering his beard again. He was more interested now than when he came in. "They're not dumb as much as they are distracted. There's just too much going on, especially at election time. You can't assume they'll figure out anything for themselves. If you have a point to make, you better grab the voters by the back of the neck and rub their faces in it. Or so says the team."

"You don't like to do that?"

"No, I don't like that. I got into this to try to get our heads pulled out of the sand and admit that timber and fishing have changed permanently and 1950s answers won't solve 1990s problems. I got into this to try to bring some reality to the table and God forbid maybe a little vision, not to treat the public like a bunch of scatterbrained hicks." He was leaning forward now, his hands slicing the air between us.

"So you tell your team that and they say?"

"They say, 'Great, that's what we want, too, so now let's get you to D.C. so you can do it.' So here I am. Nice to meet you, Jack."

"Likewise I'm sure. What do you think you should be doing right now instead?"

Arthur shrugged. "What do I know? I'm a history teacher. I teach civics, too, but this stuff isn't in the books. Elections are, and election campaigns, but not the way we do them today. Not these soap operas." He sat back in his chair and sighed. "I have three kids, Jack. The oldest is twelve. When my wife and I talked about whether to do this or not, she said I couldn't do this just as a gesture. She made me promise to listen to the experts and do everything to win that didn't absolutely make me throw up." He smiled and pulled back onto his knee the ankle that fell off when he started gesturing. "Visiting you doesn't make me throw up."

I had to laugh. "Now, there's a smooth line. Yeah, I guess this is new to you."

"The other thing, and this is something I suspect more and more the more I campaign, is the team might be right. It's sort of like playing percentages. Take this as an example." His hands were dancing again. "Say that I'm right and people see me visiting you as a cynical PR move. For most of them it doesn't really register because it's what they've come to expect. Maybe a few go, 'Oh, okay, I guess that Lane's like the rest of them,' but if they're that conscious I'm probably going to get them with what I'm saying on the issues. So, bottom line is I probably don't lose or gain any votes to speak of. Now if the *team's* right, Gina had the chance to score big points for compassion and truth and beauty if we let her up here by herself. The whole last week of the campaign we'd have to listen to how close you and she are, how she gave you her solemn promise to make things right, and they'd crank out all these letters-to-the-editor from Joe and Shirley Sixpack about what a warm and wonderful woman she is, and by the way, where is Art *Lane* when a poor honest logger gets chewed halfway to death in the line of duty? Doesn't Art Lane care? So that if I don't show up and win my stripes too, then, yes, that moves votes. It's the kind of simple clear thing that sticks up and shouts at a voter who's gotten lost in all the propaganda. In the end it's enough to make them vote one way or another."

He was probably a good teacher. "So if you don't know who's right, go with the team, because there's nothing to lose?"

"Except for my immortal soul, and that I left somewhere a long time ago."

"Score another one for the team."

"Well, yes." He smiled and traced his beard again with his finger. "But I'm not completely house-broken. I guarantee this isn't the conversation they wanted me to have with you. I think I'm supposed to be asking for your support." Which, in this way, he was. He waited.

"Well, I won't tell the team if you won't."

He didn't press me. We talked for a few more minutes, mostly about my condition — he seemed interested enough now that I told him — and the search for the spiker. He said the Zenith theory didn't ring right to him, but he didn't have any better ideas. Then he stood up and reached for my hand. "Thanks for seeing me, Jack. And send me a bill for the therapy session, okay?"

I shook his hand. "It wasn't that bad," I said. "It's an interesting little adventure you got going. Good luck to you."

"Thanks." He was on the brink of saying more, something that would let him tell his team and wife he'd given it his best shot, but he didn't. On his way out he leaned in the kitchen to say goodbye to Mom.

As the front door closed I laid back heavily to relax my back and shoulders. In three weeks I was supposed to vote for one of these two. I knew who I liked and who I didn't. I also knew that wasn't the whole story. It took about three words from me to set off a gusher of confession out of Art Lane, and I'm a total stranger. His brain is spinning with all the irony and contradictions of the game, how the process of winning it taints the prize, layers and layers of stuff that fascinates civics teachers but would just clog him up if he gets elected. I can almost hear what a speech from him on the House floor would sound like, starting with a long list of the ways that the bill he's sponsoring might not be such a hot idea after all. Woody Allen goes to Washington.

At least he's asking the right question, whether there can be a clear line between the campaign and the office, whether he can let his team pull him around until November 8, and then November 9 he can be his own man. How many of these guys tell themselves they can do that, they'll just play the game to get in, but once they're there it'll all be straight and clean? All of them, maybe? They start out with their own package of ideals and great intentions, then they shave off a little here for this bunch of voters and pretend to care about some ridiculous program for that interest group, then wave the flag to cover the patriotic bases, and if it all works and they win, they expect they can toss all the rhetoric and fudging aside and march straight towards what they set out to do? Put them all together in a big room and it's called the

U.S. Congress. Did Gina Arnstead have that kind of illusion? I doubted she even thought about it. She wasn't someone prone to confusing herself.

Mom set a pot of tea and two cinnamon rolls on the table next to me. "I was going to bring this while he was still here, but you two looked too serious to interrupt," she said in a cheery singsong. It was a hidden question: were she and I back to normal yet? With strangers coming in our house she needed to know.

"Mom, that smells great," or yes, we are.

She handed me a steaming cup and sat down where Art Lane had been. "What do you think of those two, Jackie?"

I blew the steam off the surface of the tea. "I think they're vultures. And I'm the meat."

"He seemed nice."

"He is. He's the nicer vulture." I broke off a sticky flap of the roll. It was still warm. "I think he uses a napkin."

34

THE "BOOKENDS" PICTURES GAVE THE *OREGONIAN* EDITORS A REASON TO run a bunch of stuff they must have been collecting about the spiking. Lower down the same front page was a small bordered box with a tiny picture of a pine tree on the left side, a railroad spike on the right and a teaser: "Lewis County War of Words Continues, page D-1."

Section D was the *Downstate* section, and everyone looking out at me from its first page that morning was someone I knew. There in a row were matchbook-size pictures of Mel Raines, Stanton Freed and Zenith McPherson. Zenith looked absolutely guilty of something, maybe because he was wearing Lewis County overalls and held a slate of numbers against his chest.

The bottom righthand corner of the page was covered with a larger picture and a caption that began SPIKER & VICTIM? It was from the demonstration at the Falls road gate a month before. It felt more like six months to me. There in the foreground was Zenith holding the 6-foot wooden spike over his head. In the upper right hand corner, too shaded and fuzzy to pick out if you weren't led to it, was me. I wasn't looking at Zenith. I was talking to Stanton, whose back was to the camera.

Winding around the pictures was a feature story with the headline NOW THEY BATTLE WITH WORDS. The first three paragraphs were a rehash: Lewsco's history and the OO buyout, a little on me and the accident, a description of Zenith's arrest up at his bus. Except it called him Ralph McPherson. "Ralph" would make me use a nickname, too.

201

There was more I didn't know: he was from Montgomery, Alabama, the oldest of six kids, and his dad had been commander of the state police for twenty years. According to Ralph's mom, Ralph enlisted in the army the day of his eighteenth birthday and she hadn't seen or heard from him since.

Most of the rest of the article quoted Stanton, "widely regarded as the leading spokesman for old-growth forest protection in the Pacific Northwest," and then Mel.

> Freed challenged authorities to bring forward the evidence that led to the arrest. "This burned-out victim of our past greed and folly is certainly convenient for them to have around," Freed said in a reference to Corporal McPherson's four tours of duty in Vietnam, "but where is their proof?"
>
> Freed said he would be "astonished" if the government can put together a convincing case. "But if they somehow can, it would be one more ironic legacy from Vietnam," he said. "[McPherson] would stand before us as a true patriot: a man who gave his fullest measure twenty years ago because of what he thought his country stood for, and who is doing the very same thing today."
>
> Asked to respond in Grants Pass yesterday, Lewis Corporation Vice President Mel Raines said "It's nice to know that Western Resources Defense Council thinks it's patriotic to spike trees and practically kill one of our men. We happen to think it's cowardly and bloodthirsty." Raines said anonymous reports of more spiked trees in the area have delayed several other logging operations in the Lewis Falls area.
>
> "They couldn't stop us in court, because we only operate within the law, and on our own land," said Raines. "So they use our concern for the safety of our workers against us and terrorize a whole county instead. Now it should be clear to everybody who does and doesn't care about timber workers in Oregon."
>
> Raines said McPherson's guilt or innocence is a matter for the courts to decide, adding that McPherson's habit of brandishing the mock-up of a tree spike would be hard for a jury to ignore. "I don't know how much more directly than that he could have shown what he wanted," Raines said.

Before I'd finished the whole paper — the Opinion page wondered in one editorial why we can't just live together, and in another whether it might be time to cut off public access to the forest — I heard a tap on the front door. Mom opened it and I heard Holly's voice. A moment later she walked in my room holding her own copy of the *Downstate* section.

"Already saw it," I said. "The 'burned-out victim of our past greed and folly?' Quite the phrase-meister, your boss."

"Ex-boss," she said. "As of ten minutes ago. I just got off the phone."

"You're kidding."

"This is completely bogus." She held up the paper. "He tries to tell me he's just doing his job, but this is over the edge, this cute backhanded fanning the flames that maybe Zenith did do it. Pulling off this spiking, this wasn't amateur hour. I don't know if you or me could have pulled it off. And Zenith." She stopped and looked towards the ceiling. Her eyes were red. "When they picked up Zenith, Stanton said the reason he never takes his overalls off is he can't figure out how the buckles work." Her lips started to tremble so she drew them inside her mouth and clamped down tight. She looked at me like she wanted something. Forgiveness? Like I could find words of forgiveness for Holly that she'd tolerate.

I said, "Okay. Who did it?" Her face was suddenly hard and her eyes dry. "No, I know you don't *know*," I said. "I'm just asking what you think."

"Not Stanton, if that's what you mean." It wasn't. "This isn't what he'd do."

"Because he's such a stand-up guy? Standing up for Zenith the way he does?"

She shook her head. "Stanton doesn't take risks. He cashes in on risks other people take."

"Okay, but so what? How hard would it be to get someone else to actually drive the spike? Stanton could make it happen without leaving San Francisco."

"No." Holly was sure. "Trust me on this one." For a minute we looked over the newspaper together. Her head was close enough to me that when she shook her head her hair touched my ear. I heard her breath. "God. I can't stand this, Jack." She tapped her finger on Zenith's picture. "I can't stand that he's in there."

"Zenith?" I said. "That's the part you can't stand? That Zenith's in jail? Are you putting me on?" She took a step away from the bed and looked down at me. "Shit. How about this, Holly, how about if Zenith and I trade places? I'll take jail and my legs back any fucking day of the week."

"I know," she said slowly. "You don't get to do that, Jack."

"But that's the part that gets you the most? Zenith? Oh, man. Well, I sure hope you can forgive me for putting him in such a messy situation." I was that pathetic, in front of Holly, and I barely cared. I glared straight at her.

She didn't flinch. "Jack," she said quietly. "I don't think we're talking about what gets me the most. We haven't had that conversation yet. We're only talking about the piece we can maybe do something about. That's what *I'm* talking about. Whatever else has happened, Zenith's sitting in a cell for something he couldn't have done. Whatever else, that shouldn't be." She sat down and leaned towards me slightly. "He shouldn't be there, Jack. Aren't I right?"

The blood rushing through me began to slow down. I saw in her eyes she needed me to understand, not about Zenith, but about the helplessness she felt about me. "Yes."

She nodded slightly, her eyes wide and still on mine. "I have to go down there."

"What, to the jail?" I said. "What will you do down there?"

"See Zenith," she said. "Find out what's going on. I don't know, I'll figure it out when I get there."

I tried to imagine Holly Burgess, local traitor, going head-to-head with Port Douglas law. "I'm going with you."

THAT POSED TWO CHALLENGES. THE FIRST WAS GETTING PAST MOM, WHO practically trembled when she heard what I had in mind. She reminded me how Dr. Ford said it'd be a few weeks at home before I'd be ready to go anywhere. I'd been home about one. Holly said nothing as Mom and I argued. I think she was glad I was ready to get off my sorry butt and do something, but the last thing she'd do was undermine Mom in some way. Finally we made a deal: I could go if I got Doc Ford's blessing.

Mom must have thought that would buy another couple of days, however long it would take him to come up from Grants Pass for an examination. She hadn't been in the hospital room the day I checked out when Doc Grant told me to call any time day or night if I wanted anything at all.

"You can't bother the man like this in the middle of the day and expect him to drop everything," Mom hissed at me in a loud whisper as she watched me dial the hospital number, ask for Dr. Ford and tuck the mouthpiece under my chin to wait. A minute later Doc Ford was on the phone with me. Fifty minutes later he walked through Mom's front door. He took off his fleece-lined Pendleton, turned down Mom's offer of coffee, and strode across the living room towards my wheelchair.

"And they say you can't get anyone to make house calls anymore," I said.

"They say a lot of things," he said, putting his bag down and grasping the handles of my chair to push me to the sofa. He gently lifted each of my feet and set them on the cushion so that both legs were straight. Then he kneeled and began to squeeze my thighs and shins and the back of my legs with both hands. "Talk."

There wasn't much to say. Nothing he did gave me a particle of feeling below the top of my hips. It still was so strange. My eyes were watching his hands grab and knead rolls of my flesh so hard his knuckles turned white. And there was nothing. All I could feel was the ridge of a dull pain stretching across the lowest inches of my back, where the lifting of my legs pulled down on a web of muscles. I described it to Doc Ford and he grunted. After a while he lowered my legs back down to the foot plate, grabbed both of my shoulders and rotated my torso back and forth. "No problem there," I said. "That feels fine." He reached into his bag for a little rubber tomahawk and tapped me just below each knee, holding my feet, feeling for some kind of current. "What do you think, Doc?"

He said he wondered what the hurry was. But when I asked him to tell me the worst that could happen if we went, he puffed his cheeks up and then let the air slip slowly between his lips, a little moment for him to think.

"She'll be with you the whole time?" he asked, nodding at Holly.

"Yep."

"No stairs or curbs to get over?"

Holly had called the sheriff's office while we'd been waiting for Doc to come up the hill. They said they'd let us use the inmate elevator, a metal chamber that comes right through a steel-plated hatch in the sidewalk to load and unload inmates at curbside without having them walk around in the open handcuffed or shackled. "Nope."

Doc frowned at me for a few seconds, silent. "We have more help," Holly said. "Steve Raines is coming, too. He's driving us." Complete news to me. The sheriff must not have been the only call Holly made.

"How long will you be?" Doc asked. Mom got up from the chair behind him and left for the kitchen.

Maybe three hours, we told him, counting the half-hour to drive down there and half an hour back.

"Be back in two. And take this along." He took a tiny plastic container of my pain medication from his bag and handed it to Holly. "If your back gets heavy, or any cramps anywhere, you stop and come back right then. Clear?"

I looked at Holly, who was nodding her head at him. "Clear?" he asked me again. I turned to him. His glasses caught all the light from the reading lamp above my bed, two circles of glossy yellow so I couldn't see his eyes. "This is how it is now," he said. "From now on everything has to stay to the plan. You don't get to make the mistakes the rest of us do."

Doc didn't look at me as he zipped up his bag and headed for the door, or at Mom as she rushed to meet him there with fluttering thanks. He turned and looked over her head while patting her shoulder, sending his words to Holly. "Two hours."

35

THE SECOND CHALLENGE WAS THE LAYER OF PRESS PEOPLE STAKED OUT in Mom's yard, thinner than a few days before but still serious. Five minutes after Doc Ford left we heard a car horn tapping short bleats just outside. It was Steve trying to clear a path as he backed a Company van towards the porch. He got within about thirty feet. Crossing that stretch, I was the center of a moving four-person diamond: Steve out front, his men Larry and Roy to my sides and Holly pushing my chair from behind. I wasn't out in the open air more than a minute, but it was like we'd thrown a loaf of Wonder Bread in a pond of starving ducks.

They screamed the whole way. "Who are Jack's Avengers?" "Do you know McPherson?" "Why would he do it?" "Can you move your legs?" "Where are you going?" "Dan Rather wants to talk to you!" "Do you blame James Nielsen for this?" "What did you tell President Clinton?" "Why won't you talk to us?" "Is that Holly? Holly, did you hire Zenith?" "Do you want revenge, Jack?" "Dan Rather!" "What are you hiding?" "Are you going to Washington?" "Let's see your legs move!"

Steve slid the side door open when we stopped next to the van and I raised my hand. The noise stopped instantly. "I'm feeling stronger every day," I said. "Now you know everything I know. Good-bye." Larry and Roy lifted me in my chair through the van's side door and the yelling started again. Steve slid the door shut and walked around to the driver's door while Holly got in the other front seat. Larry and Roy got into a compact pickup and moved in front of us to start clearing the way. Whatever Holly was trying to say to Steve as he pulled the van onto the roadway was drowned out by the pounding of fists and palms on its tin sides.

"Four...five...seven." Steve counted the press vehicles behind us in his side mirror as we crossed the town line and headed west for Port Douglas. He watched them for another mile before looking for me in the rear view mirror. It felt like he was running through variations of what he wanted to say. "I didn't come see you in the hospital," he said. "I should have."

I reeled back my instinct to bail him out — hey man, no sweat, or I was too zonked for visitors anyway, or big deal, you're seeing me now — and stayed quiet. I wanted to hear this. It wasn't like I'd laid in the hospital constantly wondering when he'd walk thorough the door. When it did cross my mind I immediately wondered how it would feel to watch him and Holly meet at my bedside for the first time in years (I *assumed* it'd be the first time, anyway, before I saw Holly pick up the phone and call him for help when the press was storming Mom's house). That made me feel fine that he wasn't coming around.

But that's not how I felt now, as I watched Steve driving. The Company, his company, had thrown me away. What happened to me happened while I was doing their work, and in almost three weeks in the hospital I heard exactly two things from them. The first was from the head nurse, who said the Company wanted to be sure I wasn't worrying about all the costs mounting up, its insurance would cover everything I needed. The second was a bouquet of snapdragons and lilies, twice as big as any of the others around the edges of the room, with a card that had Charlie Brown lying on his back, Lucy holding the football she'd swept away from him, a printed message ("You *can* believe that all of us are pulling for your speedy recovery") and, handwritten below, "Love from all your friends at Lewsco." That was it.

Steve was looking in the rearview mirror for a clue from me. He looked back at the road when he started to speak. "I haven't stopped thinking about it. About you." A look at me, not much more than a blink, then back to the road. "I could tell you all kinds of jive about how it's been but it doesn't matter. It wasn't right not to come."

"But tell him why," Holly said in a voice that drew me a picture. She sounded like a woman both exasperated and completely loyal to her troubled husband. "Go on." Steve just drove. Holly turned around in her seat towards me. "Orders from headquarters. Lewsco told everybody that anyone who talks to you is history." She turned back to face the highway. "Sweet company you have there, bucko."

We drove half a mile without talking. All the big trees are still standing like a solid wall in that stretch, but if you look closely between them you can see the brown edge of clearcuts not more than a hundred feet from the highway. "Say that again?" I said.

Holly didn't move or speak. "It was from the legal office in Oklahoma," Steve said. "They didn't say they'd fire you exactly, but they said nobody's supposed to talk to you or the press except for the official spokesperson." His eyes lifted to the mirror and to me. "Which is Dad."

"Oh, yeah, of course," I said, "Mel and I talk all the time."

"Well, I mean to the media," Steve said. "I guess nobody at all's supposed to talk to you." I looked in the mirror until his eyes came up again. His face stretched into something like a tiny shrug. "To a lawyer it's a no-brainer. All they do all day long is worry about liability. They're worried we might tell you we're sorry it happened."

"What a grotesque thought," Holly said.

"And if we say we're sorry some jury is going to think we're admitting we did something wrong and then whack us for a couple million."

We passed Utility Flat, a big gravel clearing on the right that the Company uses as a staging area for shows on the west slope. All that's there now is a decaying tear-drop travel trailer that used to be an equipment shed where somebody sharpened chains all day long. When it was in use, I thought, I could walk. I said "So you say 'I'm sorry,' and then I sue you?"

His face made another shrug. "They sit in a big office in Tulsa. They're not here. But there are reasons they're paranoid. There have to be lawyers fighting to get close to you, right?"

"Maybe. I don't know. There's still a big carton of mail I haven't read at Mom's. I only look at the ones with hand-written addresses. And she changed her phone so nobody's calling us."

"Well, you open some of the fancy envelopes sometime and see what's there," he said. "There are reasons the Company's paranoid." He rubbed his forehead like it hurt and ran his hand over the top of his head.

"So how come you've come to Mom's twice now in plain daylight?"

"Yeah, well," he said, "the other thing is the Company's full of shit." We drove a while before he spoke again. I could see his mouth working, like his teeth were raking his tightly-closed lips. Then his eyes went to the mirror and stayed there, on mine. "I am so sorry." In forty years I've seen Steve Raines look cranky, frustrated, pissed off and, once in a while, anxious. But I'd never seen him look as he did that moment. He looked lost.

We passed the StageStop Store on the left, the only business between Lewis Falls and Port Douglas. Steve and Holly turned to look up the skid road behind it; up there, just out of sight, was where Zenith marooned his old bus years ago. Then we went around a curve, the store and the dirt road disappeared, and the highway began its steeper drop towards the coast.

36

STEVE DROPPED US OFF AT THE LEWIS COUNTY COURTHOUSE, A SQUAT sandstone building that covers its own block just off the main drag in Port Douglas. The basement is the county jail. Three deputies were waiting for us at the curbside elevator and they had patrol cars parked in a pattern that blocked off the cars behind us. Steve and the deputies unloaded me, then he and Holly agreed on a time to pick us up and he was gone. Right before we got to town I wondered if he'd come in with us. Like he needed to show up on the front pages next to Jack Gilliam and WRDC firebrand Holly Burgess, coming out of a visit with Zenith.

At the bottom of the elevator a woman in a starchy tan uniform met us and told us to follow her. Holly pushed me through a cinderblock maze and finally through a door at the end of the hall. The room had no windows. All four walls were covered with shoulder patches from sheriff's departments around the country, hundreds of them aligned in perfect rows and columns from chair height all the way to the ceiling. The far end had a huge metal desk with a shaky mountain range of files and notebooks. Filling the room's center was a dark-stained circular table with two men behind it. They faced us as Holly rolled me through the door. I'd never met either but I knew who they were. Anyone who follows the news would.

"Mr. Gilliam," said Lewis County Sheriff Warren Smith, butting his chair backwards with a screech as he stood up. "Welcome to our humble abode." He reached me in four heavy strides, three hundred pounds wrapped tight in the same tan uniform his deputies wore. The effort made him grunt as he stuck a big hand towards me. It felt like a row of tautly-packed sausages. He squeezed my palm twice before letting go.

Sheriff Smith was the best-known lawman in the uncitied farm and forest counties that stretched from Eugene down to Redding in the Sacramento Valley . He'd grown up in Brookings, the coast town just this side of the California line, and left before he finished high school to fight in Korea. He came back from a frostbitten tour with seven toes and a Silver Star and became half of the Brookings police force.

Fifteen years later he joined the Lewis County Sheriff's Department to get out in the woods where the first marijuana plantations were showing up. Pot and what it stood for — loose living, the collapse of rules and respect, California — were more evil in Deputy Smith's book than North Koreans. It wasn't going to infect Southern Oregon on his watch. About the time I graduated high school the Lewis County Commissioners accepted an offer from Nixon's drug office and had helicopters spray paraquat over suspect parts of the county. Paraquat is a wonder of modern chemistry that makes people who come in contact with it, usually from smoking the marijuana it's sprayed on, violently ill. I don't know if anyone died, but there were youngsters all over the West Coast who probably wanted to.

Warren Smith had no use for that. It punished too many of the wrong people, kids more brainless than criminal. It offended his sense of craft. It was the easy sledge-hammer way out for mediocre cops. It was clumsy and, worse, lazy. He believed in the old-fashioned way. He'd stake out little forest clearings studded with pot plants for days at a time, sometimes through whole weekends when he was off-duty. Over time he hauled in dozens of growers, mostly little guys producing eight or ten kilos they'd take down to San Francisco or L.A. once a year.

Smith was crouched in the bushes on an August afternoon in 1973 when two guys in their twenties showed up with plastic jugs in their backpacks to water the high-grade sinsemilla plants he'd been watching for three days. Only Smith knows what happened next, because five minutes later both growers were on the ground with bullets through their chests. The bad news for Smith was that one of them was the son-in-law of a big West Hollywood entertainment lawyer. In the TV movie that came out later, the lawyer's kid was played by the dark-eyed guy who went on to star in one of the Highway Patrol series, and I think Brian Keith played Smith.

Smith went up on a string of criminal charges, and the two families had a lawsuit going for a while, but he was able to slip off the force and out of the picture for a while. He sold cars up in Coos Bay and then came back around 1980, when marijuana madness was threatening once again to destroy everything good and decent on the South Coast, to run for Sheriff. He promised voters he wouldn't let the county turn into some degenerate California annex.

He won big and has run unopposed for re-election every four years since. When I see him on TV he's still complaining about how the County Commissioners talk a great game about protecting our kids from drugs until budget time roles around, and then they're sorry but there's just not enough money. Not enough for drug surveillance and investigation, not enough for road deputies ("all I can say to Lewis County folks who live in Bounty or Little River or Powers and need help fast is: you folks better learn how to help each other, because if you're waiting for me to show up, you've got a wait and a half coming, folks"), not enough to let him do his job.

Smith hasn't chased around any bad guys for a while. His mass has softened and slipped towards the ground and he's grown a goatee for character. Most people looking up at him as I was now would think they were looking at Burl Ives.

"This here's Dwight Hamlin," Smith said, swiveling his mass half-around towards the other man at the table, the Lewis County District Attorney, who also stood.

"I know. Don't bother," I said to Hamlin as he tried to weave between table and chairs to get around to me. He stopped and sat back down. "I've voted for the both of you plenty of times."

Hamlin laughed, a snuffled gristly sound. His only noticeable feature was a shiny bald head divided into 1/4-inch strips by gray strands of hair combed from one side all the way over to the other, like Sam did it before his hippie stage. He was a brittle-looking collection of bony edges and knobs who'd need an identical twin next to him to match Sheriff Smith's weight. "If you vote around here, it's kind of hard not to," he said with a smile. In four terms of office nobody had run against Hamlin either. It wasn't a sensible challenge for an ambitious lawyer to take on.

"That's true, isn't it?" I said. The three of us finished up a shallow laugh while Smith made a place at the table for Holly and me. The fading smiles let me look directly at both men while they checked us out.

"So, welcome to our humble abode, Mr. Gilliam, and Miss...?" Smith offered.

"I'm Holly Burgess," she said.

"Yes," Hamlin said.

"That's right," Smith said. "You're from up on the hill, too. Fife Burgess' family."

"And 'Jack' works better for me, Sheriff," I said.

"'Preciate that," Smith said. "First names all around do the job? Then Jack, we heard you was in for a visit, and we just wanted to tell you welcome and if there's anything we can do for you, you just say the word."

"Well, thanks, Sheriff. Actually you've helped a lot already just the way your deputies got me in the building. I'm kind of traveling with a crowd behind me these days."

"Oh, yeah, oh yeah," Smith said, smiling and leaning his chair back. "Those boys like a story like this, they do. A whole mess of 'em put their teeth in my butt, too. And they don't loosen up until you give 'em something, I can tell you that."

"Which is why you held a press conference right after you picked up Zenith McPherson," Holly said.

Smith frowned. Hamlin said, "That's right."

"And another one the day before yesterday, to show off all the personal things you took from his bus," she said.

"We're a public agency, ma'am. It's not our job to withhold important evidence from the public."

"And which important evidence would that be?" Holly asked the D.A.

They stared at her. Smith shifted his weight with a soft grunt and started tapping the table with his thumb and forefinger, one then the other, faster as he went along. "Let's just say," Hamlin said, "that at this stage of the investigation there's no reason to suspect that anyone but Mr. McPherson was involved."

"Really," said Holly. "Maybe you can tell me, I'm always curious about these things, where he found a spike made out of that kind of material? And when did he drive it in? And where's the hammer or whatever it was he drove it in with?"

"I'm afraid I'm not at liberty to share information like that with you at this point. If you're asking me if we have an airtight case put together right now, today, I'd have to say no. There are still a couple of holes." Here Hamlin leaned towards us, elbows and forearms on the table. "But I'll tell you something else: if it wasn't him, it's one of the crowd he likes hanging around with. We know at least that he knows something. He knows *something* that'd help nail this together."

Hamlin didn't mean the pun and nobody seemed to notice. He bit his lip and went on. "The thing is, we can't get him to talk. I don't mean we can't get him to give us good information. I mean *talk*. We've had Mr. McPherson now" — he looked over at Smith — "three days?" Smith held up four fat fingers. "Four days, and he hasn't said a word yet. I mean a *syllable*, a snort, a grunt, nothing. The man has not made an audible verbal sound in four days."

"Much longer than that, Mr. Hamlin," Holly said. "Except for grunts when he gets excited he probably hasn't made a sound in close to twenty years. He talked a little when he first came here, looking for some people, but I don't think he's said a word since then."

Another pause. Smith was watching his thumb and pinky do their two-step on the table. "Well," he said. Another four taps, then, sudden as snapped fingers, a look at me. "So then you've known this fella a long time, the two of you have?" He looked at Holly, then back at me. "And you're sure he didn't do this to you, so you don't want him taking the rap, right? You care about this fellow, or we wouldn't be here talking together, right?"

We're here talking, I thought, because you pulled us in here to talk. On the chance that wasn't the feedback old Warren was looking for, I nodded. "That gets us thinking," he went on. "Maybe he'd be more likely to let you know something than us. If he trusts you more, maybe. That's just what we were thinking."

Smith was trying hard to get his face to look casual. Hamlin was watching his folded hands on the table. "Like interrogation," I said. "You want us to interrogate Zenith for you."

"I wouldn't say we're talking about an interrogation," Hamlin said.

"No, I guess you wouldn't," Holly jumped in. "You'd say 'being alert for clues,' or something like that. Be alert for clues as we talk to this pawn, this...*prop*, this prop in the melodrama that's going into your next election brochure, this guy who looks the part perfectly for you. What you'd say is help us get him out of a jam he doesn't have anything to do with, and you know he doesn't and you're keeping him caged up like an animal anyway."

Smith bolted forward in his seat. "Oh, this guy, right! He can't get the $50 French wine and the lobster tails he's used to, and his foursome at the Country Club probably wonders where he is, too! Lady, do you know how this guy usually lives? Have you been up to that junked-out bus he lives in? Have you stuck your head inside that thing and *smelled*?" Smith scrunched up his face like a wad of fleshy paper. "Don't talk to me about animal cages. Anybody who calls my jail a cage compared to the pigsty he lives in doesn't know what they're talking about. They're flat ignorant if they say that."

Hamlin lowered the volume. "It is much better here than you probably imagine, Holly. About six years ago we got sued for jail conditions, the food, the amount of light, exercise time, how many blankets, how much space for each inmate, that kind of thing. I wouldn't have admitted it at the time," he said, leaning forward a couple of inches to take us into his confidence like close friends, "but there was some merit to what they were saying. Now, though, it's different. We have a clean comfortable operation here. I'd stack it up to any county jail in Oregon, maybe the country, for how we treat inmates."

"I'm sure it's beautiful, Mr. Hamlin," Holly said. "The difference is that Zenith's bus has a front door that he walks in and out of any time he wants."

"He can walk out of *mine* if he talks to us!" Smith shouted, slapping the table. I could feel the mist flying from his mouth. "He's suffering so much in here, maybe he can give us something more than that shit-eating grin, pardon my French. Just a couple of names. *Some*thing. Then he's free to get back to lifestyles of the rich and famous."

"The other thing," Hamlin said gently, "is just safety. We think Mr. McPherson is safer in this building than he could possibly be back up on the hill on his own. There are an awful lot of people up there upset about what happened to you, Jack. I mean really upset. We've gotten anonymous calls from a few of them about their plans for Mr. McPherson. They're positive he's the one who did this."

"Now, why would that be?" Holly said, flaring at Hamlin. "That couldn't have anything to do with the show you've put on with your press conferences, could it? Pictures of him at demonstrations, how he won't talk or meet with a lawyer, the books and magazines you found at the bus? Even though you know you haven't found one piece of evidence that a judge wouldn't laugh at? And now because these stupid 'anonymous' crackers are jumping to crazy conclusions, gee willikers and we don't know why, you have to make sure you protect poor Mr. McPherson?" She shook her head with a snort. "You guys…"

"Look," I said, "What is it exactly you're telling us to do?"

The only sound was Smith tapping the table. He seemed to be waiting for Hamlin to answer, but the D.A. just stared blankly at Holly. "We're not telling you to do anything, Jack," Smith said.. "You're here to see McPherson, go see McPherson. You want him out of here, he wants out of here, we want the cocksucker out of here the minute we get our hands on the right guy. So if you can pull out anything that gets us closer, that's what we all want, right?" He looked past me at the door and cupped a hand to his mouth. "Lattimer!" he yelled, then looked back to me. "We want the guy who did this as much as you do, Jack," he said.

The door opened and the same deputy who brought us in walked through. I turned to Holly to see how she wanted to negotiate the exit. She was locked in a cold stare with Hamlin. After another second his eyes lowered and then bounced up to mine. "Good luck," he said to me flatly, and stood up just as Smith did. A moment later Holly was pulling me away from the table and trying to turn the chair around on a tiny patch of floor. She couldn't. She pulled me backwards into the hallway instead. As we moved away I saw Smith's big arm cross his doorway and flip the door closed.

37

HOLLY AND I WAITED QUIETLY IN A WHITEWASHED BLOCK ROOM. WE WERE seated at a narrow formica counter that ran underneath a bank of large windows of diamond wire-reinforced glass. A foot-wide plywood partition jutted out from the wall between windows, separating Holly's counter space from mine. On either side of the plywood hung black telephones, an old thick style that showed no dial or buttons when you picked up the heavy receiver, just the indentation of a circle where the dial usually was. I picked it up when Holly parked me at the counter and sat down next to me. "Hellooo?" There was no sound but the open resonance of a live line.

Through the glass we could see a small room, not more than twelve feet along the windowed wall and maybe eight feet from the windows to a back wall made of square iron bars. After we'd waited five minutes Zenith walked through a metal door in the barred wall.

He looked drained and more fragile than I remembered. He was cleaner than usual, with the County's orange coveralls zipped up to his throat and his hair pulled back into a lumpy bun. His face was motionless, unclenched from any kind of concentration or focus. Everything his eyes fell on seemed to make the same minimal impression on him until he saw me.

I was sitting exactly opposite the door he came through, so he saw me first. His face jerked slightly, then his eyes tightened until they were almost shut. I wondered again, as I had when he saw me during the demonstration where he was packing the big dummy spike, where his bitter sense of me came from. He must have remembered something that I don't.

Then he took a jerky step that made me notice that his wrists and ankles were all connected by a medium-weight chain, a web of handcuffs and shackles that bound his arms down in front of him. "Oh, Jesus!" Holly said from the little stall on my left.

The glass wasn't soundproof because Zenith heard her, too. He looked straight at her and cocked his head. Then his face opened up into a smile of snaggly caramel teeth that sent fans of wrinkles outward from both eyes and down his cheeks. He turned and rushed as well as he could for the chair opposite Holly. We could hear the chain tingle as he shuffled. As he sat down Holly picked up her phone. "Zenith? Zenith." She rapped on the glass until he picked up the phone. "Are you okay?"

Zenith nodded and the way he was strapped made his whole upper body move. As one hand held the phone the other dangled in the air ten inches away, like a dog on his hind legs begging on command. "Jesus," Holly said. "Zenith, just wait a minute. I'll be right back, okay?" She lay the receiver on the counter, pushed her chair back with a screech and left the room.

Zenith stared through the glass at where she had been, the phone still to his ear. After a few seconds I knocked on the glass in my little booth to get his attention. He didn't move. I looked at his profile, his gaze locked on Holly's chair, both hands up with the phone receiver in one. I knocked again. Nothing. I backed my chair up behind where Holly had been sitting and tried to reach her phone. I couldn't; the space was too tight and the cord was too short. But I was in Zenith's line of sight now. I pointed towards my booth and mimed talking on the phone to get him to slide over to the seat across from mine. He looked right through me. He was not going to move and he was not going to let go of that phone.

I returned to my space as Holly came back into the room. She was shaking her head with her lips pressed tight. She sat down and picked up the phone. "Zenith, I want to know about the chains," she said. "When do they put on the chains?" I saw him cock his head, thinking. "Do you always have the chains on?" He shook his head. "When you're in your cell, are there chains?" His head shook again. "It's just when they take you someplace out of your cell." He nodded yes. "Every time you leave your cell?" she asked. Here his jaw clenched and he looked upward to think.

The door behind him opened and a chubby young guard walked through. He pulled on a string of keys attached to his belt and went to Zenith. He said something to him and Zenith stood up. The guard unlocked metal keepers at Zenith's wrists and ankles and lifted the chains away from him. Then he looked at Holly and held up three fingers, mouthing "three minutes" with big movements. He left and Zenith sat down rubbing his wrists. He looked at them carefully, first one, then the other, then up at Holly as if she'd touched him and made him whole.

"Good," she said. "All right. Is that okay now?" He nodded briskly, with energy, tuned in like I'd never seen him before.

"This is really stupid, Zenith. This thing has all these guys crazy. They have to have someone to blame it on and right now you're it. But they can't keep you like this. We'll get you out of here, Zenith. We can't today, but soon. All right?"

His look at her was pure concentration.

"All right?" she said again.

He nodded brightly.

"Now, when they ask you all their questions," she said, 'how are they about it? Are they angry? Do they grab you or anything?"

This he thought about for a moment, his eyes going up. He looked back at her frowning and shook his head no.

"They don't touch you at all? Do they try to scare you?"

Zenith smiled a little and shook his head again. Definitely not.

"Okay. Now, I need you to listen very carefully to me, Zenith. This is important: do you know anything about the spiking? *Anything*? Did you see anything out there, or hear anybody talking about doing it, or maybe saying *you* should do it? Anything like that?"

I looked to see him shake his head, but he didn't. Instead I saw his mouth move very precisely, making the word *no*.

"You *don't*!" Holly's voice had a yelp in it. "You don't. Okay. Zenith: do you have any idea of who we can talk to, anybody you can think of who might know something about what happened?"

His lips moved again: no. He smiled slowly. The teeth were more awful close up.

That was it. The guard came in again and said something to Zenith, whose eyes stayed locked on Holly. The guard stepped forward and started pulling Zenith's chair back. "Don't worry, Zenith," Holly said. "We'll come back soon. I promise. Be strong, because we're getting you out of here, okay?" He nodded, backing towards the door. Then with the snap of a glance at me and a last gaze at Holly, he was gone. The clang of the closing door was muffled by the glass.

"Well!" Holly said, getting up and reaching for the handles on my chair.

"Could you hear him?" I asked her. "He said 'No?'"

"Clear as I can hear you. Hah!" And as we backtracked through the basement maze I thought of the joke Sam told once about the six-year-old boy who's never spoken, whose parents are crushed and confused because he tests out fine in every other way. Then one night at dinner he says "Mother, I believe I'd like some butter for my peas, if you'd be good enough to pass it to me," and she says "Tommy, you can talk! Oh, darling, why haven't you been talking?" and he shrugs and says "Up until now there hasn't been anything to say."

"Makes me think of an old joke," I said to Holly as we reached the elevator.

"Can you believe it?" she said. "Zenith SPEAKS!"

I ONLY HEARD THE BEGINNING OF STEVE AND HOLLY'S CONVERSATION AS we rode back up the hill. Two squad cars followed us the first part of the way to give us a little distance from the media vans.

Steve and Holly stopped concentrating on their side view mirrors when we crossed the city limits and the buildings thinned out. Holly shifted in her seat and looked at Steve. "Guess what?" she said. "Zenith speaks."

"You talked to him?"

"Yes I *talked* to him. And Zenith talked to me."

Steve looked at her. "Pardon me?"

"He did. He said 'no' twice. Didn't he, Jack?" Neither one of them looked at me.

"Well, that's interesting," Steve said. "What else did he say?"

"It's a big deal, Steve. *I* think it is," she said. "I did the rest of the talking. It's what we thought. He's clueless about the whole thing. It was a bolt from the blue to him like everyone else."

"Amazing," said Steve, "how everyone's clueless."

"Well, Zenith is."

We were leaving the upper edge of the coastal bench now, passing between two big Christmas tree farms that marked the start of the foothills. "According to my Dad," Steve said slowly, "he's not. From what they've put together, if he didn't do it, he knows who did."

"Oh, really?" said Holly. "What have they put together?"

"Dad won't say. And I keep asking him, believe me, because everything I find's a dead-end. Zippo."

"But Mel's got it figured out."

Steve tipped his head to the right, then left, a little shrug. "He knows something."

They watched the road quietly as it wound around the curve that gives the panoramic view of the bay and the coast that you see on postcards. "Steve," Holly said. "Are you going to tell Mel what you did for us today?"

He paused for most of a minute. "Yes."

Holly turned to look at him. I saw the corner of a smile on her cheek. "Good," she said.

That's all I remember. I had started to feel tired just before we left Zenith, then the media jostle outside the building shot me full of adrenaline. With that washed away I was dozing off. I think, or I dreamed, that Holly was saying something about Zenith's chains and her worries about what more jail time would do to him.

When I was little and we were driving home late at night, especially from somewhere far away like one of Mom's family reunions in Yakima, I'd love to fall asleep in the back seat with Mom and Dad's conversation, mostly Mom's, surrounding my dreams. It felt wonderful then, protected and warm, certain without thought that it would end with a trip to bed in Dad's arms. It didn't feel wonderful now.

"All right, move it, buddy, end of the line." I startled awake to Steve's voice and the oiled rushing sound of the van's side door sliding open. Two Lewsco guys helped him get me into Mom's house. She kissed me and smoothed my hair down with both hands and asked how I was feeling. My back hurt like hell but I said I was fine, just a little tired.

Mom shook her head instead of saying what she was thinking. "Let's get you to bed," she said.

Holly had come inside with me. She gave Mom a little hug and put her hand on my shoulder. "Thanks for going with me," she said. "Now we know it's up to us." She kissed my forehead. "I'll call you tomorrow."

She went out the door to where Steve was. Where they went then, I have no idea.

38

I SLEPT THROUGH THE NEXT DAY AND INTO THE ONE AFTER THAT. A little after noon on Saturday Mom came in with a bowl of soup and plate of toast and asked if she should let the Chinese man in to see me. She meant Will Hayama. I had her ask him to wait until I could wake up, eat a little and get myself back in the chair.

Ten minutes later I rolled out into the living room. He and Mom were standing at the wall of Dad's old team photos. "This was the year when they almost won the championship," she was saying, "and he always blamed himself that they didn't, even though he was by far the best player on the team."

"Hello, Will," I said.

He turned around with a smile. "Jack. Mrs. Gilliam, thank you. The *details* you remember are remarkable. Thank you very much."

Mom lit up. "Could I get you one more cup of coffee?"

"Thank you, ma'am, but I'm just about right."

"It would let me clean out the pa-ott," she sang. She all but winked at him. It made me realize that Will's small kindnesses were the most attention anyone had paid her since the accident. Maybe longer.

"Well, one more couldn't hurt. It tastes delicious." He sat down across from me as Mom took his cup to the kitchen. "I didn't know any of that about your father. She's so proud of him."

"You must be a trained detective."

He laughed. "You know, my grandfather played pro ball. He was one of the first Nisei to make the high minors. He caught for the San Fran-

221

cisco Spartans, 1940 and '41. Then the war came."

"They shut down for the war?"

"They shut us down for the war." He brought his hands together on the table and looked at them. "He was relocated to Tule Lake along with the whole family. When he got out he wasn't thinking about baseball. He could barely walk."

I felt stupid. "What an ugly thing."

"Well," said Will. "That was a long time ago."

"In some ways," I said. Will turned his head slightly without taking his eyes from me, measuring something.

Mom came in and put a steaming mug on the end table beside him. "One spoon of sugar and no cream, right?" she said.

"Perfect."

"Perfect," she said. "Now I'll be in the kitchen if you need anything. I'm making a pot roast for tonight." She wiped her hands on her apron. "Do you have any plans for tonight? It's much too big for just Jackie and me."

"That is really kind, ma'am, thank you. But I just couldn't do that."

"But it's no trouble at all. We'd *like* — "

"Mom." She looked at me. "Did you hear him? He said he can't."

She nodded and drew a big breath. "Then I'll just be in the kitchen if you need anything."

Will smiled at me as she left. He sipped, put the mug down and took a small spiral notebook from his inside breast pocket. "A couple of questions?"

I nodded.

"Jack, do you know a Ray Swerdlow?"

Oh, boy. Ray Fuckin'-Ay Swerdlow. I hadn't given Ray Swerdlow a serious thought in ten years. I think he left Lewsco a year or two after I did, and not on his own steam. He was too far into the sauce to trust in the woods. After that he made his living selling meat, mostly fresh venison during the eleven months a year that weren't hunting season. Everyone knew it and left him alone, though you'd hear cracks about his elegant hunting methods. He'd lay out salt licks near a bend in the Lewis two miles downriver of town, wait for a doe or fawn to show up and blow them to oblivion with shotgun shells fit for elephant hunts. Around town they said buying Ray's meat would take care of any iron deficiency in your diet. Most of the money he made went to Sam at the Spot. He had a stool halfway down the bar, four seats down from Fife, though as an independent businessman he of course couldn't spend quite as much time there as Fife does. Having to listen to Ray rant on about the world has kept down my alcohol intake; when he was in the Spot I didn't hang around much.

"Yes," I said. "If you live up here, you know Ray Swerdlow."

"Well, Ray Swerdlow walked into the Emergency Room in Port Douglas this morning covered with second and third-degree burns. He told the nurses that his gas water heater blew up last night, but the doctor said it's been infecting for at least 48 hours."

Ray Swerdlow. "So you think...you think Ray Swerdlow is Jack's Avenger?" I tried a light little laugh but it came out twisted. "I don't know, I just don't see Ray Swerdlow as Avenger material." I looked for a smile from Will. Nothing. "I'll check my Avenger roster if you want, though, to see if he's on it."

Will scribbled a few words on his pad. "Do you think he has it in him to start that fire?" He looked back up.

"Oh, yeah," I said. "Easily. What he doesn't have is much use for me. I can't see him reaching up to scratch his nose to even the score for me."

"You've never been friends?"

"You could say we've never been friends," I said. "Ray Swerdlow's a throw-back, Will. He's ten minutes out of the primal ooze. All the contact we had was years ago, and it wasn't a bonding experience."

He scribbled quickly. "Okay. Does he have any close friends that you know of?"

"No. But that doesn't mean anything. Who you should ask about that is Sam at the Spot."

"Okay." He flipped the little pad closed and put it back in his coat. "I will. Is there anything else that comes to mind when you think of Ray and the fire?" I thought a moment and shook my head. "If something does, will you call me?" he asked, standing up.

I nodded. "Before you go, though, what about the spiking? What's going on?"

Will shrugged. "I'm not really tuned in. We get pretty compartmentalized and right now I'm the guy on the fire."

"You don't know anything?"

"Oh, you hear things. Supposedly they discovered something this week that they're discussing whether or not to make public."

"About Zenith?"

Slowly, without really stepping, he was moving towards the door. "You know, you hear things. I think they've decided they have to put the pieces together a little tighter before they can really move."

Mom must have heard our rhythm change because she came into the room. "More coffee? It'll let me clean out the pot."

"Thank you, ma'am, but I think Jack will have to help you out there. I'm afraid I have to be in Grants Pass in about forty minutes."

"Then you'd better get going this minute!" She fussed him towards the door, pulling out a promise he'd be back soon. He waved over her shoulder at me from the doorway. When he was gone Mom came over to pick up his cup and wipe the surface of the end table. "You know, I don't feel right calling him by his first name," she said, "and I can't say the second one right. Heroma?"

"Hayama. HI-YAA-MA. Will Hayama."

"Hayama," she said, taking the dish back to the kitchen. "Hayama. Hayama. Hayama."

39

PAST A CERTAIN POINT IT'S HARD TO BE SURPRISED ABOUT ANYTHING. I thought I'd passed that point around the time I was entertaining my friend the President with hilarious jokes. But I hadn't.

Other than a couple of short check-ins from Holly and a grocery delivery from Sam's, we had no more visitors for a few days. Mom rented some old James Bond movies at Sam's Store. I don't like them, but for thirty years she's pretended I do so that she can see them. Especially the Sean Connerys — she'll watch Roger Moore or the later imitations, but they don't make her brain go soft. It used to be sort of funny, a running joke between us the way she used me to justify her 007 habit. Not anymore. She was so desperate to shove some of what used to be normal into our completely changed lives that I could hardly stay in the same room with her. I felt a pang for Dad, who I used to blame for the hard times between them. This woman could drive you crazy.

I tried watching with her. I leaned forward towards the screen with an annoyed expression when she made side comments. I made it through *Goldfinger* and ten minutes into *From Russia With Love* and then couldn't sit there anymore. I rolled into my room, shutting the door behind me on her and Sean, and spent most of two days writing. Mom kept watching and hoping I'd come back out.

I did only for meals. On Wednesday morning I was finishing breakfast at the kitchen table when a brisk tapping sounded on the front door. Mom opened it and Steve stepped inside. "There's someone outside who wants to talk to you," he said.

"Steve, there are lots of people outside who want to talk to me."

He shook his head. "This one you want to talk to."

"Why's that?"

"You'll see." He walked over to grab the handles of my chair. "Let's go."

"Go where? Why? You just said he was outside."

"He is."

"Well, tell him to come in."

"No," Steve said. He opened the front door and pushed the chair out to the porch. The media crowd was smaller than before, less than a dozen now, and they were divided in two by a cordon of state troopers who formed a pathway for us from the bottom of the ramp to the graveled turn-out by the road, where one vehicle was parked. It was a tired-looking one ton pickup from the 1970s with a big cab-over camper on it, the kind that was common before sleek RVs took over. An oversized door had been cut into the back end, big enough for Steve and two guys to hoist my chair through. They pushed me forward towards the middle of the little enclosed space and closed the door behind me.

Coming in from the bright daylight, I needed a moment to see clearly. Straight across from me, sitting up on the bed above the cab with his feet dangling down, was a paunchy guy of about 50 in a tan leisure suit. He wore a red ball cap that they sell in the tackle shops in Grants Pass with a shimmering steelhead above the brim jumping through the words "I FISH THEREFORE I AM." He nodded at me and then looked down to my left.

I looked there too, into the face of a second man who sat on one of the two upholstered benches flanking a narrow formica table. He was smiling warmly. "Well, imagine meeting you here," he said. "Are you comfortable? I apologize for the tight quarters, but I think we can make do."

I was sure I should know who he was. He was probably sixty, but he could have been an extra-fit seventy, tan, salt-and-pepper hair parted neatly, a smooth-shaven face bland and angle-free as a potato— I wouldn't want to have to describe him to a cop. He wore a red plaid shirt he'd probably worn for twenty years with the neck button open to show a bright white undershirt. "I came to see how you're doing," he said.

"Uh-huh. Have we met?"

"No."

"Well, I'm sorry if I'm supposed to figure it out for myself, but who are you?"

"Jim Nielsen," he said, "Oklahoma Oil." He reached out his hand for mine.

"Yeah, right." I started to move my chair back towards the door. "Steve!" I yelled. I wondered who'd think this would be funny enough to go to the trouble. "Steve!" The guy in the fishing cap on the bunk was laughing and the friendly one next to me kept his hand outstretched, patiently waiting for me to take it. I looked past it into his face and remembered the picture in the Lewsco maintenance office, the one of Reagan signing a bill on the White House Lawn in front of Mel and — this man. I reached for the hand that ran the fifth biggest company in the world, along with Lewsco and most of the South Range forest and our lives, and I shook it. "I...don't... have any idea what to say."

The fishing guy snickered again. Nielsen nodded and smiled. "Well, we didn't exactly call ahead."

"But...who's with you?"

"Just us," he said. "Leonard and me." Leonard raised one hand from the bunk and wiggled his fingers in a dippy wave. "Leonard helps me out with everything."

"Who brought you here?"

"We brought us."

"You *drove* here?"

"Well, from Grants Pass. Leonard flew us in there. We thought about trying to fly into Ben Tyler's old place, but my plane's a little bigger than his was. Plus it's my first chance to see the country here. It's beautiful, Jack, you're lucky."

He was so relaxed that I was starting to be able to think. "In this thing?" I said, looking around the musty little compartment. "Is this a style statement or something?"

"It's more of a practical thing," Nielsen said. "We weren't interested in making a big splash."

"Why did you come?"

"To see how you're doing. To see if there's anything you need."

I don't know how to explain it now, but sitting there two feet away from him then in that funky aluminum box, he had this way of opening your mouth so that what came out was what you really thought. I've been tongue-tied around people with 2 percent of James Nielsen's money and clout. His, right then, made no difference. "You know, you've changed a lot of lives up here," I said. "With what you've done to this town, to this whole part of the world — well, I'm sorry, but I don't believe you came all the way up here to pay me a courtesy call."

"I can see that," he said. "It's interesting, this idea of yours that this has been the handiwork of one person by himself, doing what he does for whatever reason he has. You make it sound like some kind of isolated accident instead of an event that came from everything before it. But that's not your question. Your question is why I came, and the answer is to see how you're doing and to find out if there's anything you need. Would you like a beer, Jack?" I didn't say anything, but Leonard slid off the bunk and reached down to open a tiny refrigerator. He came back up and set two cans of Hamms on the table next to Nielsen. I can't stand Hamms.

Nielsen opened both cans and handed me one. "I came to tell you I admire you, Jack," he said. "I believe the first responsibility we have is to do the job we say we're going to do. You're never going to walk again just because you were doing your job. I have to admire you for that."

"And you don't plan to take any pictures of you admiring me?" I asked.

He laughed. For some reason, maybe to slow things down, I started to tell him about the *Oregonian* page with Gina Arnstead and Arthur Lane rushing up to see me from opposite directions. I didn't get very far before he put up a hand. "Leonard?" he said. Leonard reached to a far corner of the upper bunk and pulled down a box of newspapers. "Right here," Nielsen said. Leonard put it on the bench seat next to him and, two papers down, Nielsen found the page I was talking about and pulled it out. "This one?"

"That's it."

He spread the page across the table. "Well, we try to keep up," he said. "You're right, this is a classic." He studied the two faces as carefully as a stamp collector at a swap meet. Then he turned the page around in my direction. "What did you think when you saw this, Jack? Besides that it's funny?"

"Well," I said, "I thought it was kind of cold."

"Why?"

As I thought about it Nielsen folded up the page and put it back in the carton. Leonard took a step forward and lifted it back out of the way.

"Well, it's obvious," I said. "They were pretending to care about what happened to me when they didn't. That wasn't their purpose for coming."

"Sure," he said. "What do you think their purpose for coming was?"

"To look compassionate and caring so more people would vote for them."

"I think that's exactly right," Nielsen said.

"But I was just a tool for them to do that."

"Of course you were. They did what we all do, didn't they? Figure out what tools we need to accomplish our purpose, and use them. I don't mean we *all* do it. Hardly anyone even goes out there to try anymore. But the ones that do, don't they grab the tools at hand and use them?"

"Yes, but tools are *things*," I said. "I have boxes of tools in my shop, and there's a toolbox in my truck."

Nielsen smiled and nodded slightly. "Sure. Of course. Let's take another example. When you went on the *Today* show after you got hurt, what were you trying to do?"

"They asked me to. They really wanted me on."

"Yes, I know what they were trying to do. What were you trying to do?"

I had to think. It seemed like a long time ago. "Well, it wasn't something I asked for. They were pushing me for an answer and I went back and forth before I said yes. I think it was deciding that the most important thing was to start bouncing back right away. It felt like if I started feeling sorry for myself I'd drop into a spiral I wouldn't climb out of, so I kind of wanted to show the world I wasn't feeling sorry for myself. Then I'd believe it, too."

"So your purpose was starting to bounce back from your accident. Did you realize that before or after the *Today* show called you?"

"Afterwards," I said.

"Okay," he said. "So it's the same as our politician friends, except for the order. They had their purpose and then came upon a useful tool: you. You had a useful tool handed to you when *Today* called and then you figured out a purpose for it. It's a little different. But it's the same. To accomplish your purpose you need the right tools and you need to be willing to use them."

"So when somebody interviews you and asks you the key to your success, that's what you tell them?"

"Well, interviews aren't what I do," said Nielsen. "But I might say something like that. Would I say something like that, Leonard?" Leonard made a sound between a laugh and a hoot. "More likely I'd just say stick to your purpose. A lot of people hop from one purpose to another every time they see a shiny new tool, like a drunken monkey."

"'Drunken monkey.' That's a line from Baba Ram Dass."

"One of his best."

"You know *Ram* Dass?"

He closed his eyes for a moment and breathed slowly. "'You are a totally determined being,'" he said, opening his eyes. "'The very moment you will wake up is totally determined. How long you will sleep is totally determined. What you will hear of what I say is totally determined. There are no accidents in this business at all. Accidents are just from where you're looking. To the striving brain it looks like it's miracles and accidents. No miracles. No accidents.'"

"'To the ego,'" Leonard said.

"What?" said Nielsen.

"It's 'to the ego it looks like it's miracles,' not 'striving brain.'"

Nielsen shook his head. "Not there. It's 'striving brain' there."

"It's 'ego,'" said Leonard.

"Fifty bucks?" Nielsen said.

"Hundred," said Leonard. He took a little pad out of his breast pocket and wrote on it.

"What else do you read?" I asked.

Nielsen shook his head. "Maybe that's our topic next time, Jack. Now I have to go." He put his hand on the arm of my chair. "Last question: can I do anything to make this easier for you? Is there anything you want?"

"You could tell me who did the spiking. And who burned down the co-op in Port Douglas, if you know."

They looked at each other. Nielsen took a $100 bill out of his wallet and handed it to Leonard, who was humming. "Leonard said you'd want to know. I don't think it really matters, but I can see how it would to you. And if I knew either answer I'd tell you right now. Do you believe that?" I nodded. Naive or not, I just believed him. "And now that we've had this talk, I'll make it my own business to find out. We can do that, can't we, Leonard?"

"We can do that," Leonard said.

That sounded like a conversation ending. As Nielsen looked at me I raced to think of what I'd soon regret not saying to him while I had the chance. "And I guess I'd like to know why this," I said, slapping both wheels of my chair, "would be anybody's purpose."

"I don't think it was," Nielsen said. "The purpose wasn't hurting you. The purpose was one of two things: to scare us off, or, if they can hang it on one of our people, to disgrace us so much we'd go away."

"I know some people who'd say neither of those is a bad purpose," I said. "Some pretty good people."

"You're putting it too mildly," Nielsen said. "Maybe you're trying to be polite. There are people who'd say both of those are great purposes." He spread his hands wide on the table top as if to show how great. "And I'm not going to say if they're right or wrong, because I don't know. What I know for sure that nobody will argue with is this: if those purposes succeed, mine fails."

Leonard knocked on the wall above where Nielsen sat. The back door opened and a state trooper reached in to pull my chair back. Nielsen reached down to the seat beside him and set a cellular phone on the table. "I carry this all the time, Jack," he said, "and that" — Leonard was leaning over to hand me a scrap of paper — "is the number. If you ever feel like calling, use it." He nodded to the cop behind me and then looked at me one more time. "I knew I'd be glad I met you," he said.

Leonard followed me out the door as my chair was lowered to the ground and seconds later the truck pulled out of the yard. "Was that the FBI again?" someone yelled. "What did they say?" "Dan Rather wants to talk to you!" "Zenith confessed, right? Did he have accomplices?"

As the Lewsco guys pushed my chair towards the house I took a good look at the reporters. For the first time I saw individual faces, weary faces. What hit me is they're stuck in this drama, too, stuck like me in roles they didn't want, while he just dances on the surface, touching down a toe when he feels like it to muse his musings, then pulling out to skitter off to whatever else he feels like doing. Like he doesn't have the slightest thing to do with what happened.

When we were on the porch I told the guy pushing me to wait a moment. The shouting stopped when the press saw me turn my chair towards them. The three troopers still on the scene blocked the ramp and the steps, and the videocams surged forward to get their best shot at me.

"That wasn't the FBI," I said loudly. "The person in that camper is James Nielsen." I looked up at my helper. "The door, please." He opened the front door and as he pushed me through I didn't hear the slightest sound behind me. Mom was standing at the kitchen table with one hand over her mouth. As I rolled towards her I heard the front yard explode into shouts and the clatter of fast movement.

I rolled back to the table and asked Mom if there was more coffee. She brought me a fresh cup and sat down. "What did he say to you?" she said carefully.

"That there's a purpose to everything," I said. Mom nodded. Mom and James Nielsen share some theology. "He said he was glad to meet me. And he gave me this" — I handed her the slip of paper Leonard had given me — "in case we need anything. It's his private number."

"We can *call* him?"

"Probably not now," I said. "Back when he gave it to me we were still friends."

40

THOUGH SHE WOULDN'T ADMIT IT, THAT VISIT BOTHERED MOM MORE than the others. All she said was that things were feeling like Grand Central Station, which was not the place to get better. She tipped her hand two days later when she asked how I'd like it if we went to the LFHS football game that evening. "You know it's the Festival game, right?"

Even in my weird cocoon these days I knew that. The Friday night game before Halloween was the biggest game of the season because of the Pumpkin Festival at half time. Growers and amateur gardeners from all over the South Range brought their best pumpkins to compete in the Heaviest, Tallest, Fattest, Most Orange, Funniest and Most Sincere categories. They'd cover a whole end zone at halftime for the judging, a band of solid orange bright against the bright green. Then before the second half the Lewis Falls Lions Club would load them up and haul them down to the Methodist Church basement in Port Douglas. The next morning people who might otherwise go without could pick them up for jack o'lanterns and pie filling for the holidays.

"The outing will be good for us, don't you think?" Mom said.

"Weren't you the one blocking the door when we decided to go see Zenith?" I asked her. "What happened to how I'm trying to do too much too fast?"

"That was all the way down to the Port," she said. "This is practically across the street. And we'll just go for a little while. I'll call Steve to drive us, he said we should call anytime."

He had. But he couldn't have expected her to do it. Mom would rather open a vein than do anything that might bother others. And her definition of a bother was anything anyone did that had anything to do with helping her.

Now she was ready to pick up the phone and call Steve to get the Lewsco squad to take us to the football game? What was this? Tradition? Pumpkins are a big deal up here. You should see the bruisers that get hauled into town for the Festival. Mom's definitely into tradition. But she's more into not bothering people.

"You really want to do this?"

She looked down at the soapy dishes in the sink. "I just think the outing would be good for us. With all that's been happening, the pressure on you and the big people that want to see you every day and no time for you to be a normal person." The last few words were a whisper and when she turned to me, her hands still in the water, she was crying. "I don't want you to go away."

There it was. She thought maybe the Festival would remind me how to live in Lewis Falls. "Right, Mom. Where would I go? Hollywood? Maybe they'd make me the new James Bond." Now she was crying hard, her face and chest jerking in little sobs. "Come here." She stayed by the sink. I rolled over to her and reached around her waist. "Look at me." She shook in my arms. "Mom." She looked down at me. "Now, listen to me: this is my home, right here. Period. I'm not going anywhere else, no matter who comes to talk to me. Except to the game with you tonight." Her smile squeezed out a last built-up tear. A minute later she was ploughing through the dishes again, talking about the game and Festivals from my high school years and whether she should call Holly and her mother to go with us.

I didn't want to lean on Steve anymore. But we would. Something in the conversation with Nielsen made me see how pitiful it had been for me to bitch at Mom. Cowardly is the word, probably. This was the first thing she'd asked for plainly since the accident, and it was going to happen.

As his guys lifted me into the van that evening — Steve didn't come himself — the little media herd made way for us with less commotion and shouting than before. We drove to the far side of the Square, where the LFHS football field bordered the old Field of Dreams diamond to take advantage of the lights. The van crossed the grass and pulled up to the side of the aluminum grandstand, where the guys set me down and pushed me to the center of a little patch of ground marked off with red timber-survey tape. They already had a folding chair set up for Mom and four others for themselves to make a buffer around Mom and me.

The game was intense by the time we got there. We were down 13-6 to the North Port Douglas Mariners late in the second quarter, deep into a drive that could let us take a tie into halftime. Gradually a few people started drifting down off the grandstand to circle me and my little squad.

"Jack!" Marcy Bates yelled over the shoulder of one of the Lewsco guys. "You look *won*derful!"

"I can't believe it!" said Toni Figuera, Ray's wife. "Look at you!"

"Well, hell, hon," said Ray, right behind her, "don't make fun of him. He always looked that gnarly."

The loosely-tacked red barrier tape fell to the ground as people pushed in, and all four Lewsco guys around me stood up with outstretched arms to nudge them back. "Okay, okay, easy now," I heard the one on my left say. "Let's watch the game."

"A little space, people?" said the guy in front of me. His name was Larry and I remembered him operating the crane on shows I'd been on years ago. The past week he'd taken a shift guarding Mom's almost every day. "Come on, let's keep some space here." I heard about half of what the guy to my right was trying to explain to the Figueras, that I'd been locked inside by all the attention almost like I was in jail and they really needed people's cooperation in order to get me out. There was a little jostling, a little buzz of whining, but the inward pressure eased as people moved back into the grandstands. They shouted good wishes and I waved back as they went.

A few people still lingered around us to watch the game. Lewis Falls had the ball on the North PD 12 yard-line with less than a minute left in the half. I could see the important things hadn't changed. We looked like a bunch of bony-elbowed boys and the other guys looked like they were from Ohio State, just like when I was in school. North PD threw our small-but-slow quarterback Mark Ferrin (Dougy's boy) for big losses on the last two plays of the half, and both teams jogged off the field while the four horns in our band played some college fight song. Before they were completely off the field a huge stake-body truck backed up to one end zone and a half-dozen Lewis Falls Lions stepped forward to unload pumpkins. I had a little trouble seeing them through the stream of fans that started to spill from the grandstand.

There was a quick screech of sound-system, then the voice of Lou Figuera, Ray's uncle and Lewis Falls' mayor since about the War of 1812. "LADIES AND GENTLEMAN! WELCOME! WELCOME TO THE GREATEST HARVEST FESTIVAL AND PUMPKIN EXHIBITION IN THE KNOWN WORLD! SOON WE WILL ALL KNOW THE NAMES OF THE GREATEST PUMPKIN GROWERS THROUGHOUT THE LAND, BUT FIRST IT IS MY GREAT HON-

OR TO INTRODUCE TO YOU THE MASTER OF CEREMONIES FOR THE EVENING, OR SHOULD I SAY *MISTRESS* OF CEREMONIES FOR THE EVENING, MY VERY DEAR FRIEND AND A FRIEND TO THE TIMBER INDUSTRY AND EVERYONE IN IT, SO LET'S SAY A BIG SOUTH RANGE HOWDY TO THE HONORABLE COMMISSIONER, GINA ARNSTEAD!" It was obvious how much Mayor Lou liked his job.

The little marching band played again as a shiny red Dodge pickup with ARNSTEAD FOR CONGRESS signs on the doors drove toward the mayor on the 50-yard line. Gina stood up in the bed, one arm braced on top of the cab and the other waving to the crowd. When the band stopped playing you could hear the last fading of a barely polite ovation. Gina waved and smiled like the solo star of a ticker tape parade. Then with a little help she hopped down from the tailgate and gave the mayor a little hug that moved him out from behind the microphone.

"ISN'T THIS A GREAT *GAME*!" her voice boomed out. A few people clapped. "TELL ME IF YOU THINK THIS IS A GREAT GAME!" A lot more clapping. "THAT'S *RIGHT*! YOU KNOW, THIS MOUNTAIN, LEWIS FALLS, IS JUST A LITTLE DIFFERENT FROM OTHER PLACES. IN THE LAST THREE MONTHS I'VE BEEN TO EVERY TOWN AND CITY IN THIS CONGRESSIONAL DISTRICT, NOT FOR ANY PARTICULAR REASON EXCEPT THAT I JUST LIKE TO TRAVEL." She paused hopefully for a laugh and got a small one. "BUT LET ME TELL YOU SOMETHING ABOUT LEWIS FALLS."

I don't know what she told us about Lewis Falls. I was thinking instead about how methodically Gina followed her purpose, no wasted movement. Tomorrow and Sunday she'd tell other crowds she'd been all across the district and how Port Douglas, or Bounty, or Brookings, or Powers or Grants Pass or Wetherford or Thomasville or Central Point, is just a little different from other places. After a while it sounds like elevator music. Most people passing around me on the way to the snack stand and portapotties didn't notice she was there.

"Hey, Jack!" I looked up and on the edge of the grandstand, their feet a foot or two higher than my head, was a little knot of people I knew — Dougy and Bonnie Ferrin and their daughter, Bobby and Karen McInteer, Barb Macy, a few others. Their greetings lapped one over the other.

"Jesus, we're glad to see you."

"Speak for yourself, Doog."

"Stop it, Bobby! Jack, we've been thinking about you every day..."

"And praying every day."

"...and praying."

"We couldn't believe it. We just can't believe it."

"How are you holding out, Lois? Is there anything we can do?" Mom smiled up at them, shook her head.

"How do you feel, Jack? Is it, are you okay?"

Larry and another one of Steve's Lewsco guys had climbed up into the grandstands and were urging them away from us now. "He's fine, he's fine," Larry was saying, "now we're gonna leave him be and just let him enjoy the game, okay?"

"Hey now, wait," I said to Mitch, a soft heavy guy standing near me and watching the movement. He was foreman at one of the mills and seemed to be the honcho when Steve wasn't around. "Why don't we lighten up, okay? Get your guys down here and tell them to lighten up."

Mitch's fat cheeks almost closed his eyes as he looked at me. "Steve said not to let anybody bother you."

"They're not bothering me, they're my friends. They're just saying hello."

"Steve was pretty strong on it."

"Yeah, I'm sure. And I'm pretty strong that you're not pushing my friends around. Get those guys down out of there and chill them out."

Mitch looked at me another moment, two dark slits beneath bushy eyebrows and a Stihl chainsaw cap, then looked up to the grandstands. "Jim. Larry. It's okay." Mitch made a come-here gesture with his head and the two started stepping down the benches to the ground. My friends came back towards me.

"Those your boys now, Jack?" Dougy said. "'I got a offer you can't refuse?'"

"Sorry," I said. "It's supposed to be for them." I gestured towards a band of reporters off to the side, kept at a little distance by a chain of three other Lewsco guys. Cameras kept clicking and whirring and every few minutes someone loudly threw out a question that sounded mechanical, bare of hope that I'd answer.

"They been all over the place," Bobby said. "At church, at the Spot, anyplace there's anybody might know you. They already been through all of us. 'What's Jack Gilliam really like?'" He grinned the same unhinged grin he had in first grade. "I told 'em good."

"Thanks, Bob," I said. The loud drone of Gina's voice stopped so suddenly in the upswing of a phrase that we all turned to look at her. She'd pulled her head from the microphone towards someone whispering in her ear, a man who was pointing across the field straight at us. She was following his gesture, squinting towards us against the powerful lights.

She nodded and leaned back towards the mike. "AS MUCH FUN AS WE'RE HAVING TONIGHT LET ME BE SERIOUS FOR JUST ONE

MINUTE. WE HAVE WITH US SOMEBODY VERY SPECIAL TO CEL-
EBRATE TONIGHT, SOMEONE YOU ALL KNOW AND SOMEONE
I FEEL PRIVILEGED TO COUNT AS MY FRIEND AND AS REALLY
KIND OF MY *PART*NER IN STANDING UP FOR THE WORKING
MEN AND THE WORKING WOMEN OF SOUTHERN OREGON.
SOMEONE WHO WHEN THE ENVIRONMENTAL EXTREMISTS
SAID YOU BETTER BACK DOWN, HE SAID *NO,* I WILL *NOT* BACK
DOWN, THIS IS MY HOME AND MY WAY OF LIFE AND I WILL
NOT LET YOU PEOPLE TAKE IT AWAY FROM ME. AND HE DID A
LOT MORE THAN SAY IT, HE PUT HIS LIFE ON THE LINE FOR
EVERY SINGLE ONE OF US WHO'S HERE TONIGHT, AND NOW
IT'S TIME FOR ALL OF US TO STAND UP FOR HIM AND I'M JUST
PROUD TO COUNT HIM AS MY FRIEND, MR. JACK GILLIAM!"

And the place went nuts. My friends yelled and the grandstand
clanged as they jumped up and down, Gina and her sidekicks clapped
with their arms stretched unnaturally towards me, my Lewsco guards
all faced me with applause and earnest looks, with the roar of a thou-
sand mixed voices draped over it all. The little brass band started to
play either "This Land is Your Land" or "Dixie"; there was too much
noise to tell which. With no attention on them, the gaggle of media
pushed closer towards us.

Only Mom and I were still sitting. I turned towards her. "This what
you had in mind?" I yelled.

Her eyes were wet and her chin trembled. "They all love you so much,
Jackie," she said. "Everyone here loves you." She began looking around
like a little girl inside a jeweled castle. I looked just behind her to
where Mitch, the Lewsco foreman, was still clapping. A video camera
lens was creeping over his shoulder like a serpent, inches from his ear,
straight towards Mom and me. I pointed at it for Mitch to see. He
turned around and with two other guards moved the edge of press
people back to where it had been.

The paper the next day said the cheering lasted for five minutes, but
I don't think it was that long. It would start to fade, and then a few
people would yell extra loud and rev it back up. After watching it stu-
pidly for a while I lifted my arm and waved. That set off a shot of noise
that then tapered off until Gina could be heard again. "THAT'S
RIGHT...THAT'S RIGHT...HE DID IT FOR EVERY ONE OF US.
THANK YOU, JACK GILLIAM."

As the ovation faded out the judges handed her the names of the
pumpkin winners. She read them as if they were Oscar winners, a mix
of drama and solemn pride with every one. I knew most of the names.
One of them was Peter Thomas, the town's mad organic soil scientist,
who took the Most Orange title for probably the tenth year straight. It

was one of Lewis Falls' favorite inside jokes, how seriously Peter, who took nothing else but his books seriously, guarded his secret starting-soil recipe, how he mounted his expanding awards collection, half dollar-sized pumpkin images cast from lead, on his living room wall. For his birthday a few years back we got an oversized can of hazard-orange spray paint from the Department of Highways garage and gift-wrapped it with a note saying "Because yours is probably used up by now."

Peter was on the field now, his newest medal around his chest while Gina shook his hand. As the winners marched past her one by one, some of the Lewis Falls Lions were parking their pickups next to the end zone to load all the pumpkins so the game could continue. One of them was Steve's four-wheel drive Ford — he's Lions president this year. Steve got out and then his passenger door opened and Holly got out. I watched them start to load pumpkins into the back. They moved fast and efficiently. After a minute Holly stopped to take off her barrette and reorganize her hair. Then she was back at it, a little faster than before as if making up for her break.

The pickups were soon loaded and gone and the second half began. After the first minute the crowd's whole focus was back on the game. Only Dougy, Bobby McInteer and Ray Starcher still hung around at the grandstand rail to talk.

"Hey, Jack," Bobby said, "has that Jap guy been to see you? The FBI guy?"

"Yeah."

"What's his deal? He keeps coming around asking questions, the same ones over and over."

"Like he doesn't believe us," Starcher said.

"Like what questions?"

"Like who was in the Spot on the nights before that PD fire, and what everybody said and who they said it to and where they were sitting," Bobby said.

"Like we memorize who sits where every night," said Starcher.

"Well, it's not that hard, Ray," I said. "You'd have a seizure if you had to sit on a different stool one night. So would you, Bobby. It's not what you'd call an unpredictable place."

"Yeah, but the thing is," Bobby said, "he keeps asking about guys who were there that we don't know."

"Oh, right, I forgot," I said. "There's always all those mysterious strangers at the Spot that you guys don't know anything about."

Dougy said, "Actually, there are, Jack, since all this happened. Those radio and TV guys hang out in there, shooting the shit, waiting for something to happen, playing poker."

"Big-time poker," said Bobby.

"Whining about what a bum-fuck town we are," Ray said, looking behind me tensely. I glanced over my shoulder and saw a couple of media guys sauntering closer. Mitch and Larry and the others were watching the game.

"So what is his deal?" Bobby said. "The Jap. I mean, he's got Swerdlow already for torching the place, right? What's he want with us?"

"I guess they don't have it all tied together the way they want," I said. "He's kind of a details guy."

"So he's come to see you?" Dougy said.

"Twice," I said. "He and Mom kind of have a thing going, right, hon?" Mom's chair was a few feet away now. She was watching the game between two Lewsco guys.

"Hmm?" she said to me with a smile.

"What do you think of Will Hayama, Mom? Want him over to visit again soon?"

"John Gilliam, you hush your dirty mouth. You're not too big to spank, which I promise to do if you don't leave me alone." She gave a happy little humph and turned back to the game.

"Like I'd feel it," I said to Dougy. "Anyway, even with Swerdlow, I think he's still putting pieces together."

"What's he told you?" The voice came from behind me, a woman's, unfamiliar. "What did Hayama tell you about?" I turned around as far as I could. A shotgun microphone was pointed at me from three feet away and behind it was a reporter I recognized from network TV. "What did you tell him about the fire?" Behind her was a black cameraman. Close up he looked like he could have played NFL ball. He shouldered a massive Hitachi videocam like it was a trinket.

"Lady, do you mind?" Dougy said. "We're having a conversation here."

"I can see that," she said. "Jack, tell us what you know about the fire."

"Beat it, lady," Bobby said, loud enough to pull Mitch's attention from the game. He tapped two guys on the arm and they moved past me towards the reporter. Another few press people crowded closer, too.

"Shut up," she said, trying to twist around Mitch. "Jack, what is going on now? Tell me what really happened with the fire. Who's Jack's Avengers?" She was rushing her words now, shouting and desperate as bodies came between us.

"*You* shut up!" Bobby was yelling. "You goddamn parasites! Get your goddamn asses out of here!"

"You *kiss* my ass, you dumb Okie!" It was the cameraman. He was shooting with one arm and using the other to brace the woman as she was being pushed back against him. I could feel the tremor of bodies shifting against each other behind my chair.

"Fuck you, coon!" Ray Starcher yelled from the grandstand, and he heaved a small Igloo cooler like a shotput straight over me. It hit the cameraman on the side of his head. He bellowed and moved forward like a mad bull, and then it was just pushing bodies and angry shouts and grunts, a close-in chaos electrified by the fear rushing through me. Someone ploughed into my side, knocking my chair over. I gripped the arms of the chair to keep attached to the seat. A few seconds later Mitch righted me and pushed the chair back out of the way.

"My Mom!" I yelled at him, and he ran faster than I thought he could around the edge of the fighting. Less than a minute later, two Lewsco guys brought her around to where I was. She hugged me hard, pulling my head into her chest where I heard her heart pound wildly. "You okay, Mom?"

"Oh, Jackie?" she sobbed. "*Why?* It was perfect!"

She pushed my chair further away and we watched a moment of the dense frenzy on the side of the grandstand. Dougy and Bobby had climbed down to join the shoving while Ray stayed above, grabbing for more things to throw down below. The Lewsco guys were moving the press back hard, throwing forearms and kicks as they went. One of them had gotten hold of the Hitachi camera. He clasped the long barrel of the lens like a handle and was swinging it around like a boxy club. With a big backswing he stepped over to the grandstand and bashed the camera with all his might against a metal upright. The sound was horrible. He took a second crashing swing, then a third, then heaved the camera away to the side. The moment after he let go, the black cameraman hit him with a flying block and they sprawled under the grandstand, growling and rolling around like rabid hounds.

That was the center of the fury. The other Lewsco guys, reinforced now by my friends, locked themselves together in a wall solid enough to push back the rest of the press guys, who were still yelling but weren't interested in a serious fight. Then a couple of guys crawled under the grandstand to start pulling the fistfight apart while Dougy and someone else came over to help Mom and me into the van. As Dougy drove us away I could see the grandstand through the back window, with three men struggling to hold the black guy back and two others hanging on to the guy who broke his camera.

When we reached Mom's the quiet was stunning. For the first time since I'd come home her yard was empty. Dougy came inside with Mom and me to see if we needed anything. He turned down her offer of coffee and headed back towards the Square. Mom put on the tea kettle and sat down next to me at the table. She was crying softly. I reached towards her and she shook her head. "What do we do, Jackie?" she said. "How do we get it to be like before?"

I looked at her hands on the table, more spotted than the last time I noticed, and touched one of them with my fingertips. "It'll be safe again, Mom. I promise." She tried to smile and looked into my eyes for a second, then down at our hands.

41

I ONLY MADE THAT PROMISE BECAUSE I DIDN'T KNOW WHAT ELSE TO SAY. But as I was saying it — in the same hour anyway — things were already happening. Somebody called District Attorney Hamlin at home before the game was over (North Port Douglas beat us 26-10, after a half-hour game delay to clear out the riot, which the PD newspaper pointed out as a splendid example to set for our high school youth), and before midnight he had the Circuit Court judge on the line to grant a temporary restraining order keeping members of the press a minimum of one hundred yards away from me. While we were sleeping two Lewis County deputies parked their prowler in front of Mom's to enforce it. At least one deputy has been here around the clock ever since. There's supposed to be a hearing next week about a permanent injunction, which would be fine with me.

Actually it wasn't while I was sleeping, because I didn't that night. The adrenaline that pooled up somewhere while we came home and drank our tea broke loose a minute after I'd pulled myself into bed. We could have been crushed. Mom could have been crushed. So much for pretending we can do normal little things like normal people. I'm not just a gimp, I'm a gimp who has to live this bullshit drama. So does Mom, who's done *nothing*. It's complete bullshit.

The anger ground me down to exhaustion long after midnight. I drifted down through softer layers to where Holly was. There a cold steel hook jerked me back up: Holly had driven off with Steve and his load of pumpkins. She was with Steve. Awake again, I thought of parts of her, the blond down that makes her smooth arms glisten, the thrust of her full upper lip when you see her from the side, the silk spirals of hair just behind each ear, swirling around themselves in a perfect softness that used to weaken me when I stared at her in class. And now as I lay too tired to steer my thoughts, he could be touching them right now with his lips or his fingers. What were they doing right *now*, that second?

I know that I eventually fell asleep only because when Mom came in to tell me Will Hayama was waiting out in the living room, she woke me up. It was about 9:00 a.m. She set a hot mug of coffee on the side table and picked my pee pan and hose off the floor while I tried to focus on what she'd said. I told her to have him wait five minutes before coming in.

He did, carrying Mom's favorite mug with a gust of steam over the top. He took off his dark suit jacket and draped it on the back of the chair at the foot of the bed. His movement made everything seem a little less out of control.

"Well," he said, "I suppose things got so boring around here that you decided to go out and liven them up a little bit?"

"Oh, yeah," I said, "*we* livened them up. When you told me to stay away from reporters you forgot to mention they'd turn into psychopaths."

"I didn't mention that?" He sipped the coffee and set it down on the dresser next to him. "Not psychopaths, exactly. They just know if they don't get their job done there are plenty of people waiting to take their place. So when the job's not getting done, they get scared. One more suggestion?"

I nodded.

"Don't go anywhere for a while. What happened last night, and the order keeping them away, that just raises the ante. Talking to you would be even a bigger plum than before."

My hands went into the air on their own. "Geez, I'd like to help you, but I've got so much planned. This afternoon I'm running a fucking marathon and then tomorrow I leave for Nepal to trek in the Himalayas. You don't really expect me to sit around here like a bump on a fucking log, do you?"

Will watched me calmly. "It's hard, isn't it?"

"It's bullshit! Because they're all crazy out there I'm the one under guard?" I tried to shift to sit straighter in the bed. My back was sore. "If I can't go anywhere how much different am I than Zenith?"

"Different," Will said. "This won't last long, Jack. It won't. We're putting the picture together, and once we do and they've got their punchline the press will move on. They'll be off to their next fable.

Give it a week, two, maybe, and then you can get back to your swinging lifestyle." He paused, watching. "I've been to Nepal, Jack. You'd like it. You could go."

"Right," I said. "They have gimp ramps up and down the mountains for people like me, right?" I don't know what I expected him to say. A pep talk, maybe some Power of Positive Thinking? He didn't say anything. He watched me quietly and I was too embarrassed to look back. At this rate I'd soon sink in his eyes to nothing more than human debris from the crime. And get nothing in return. I took a deep breath and lifted my head towards him. "Did you say a week? You must be seriously on the move."

Will nodded. "I want to finish this."

"I hear you've been putting in your time at the Spot. That's really the Lewis Falls Way, Will. We always go to the Spot when we need to get the job done. You're going native."

He smiled. "I'm trying, yes. But I think they're beginning to suspect I might not be from around these-here parts," he said. "Pilgrim." He made it a perfect mix of Charlie Chan and John Wayne. I laughed, a shaking that loosened me inside. "I think it's your wing-tips," I said.

"I shine them more than you people do, right?" He held both feet up for me to see. He was wiping the slate clean for me with his clowning, lifting me back to his level. He took the steno pad from his pocket like he had to record this new insight.

"So why?" I asked him. "What' s at the Spot for you?"

"Ray Swerdlow's cronies," Will said, turning to a fresh page in his pad. "The people who listen to him drink. Somebody who can tell me who put him up to the fire, I hope, because somebody did. Yesterday when his wife came into the hospital..."

"Ruth," I said.

"Ruth came in with seventy-five $100 dollar bills. She says she found them wrapped in a bandanna at home." He jotted something on his pad and looked up at me. "Who can you think of who has that kind of money?"

"Up here? I can't. Why don't you just ask Ray, Will? He's not going to be the tough guy on you. Give him the old Sergeant Friday stare and before you blink he'll give you whatever you want."

"He's been unconscious for two days now. Ruth just came in with the money yesterday."

"What does she think?"

"She can barely talk. She just showed up in Ray's room waving this big bundle of bills in front of her with both hands."

"So that leaves you working the Spot," I said.

"I have to. This isn't complicated. We know Ray lit the fire and we know he did it for somebody else. I spent time talking to Sam, back in his office by ourselves, and he says Ray was obviously the man for the job. Evidently after you got hurt Ray kind of went a little crazy about tree-huggers and what he'd personally do if he ever gets his hands on whoever did the spiking. What Sam said was that Ray may as well have sat at the bar with a sign around his neck, 'will do stupid things for food.'"

"So the piece you need is who hired him?"

"That's it." Will nodded. "Until Ruth comes back to Earth all I can do is go through Sam's list of who heard Ray carrying on at the bar about getting even. Sam's trying. He's called me twice to add to the list, but he says there were a couple people there he doesn't know." He pulled a sheet of paper folded in thirds from the pocket of his coat. He handed it to me and watched me unfold it. It was a Xerox of a piece of lined notebook paper with about a dozen names listed in Sam's blocky longhand, which I knew well from notes on the FUN-NIES. Underneath were three other names in almost electronically-neat printing, Will's. "Do any of them jump out at you?"

I knew all but a couple of the names and could easily picture most of them. Put them all together and I doubt they could come up with $7500. I refolded the list and handed it towards him.

"Keep it," he said, standing and reaching for his jacket. "Just think about it. Think about who these people are. Take your time. Read it before you go to sleep and then write down your dreams when you get up." He put on the jacket without taking his eyes off me. "But without thinking, just right now, top of your head: any ideas?"

I unfolded the list again. "Bam, off the top?" I said, looking over the top of the page at him. He nodded, pulling at the lapels of the coat to square it with his shoulders.

"I don't have the vaguest idea. I don't know anything that you don't, Will. Being around these guys all my life doesn't mean I know them."

"But if you *did* know, Jack. Just if you did...who would it be?" I looked at the sheet once more. They were just a scatter of words across the page, clumps of letters that told me as much as an Egyptian shopping list. I closed my eyes and seconds passed. "Who would it be, Jack?" he said softly.

"You need to talk to Mel Raines." The words were out of me before I thought of them. They must have registered in my brain and Will's at the same instant.

Will was nodding slightly, his face blank. "Why?"

Why. "It's...he doesn't know everything that goes on up here, not quite. It's more like he's the one who makes things happen more than anyone else does. I don't know. You should just talk to him."

"Um-hmm." Will put the little pad back in his coat pocket. "We're trying. I was supposed to meet him yesterday and he canceled. He said Monday, maybe. But maybe today would be better than Monday." He moved the chair back to the wall. "Do you want me to call after I talk to him?"

I wondered why he asked that. Would it mean something to him if I said no? Or yes? "Whatever. I'll be here."

He stepped to me and reached out his hand. I shook it. "Right. You will. For a little while. Thanks, Jack."

"You too," I said.

He looked back at me from the doorway. "I think you already know this," he said. "You can go to Nepal, Jack. Like I can go to Lewis Falls. If you want, let's talk about it when this job gets done."

"Pilgrim," I said.

He lingered an extra moment at the doorway to smile. Then he was gone.

42

THERE WAS AN UNDERWATER FEEL TO THE REST OF THE DAY, WAVY AND slow because of how little I slept the night before. Mom made me her Scottish turkey pie and we watched a Hepburn and Tracy movie together. I dozed through most of it, but the minute I went to bed I buzzed again with imaginary memories of Holly and Steve playing with each other. The prospect of another eight dark hours like that scared me. But we come wired, I think, with circuit-breakers that trip to prevent meltdown at dangerous times and mine did. I was asleep in minutes.

Then instantly I was awake, my back searing with pain. Reflex had tried to jerk me up from the bed and failed. Someone was standing over me. There was just enough light to know it was a man, someone — I felt more than saw this — I didn't know. I saw only his head and the bulk of his shoulders, haloed from behind by the collected glow of scattered porch lights from houses close by.

"Whaa waa WAAH??" It was my voice, raw and shuddering.

"Shhhh," the shadowed head said.

"Ohhh, who is it?"

"Shhhh," he whispered. "It's okay. Shhh."

"Who is it? Turn on the lamp!"

"Shhh. You have to be quieter. Where's the switch?"

"A chain, on the lamp. On the table. Right there."

He groped around and a cone of amber light burst downward from the shade to show two big hands and forearms covered with the sleeves

247

of a black windbreaker. The softer light through the shade fell on a stocky man about as old as me with a pale mustache and goatee and deep sunken eyes. His head was wrapped in a black bandanna with some kind of dots on it, Aunt Jemima style. He looked me over head to toe and smiled. "How do."

"Jesus! Who the fuck are you?"

"I just knew you'd ask that. Lars Thorndyke. Alternative Radio Network." He reached back for the chair behind him. "Can I sit down?"

"No you can't sit down! Get the fuck out of here!"

He sat down heavily, like he'd finished a hard journey. "Yeah. That'll happen in a couple minutes, Jack. After we talk."

"Talk?" The burst of shock calmed a little, like the instant after a fall when you realize you aren't hurt. I wasn't about to die. I didn't know anything else. This guy in black was calmly sitting next to my bed with his legs crossed. "You want to talk, come back like a person instead of some kind of, kind of..."

"Yeah, but you see that's it, Jack. I'd like to do this the polite way but they don't let us. I've been sitting outside almost two weeks waiting to talk to you."

"What?" Pieces of daytime life were coming back together. "How did you get in here?"

He smiled. "Magic. Actually if we're only going to talk a couple of minutes let's not talk about me."

I had skootched myself a little higher in bed, half-sitting with pillows bunched behind me. It felt less helpless. "Tell me how you got in here."

"Then we'll talk about what I want to talk about?"

"Tell me." This felt better.

"Okay." He closed one hand around his goatee and squeezed it. "Trade secret, though. When you all left for the football game Friday I started to follow along like everybody else, which sucks, until I realized I could probably have this place to myself for a little while. I let myself in the back door and took a look around. I wish I lived somewhere you don't have to lock the back door. Then I got my tools and cut a little hatch between the joists in your closet floor." He pointed across the room to the closet door near the corner. "Don't worry, you can't even see where I cut, hardly. I do beautiful work under pressure. That's why I get what I get." He pulled his goatee. "You probably think that's bragging."

"So then tonight you crawled under the house and came through the hatch?" I said. "The only way through the foundation is a crawl space right by the porch. What about the cops?"

"Not quite. It took more patience, which usually I don't have lots of. After I cut the hole Friday night I packed some food and water and my notebooks and a light and camped out under there. I thought about coming up last night, but I didn't know what your drill was here, whether one of your logger buddies sits right here with you at night or what. I didn't come here to get busted. I don't mind jail, especially here in the good old US of A. Sometimes it's good for getting your head together. But it'd mean I blow this story. And this story is mine."

"You've been under my floor since Friday night?" I looked at the red numbers on the clock radio. 2:18. "Twenty-eight hours?"

"Shit, I don't know how many hours. A lot." He put two fingers around his goatee like scissors blades and pulled down. "So that's good for something, right? All I want is to talk for a couple of minutes." He reached into the pocket of his windbreaker and pulled out a tape recorder the size of a cigarette pack. He clicked a button. "Test. Test test."

"No," I said. "No taping. I'm not doing that."

He clicked again and we both heard *Test. Test test.* "Sure you are. Nothing heavy. I just need your voice for one minute. Say whatever you want, read the washing instructions on that blanket, I don't care. Forty seconds. Just tell me how it's feeling now."

"Put it away."

"Come on, Jack. Didn't I earn it? Just thirty seconds, anything you want to say."

"I'm not doing it. Put that thing away."

"Shit." He dropped it back into his pocket. 'Do you know what it's been like out there? Ten days I've been sitting out there with those assholes listening to drivel you wouldn't believe. Ten *days.* Do you know what I've been filing? I did a story on your buddies from high school. I did one on a woman whose fucking *washing* machine you fixed. One of the network hacks heard me phone it in and congratulated me on the *scoop!* Jack, you have to give me a break here. Let's do thirty seconds, just tell me how you feel, who you think did the spiking and what you know about the fire, and I'm gone. Swear to God." It sounded like nobody ever wanted anything so much.

"You're nuts," I said.

"Yeah," he said, taking the recorder out of his pocket and setting it down between us on the blanket. "But crazy people have rent to pay, too."

"I'm not talking on tape," I said. "Because it won't be just you. It's finally quiet out there and maybe my mother can sleep like a normal person. If I do an interview with you it'll start all over again. Show me that thing one more time and you're out of here."

"Ten seconds?" he said. I stared at him. "Shit." He shook his head and put it back in his pocket. "You're cold, Jack. But can we talk a little? Tell me what's going on, help me find something I can use?"

Minus the bluster he was ordinary. "You can't tell anyone else you were here."

"Don't worry about that," he said. "A couple of notes?" He had a writing pad on his knee. He gave a little snort, like come *on*, you can't object to that.

"Just let's go," I said. "What do you want?"

"Tell me what you know. Spiking or fire, either one."

"Nothing," I said. "That's the thing. Breaking and entering and playing with yourself down in the crawl space all day and night is all a waste of time." He bent his head down and looked at me through an eyebrow. "I don't care if you believe me or not. I don't have what you came for."

"Okay," he said, sighing. "Let's do this: I'll tell you what I know, and you kind of nod your head a tiny bit when I get warm." He stuck his pen behind his ear and leaned back in the chair. "I have a couple of partners working with me on this. One of them's made a friend at the crime lab in Salem that has the spike. You know about the spike?"

"It was ceramic," I said. "not a big nail like you guys keep saying on the news. It was about like that." I spread my thumb and forefinger as far as I could to show about six inches.

"Well, it wasn't really a spike. They don't make spikes out of the stuff. They make square rods three-feet long that get cut to length for manufacturing satellite relay systems. What you hit was a piece snapped off one of those rods."

"Okay," I said slowly.

"You really don't know this, do you?" He was pleased. "What matters is you don't buy these things at Seven-Eleven. There's four or five companies around the country that use them and only one place on the west coast where they're made. It's up in Gresham, out of Portland. So my other partner up in Portland went to work on that, and it seems they had a little excitement in September, about two weeks before you ate it. Somebody broke into the warehouse after midnight and the only thing that was missing of all the expensive stuff laying around was one of these ceramic rods. Somebody broke into a crate of them waiting to get shipped out, and all they took was one piece."

Something like dread was building in me. What he was saying was real. Maybe he had the facts right, maybe not, but the idea that this started with a warehouse theft 300 miles away gave the spiking an uglier feel. It wasn't a force of nature. Somebody took deliberate steps, a bunch of them hooked together, to make it happen. They had to watch where we were cutting, they had to figure out what material they needed, they had to find it and make a plan to get it. Then they had to actually get the spike, or the rod or whatever it was, and break it to length, then they had to go in and pick out a tree, then drive the spike in and try to hide it and then get back out without being seen. Five steps, ten steps, I don't know. But each one was deliberate, it was physical in the world instead of a theory to argue or defend or regret, and the last step was me lying there in bed, real and crippled as anyone could be.

"So all this place has at night is one watchman," Lars went on, "and he's not even really that. He's an old guy who sits out in a booth at the entrance to the parking lot. My friend got his name and went to talk to him. They didn't report it to the police because there was no real loss and because it's a public company that probably didn't want its stockholders all freaked out. But my friend, who's almost as charming as me, got the old guy talking. He swears nobody drove near the building that night — my friend thinks he probably fell asleep and doesn't have a clue who was or wasn't in the building — but he says towards the end of the shift he saw an old van idling at the stop sign where the driveway he's supposed to guard meets the highway. He says it turned very slowly onto the road before driving off, and there was high-intensity streetlight on the corner that gave him a good look at it." Lars tugged at his goatee and smiled. "He called it a 'hippie van.' Big patches of rust all over it, with some kind of tree-limb bolted on as a rear bumper." Lars took the pen from his ear and tapped his chin with it, watching me.

"Well, there you go," I said. "Case closed. The watchman saw a hippie van. That proves a crazed band of armed hippies did the spiking. If they're breaking six-inch pieces out of a three-foot rod they probably did *six* spikings and I just ran into the first one."

"I don't know about a whole band. One guy alone could do it, especially if he had combat experience like your silent friend, don't you think?"

"Oh, please," I said.

"What did he tell you about the spiking when you saw him in jail?"

"Zenith didn't say anything about the spiking because Zenith doesn't know anything about the spiking. Jesus, is the whole world ready to chew the guy up because he's a little strange? I can see why the big timber boys would want to, but what's your story?"

"Whoa, down boy," said Lars. "I don't have a story. I just tell other people's."

"Oh, right. You are full of shit."

"And the rest of the story, not verified but we're working on it, is a week ago they found a rusty VW van in the little wash up behind Zenith's bus. Its rear bumper is a tree limb."

I closed my eyes and saw Zenith at his calmest, like he was across the glass from Holly at the jail. The certainty that he didn't do it — was it mine or just hers? What would she say right now, hearing this? I wanted her to be there, convincing him — convincing me. Lars was plundering my tiny supply of clarity. "You've seen it?"

He shook his head. "I said we're working on it. There are uniforms crawling all over that bluff where his bus is and none of them are talking. We're working on it."

"That's fine," I said. "You do that. And if you want more weird juicy Zenith stories, just take your pick. There are hundreds of them up here, but if you believe a single one of *them* you're a seriously disturbed individual."

"I thought we'd established that." Lars wrote something on the pad. "So you don't believe the hippie van's up there?"

"You better go now."

"Why? We hit on something you don't want to talk about?"

"I'd never *heard* of a van before two minutes ago, and now you want my serious opinion about where it is? You are completely full of shit." Lars' eyes and mouth opened, both hands touching his chest, a wronged *who, me?* look. He even sputtered a little. He watched me closely, seeing if I'd flinch. "Get out of here."

"If I can prove the van's up at Zenith's, will you talk to me about it?"

"We're done with the bargaining." I pointed towards the closet. "Get out of my house."

He believed me. He got up from the chair and put the pad in his pocket. He walked around and put a hand on the closet door, the other pulling his goatee. The light from the lamp barely made it to him. "I'm trying to remember," I heard him say, "which thing it was I said that got you all weird."

What do you say when someone leaving your room through your closet floor calls you weird? I didn't want to say anything that might slow him down. "Don't come back."

He stepped into the closet. "I don't make promises I can't keep," he said. The door closed slowly. I heard the latch's crisp click, some muffled bumps and then nothing.

43

YOU CAN PROBABLY GUESS HOW WELL I SLEPT THE REST OF THE NIGHT, knowing Lars was lying in the dirt ten feet away and four feet below me. My ears tuned in to every tiny creak and rustle, and Mom's old house had plenty, hearing him probably long after he slipped away.

I dozed. It was late morning when Mom brought in coffee and started tending my overnight gear. She was chatty and calm and didn't need to know that the media that was supposedly pushed out of our lives was now bursting through the floorboards of her house. "Do you want to get dressed and eat at the table, hon, or should I bring you in a tray?"

I got up and washed and rolled into the dining room. Waffles, like we'd had every Sunday morning I'd ever been in this house. These had slivers of pecan in them and were covered with her canned wild blackberries, both treats. I asked her to sit and eat with me. Not likely. She figures it would taint her service to share the breakfast she made just for me. The hard time I've given her about it for years hasn't made a dent. She sat across from me long enough to put down a last swallow of coffee, then saw the clock and jumped up like the chair was on fire. "I'll be late for church! Betty and me are walking over, I have to get dressed!" She went into her bedroom, then looked out from the doorway. "What else would you like?"

"I'm fine, Mom. This is great."

Five minutes later she was back in her somber black-and-white dress, fluffing up her hair with one hand and clearing dishes with the other.

A knock sounded on the front door. "Coming!' she yelled, rushing the dishes to the kitchen counter first, then hurrying back towards the door with a tumble of passing words — "Sorry about the mess, sweetheart, I'll get to it quick as I get home, don't you be trying" — until she opened the door.

I couldn't see outside from where I sat. I saw Mom's posture change and heard her voice brighten. "Ohh! Look at those! Oh, you shouldn't do that. They're *beautiful!*"

"Well, they're *big*, but I don't know about beautiful." Holly's voice. "They're just ugly ducklings from the festival. Don't you look nice?"

Mom stepped aside to let Holly come in, twisting a little to get through the doorway. Under each arm she had a pumpkin almost as big as a beachball. Mom's hands wiggled and jerked until Holly handed her one.

"This isn't generosity, Lois," Holly said. "I know who makes the best pie in this town. Your pie, the smells around here when it comes out — well, look for me about ten seconds later coming through the door."

"Look at this!" Mom said, like she was holding a baby grandchild. She carried it to the kitchen with Holly behind her. "I can feel how full they are, they're so sweet like this I'll cut back the sugar, I just didn't have time to get one this year and both of these are so *beautiful!* Here now, honey, I have to go, but here." I heard coffee hitting the cup, then Mom was flying past me. "Back before noon, Jackie, okay? And don't you try to clean up any, I mean it!" The door slammed behind her.

Holly stepped in from the kitchen with a steaming cup and sat down at the end of the table. "She means it," she said. "You so much as take your fork into that kitchen and I'm telling." She took a sip. "She is something. Makes you wonder what she'd do if you did something really nice for her."

That hung in the air until it started to take on weight. "Thanks for thinking of her," I said.

Holly put down her cup and looked at me closely. "You don't look any worse for the wear from your rumble at the game. I wanted to come over yesterday to find out exactly what happened, but the whole day went crazy." So her day went crazy. Too bad. She went on before I could say anything. "Friday night right after halftime Steve suddenly decides he has to take the pumpkins down to PD right away, just down and back because he was supposed to go fishing up at the Lakes first thing in the morning. We'd started this conversation that had to get finished, so I went along with him. I was trying to get him to give a rip about what's happening to Zenith because he'd have more pull downtown than I do, if you can imagine anyone having more pull in Lewis County than me."

She smiled at me. She waited. "It is a stretch," I said.

"So Steve's telling me it's not a time to scatter our efforts, that what we have to do is stay on task to find out who did the spiking, and that's the best way to help Zenith, too."

That's when I knew for sure that I wasn't going to tell her about Lars. Not now. My way has been to say anything that came to mind that might interest her. Crafted or not, I'd just say it. And I figured the tale of the rusty van discovered behind poor innocent Zenith's bus might possibly interest her. But it could wait. Knowing this piece when she didn't might be an advantage. It sounds lame when I put it into words, but sitting here picking my nose while she and Steve run all over the mountain doing God's work, I wanted any advantage that came up.

"So we're driving down the mountain and I'm trying to make Steve see fine, the spiker has to be found, but who knows how long that will take and in the meantime Zenith is losing it in there. Steve finally gets it, because he agrees to blow off his fishing trip — you believe that? — and stay over in Port Douglas so we can go together to see Zenith in the morning."

Stay over in Port Douglas. That was Friday night, while I was lying in the dark with images of the two of them suffocating me. "So yesterday morning you went to see him."

"Mmm-hmm." Holly dipped a spoon into Mom's flowered sugar bowl. "But not for very long."

"How was it?"

She looked down into the cup as she stirred. "Well, Zenith likes me."

"No! Honest to God?"

"It's probably because I have a minute of time for him like nobody else seems to. I think one of the reasons he never talks is that nobody talks to him. He's a curiosity, like an albino deer or something, something to point at. You show him the tiniest little kindness and he's so amazed and so *grateful.* I haven't done a thing for him really, but you should see his face when I walk in there."

"I have, remember?" I said. "Did he say anything?"

She shook her head. "He closed up the second he saw Steve was with me and he got fidgety. I guess he still associates Steve with all the clearcuts."

"Well, go figure. The poor guy really is disoriented, isn't he?"

She ignored it. "It was enough for Steve to see what I meant. It's bad, Jack. He's gone downhill just since we saw him last week. His face looks like a skeleton with eyes bugging out. I asked him if he was eating but with Steve there he wouldn't tell me anything. And the guards claim they don't know. They said come back Monday and talk to some sergeant." She swept the edge of her hair back around her ear and looked at me fiercely. "I'm not sure he can make it through Monday. Maybe that sounds dramatic, but that's what Steve thinks too." Well, then it must be true. "So we leave the jail," Holly went on, "and start calling around to find a good lawyer, somebody who can make something happen over the weekend."

"What about the lawyer he has now?"

"It's a guy named Comstock, from the Public Defenders office, and he's a joke. I called him after you and I went down and then again yesterday. He's been to the jail twice and says it's a waste of time to go talk to a mute. He's filing some papers to get Zenith moved to the psychiatric hospital in Grants Pass, but he doesn't know how long it'll take. That's all he'd tell me because I'm not family." She shook her head and pushed her hair back again. "This system, the whole thing sucks." She looked inside her cup and took mine. "You want some more?"

She moved to the kitchen before I said anything. Her voice drifted through the doorway. "So from the jail we go to the greasy spoon next to where PDEC was — boy, that's a sad sight. Big piles of rubble they bulldozed together with yellow tape around the whole thing — and we start looking at lawyers in the yellow pages." She came back in and set both cups on the table. "Steve knew a couple of them, but they've both done work for the Company. So we start calling, and of course on a Saturday just get machines and answering services, but while we sit there having a long breakfast two of them call us back. One says he doesn't want to come near it and the other's interested but wants major bucks up front before he does anything." She stirred her coffee with a lot of thought. "I don't see why somebody wouldn't be willing to do this *pro bono*. I know a couple who might in the Bay Area, but from what I've seen of Lewis County justice a local attorney is going to do better than somebody from San Francisco, so Steve and I start scheming on where to get the retainer money this guy wants. I ask Steve if Lewsco would just pay for it and he sort of laughs. He asks why the Company would want to do that, and I say because it's so obvious that Zenith didn't do it that it looks like everybody's trying to bury this thing under the rug, Lee Harvey Oswald style. The Company could look good, which with all the rape and pillaging might be a refreshing change, just by stepping up to the plate and saying they want to find out what really happened, we owe it to our worker. If the Company helps out the fall guy instead of watching him rot, people will know they didn't do the spiking themselves."

Holly could make whatever she was saying seem like the only alternative that made sense. Sam would say she could talk the bark off of trees. "So what did Steve think of that?"

"Well, he stopped laughing. So then I say, and don't ask me where it came from, how about if Lewsco puts up half and I get Western Resources Defense to put up the other half? I tell Steve he could get out in front of the enviros in one minute flat, just throw down the challenge that if environmentalists are as concerned as they say they are about tree spiking, here's a chance to do something about it. So while Steve's chewing that over I get up and call Stanton at home, who I haven't talked to since right after he visited you in the hospital, and he says, exactly like Steve five minutes before, 'why would we want to do that?' And I think this should be easy, these guys are on the same wavelength already. I tell Stanton what's in it for WRDC is number one, doing right by Zenith and number two, strategy, showing they're more interested in seeing the real perpetrators brought to justice than carrying old grudges, even against an industry that is trashing the forest communities of the Northwest, which was fun to say with Steve listening ten feet away, that WRDC wants to put aside our differences for the higher purpose of fighting terrorism that injures innocent people." She sipped her coffee. "I told him this was a chance to look big."

"And he said what?"

"He said 'Look big to who?' Actually he said 'whom.' That I was forgetting that it's only the membership that he has to look good to, and if the membership found out he was partnering with Lewsco, with Oklahoma Oil and James Nielsen on anything, it didn't matter what, he'd be toast." She shook her head. "Stanton Freed. What a piece of work. You know, when I met him . . . no. But it's really ironic, you know? Here's Stanton, completely right about the insanity of tearing through the forests the way we do, and here's Steve with his head still all the way up his butt about 'managing' forests and super-seedlings and just plant three of them for every one you cut and everything will be hunky-dory. And which one of them is ready to stand up when it counts?" She shook her head. "The world would be a lot simpler place if the really good people were the same as the people who see things clearly, instead of this big scramble of good people having shitty ideas and vice-versa."

I wondered where I fit in the scramble — what she'd think about the conversation I had the day before with Will. I wanted her to say there was nothing wrong with telling him to check out Mel. But what would she make of it, as she sat there musing on the nature of Good and Evil? That the morning after I see her rolling pumpkins around the football field with Steve, I decide the appropriate response is to turn his Dad into the FBI? However little use she has for Mel, that's not how to make it into her category of stand-up guys.

Holly was looking at me with her head tilted. "What?" she said. A second passed. "What?"

I was about to make a mistake. I couldn't avoid it. "The 'really good people'," I said. "So that would be people who do what you think they should at the moment, no matter how they treated you in the past?"

Holly stood up and took her cup to the kitchen. I heard the water run, the ping of silverware. Then she was in the doorway, pushing her hands against the jambs. "Who do you think this is easy for, Jack? Please. I know who got the worst deal. But think for a minute about how this all is from where Steve's standing. He hires his best friend to come back to the woods," (is that what I am?) "and the next day you're crippled for life. And he knew there'd been threats. It's done, Jack. It can't be undone. What you have to live with now is shitty beyond words. But have you thought one time about what it's like for him?"

My chest felt heavy. "I think I got this, but let me make sure: you are standing there," I said very slowly. "You are looking at me, and you are feeling sorry for Steve. Is that right?"

Her lips pressed together and she looked down at the floor. Then she lifted her head. "Yes," she said. "I feel sorry for Steve." Her look was hard as metal. "How long have we known Steve, Jack? Thirty-five years? More than that. And you don't know him. You know a jock. A shallow jock who cares about you when it's easy and it doesn't cost him anything. Right? That's what everybody who thinks they know Steve thinks."

"And they're all wrong, right? Like I'm wrong?"

"You don't know him. You don't know how many times he's tried to break through the surface, how close he's come, and how he's always pulled back because he couldn't be soft or weak, which for him was being anything that Mel thought was weak. Or anything Steve thought Mel *might* think was weak."

"Well, that's the piece that covers everything, I guess: Mel's an asshole," I said. "And poor Steve, he's the only guy since the cavemen whose father's an asshole. How could I be so blind?"

"Well you know what? Steve's finally figured that out. You know the Company rule about nobody talking to you or the press? That's not from the lawyers. It's from Mel. He's crazed about it. He wants Steve to pretend nothing happened, just move on like he never heard of you. So what does Steve do? First he makes this security detail for you out of Lewsco workers, then he takes you and me down to see Zenith with all those reporters following behind, then he walks into the jail himself to see Zenith. And I haven't even talked to him yet about the riot Friday night — I didn't even know about it until I got home last night — but think about the stroke Mel had when he saw *that* in the paper. Lewsco workers roughing up the press, smashing their cameras when they're trying to get to the bottom of the spiking story?"

"Yeah, like hassling my friends and me at the fucking game is getting to the bottom of the story," I said.

She shook her head. "You're missing the point. It's like 'the whole world is watching,' goons with something to hide beating up the press. And they're Mel's goons."

The bark off of trees. "But that's stupid," I said. "Why doesn't Mel stop it? He practically runs the Company and Steve's a peon."

"Mel's going to make a public stink about Lewsco helping you out after what happened? I don't think so."

"Not public. Just jerk Steve's leash back the way he does."

"He tried! That's what I'm telling you!" Holly said, pulling her chair over to sit a foot away from me. "He can't anymore! It doesn't work. He rants and raves and threatens Steve like he always did, but Steve's ignoring him." She put her hand on my forearm. "Look, Jack, when he drove you and me down to see Zenith, did you notice anything? You had to. What was he like? We were talking about the accident and how Lewsco, his company, wanted to deal with it, and what was he like? Full of jive and all his eye-batting, like he does when he's trying to skate? No. None of it. Not one single excuse. Since you know him so well, have you ever seen him like that before?"

My mind sped through a lifetime of experiences in about three seconds, looking for one to damage her point. I don't think there are any. "So this huge transformation," I said, "Jesus just smote him in the middle of the night or what?"

"It's lots of things," Holly said. "I don't know all of it, there's a lot he doesn't tell me. But the biggest one is what happened to you. All Steve wants is to make it not have happened, and since he can't he's flailing. So he zeroes in on finding out who did it; he said he'd find a way to get Zenith a good lawyer, by the way, and probably a private eye to work the case independently. And it doesn't matter how much Mel screams at him that he has to stay out of it. He's not going to." She touched me. "Do you know how hard that is, Jack? Maybe not. Your father was different."

What, kinder? Easier to please? "It's really been hard on him, huh?" I said. "He must really need a lot of comforting." I closed my eyes to breath deeply, a last try to hold back.

"Jack..."

"Look," I said, "Steve's breakthrough just warms my heart, you know? Finally getting in touch with his fucking inner child. It's just so thrilling. But you know what, Holly? I've seen this movie. I've seen it a hundred times. Sensitive Misunderstood Steve Meets Understanding Holly, Part Ten. I know the whole fucking script by heart, I swear to God I don't need to hear it again."

"Jack." Holly's eyes were closed, then moist as she opened them. "What do you want me to do, Jack?"

To choose me, I thought. I said, "To do what's right."

"What's right," she said, slowly standing. Her lips disappeared as she bit them from the inside. Her eyes shuttled back and forth like they were winding a spring inside her. "All you want me to do is what's right." She walked behind me towards the front door and turned at the entryway. Tears clotted her throat. "The two of you are sucking me dry! You guys make this goddamn fucking mess and then expect me to make it all better. I can't make it better! Why can't you get that?" She stood shaking with a hand over both eyes and walked out the door. I heard her sandals clop across the porch and down the steps.

MOM CAME HOME FROM CHURCH AN HOUR LATER CHIRPING ABOUT THE fuss they made over her because of the riot, and the wonderful prayer they did for me. She asked me how the visit with Holly had been and without a pause moved into the kitchen to see the pumpkins again. "I'll bet they'll make six or seven pies," she said, "which is wonderful, because I want one for Betty and I told Reverend Franklin I'd bring him one and I think I should take Holly and Isabel at least two, don't you, though I'm sure Isabel is doing her own..." I listened from the dining room until the words gave way to the sound of metal bowls and implements clicking and the cheerful humming of a hymn she must have just been singing at church. I rolled to the bedroom.

I wrote through most of the afternoon and into the evening, a whole sheaf of pages, until I felt the acid racing inside of me cool down. When I can get a pen's distance from this mess I start to breathe again. After midnight I felt calm enough to lay down. The exhaustion built up from the turmoil of the past two nights slipped over me.

It wasn't a quiet sleep. Shreds and patches of dreams flew at me one after another like debris in a hurricane. I can only remember one, the last one before I awoke. Holly was there waiting for me. She had been waiting calmly for a long time.

I knew it before I recognized her. She was on a grassy ledge by the river, and the grass swept up to become a long gown draped over her shoulders. As I approached she was looking away, her hair flowing like warm honey down her back. Then she slowly looked over her shoulder. I saw the corner of her smile and she swept her hair back around her ear. She kept turning until she faced me, and her smiling face glowed as if it were a silk shade around a lantern. She had waited so long for me that joy spilled from her eyes, her smile, her strong soft arms as she raised them to greet me. Her grass gown parted down the middle and she took the edges in both her hands, spreading them wide to wrap them around me like a soft fresh shroud. I came to her and her breasts pushed as firm as gorgeous fruit to my chest. She was so warm, her smile pouring over me as we kissed deeply. My face drew back to see her again and the smile had melted to full-breathed yearning, her tongue stroking her moist lips until she had to have me again, pulling me closer still. My hands rested in the smooth hollows on both flanks of her bottom, then moved back slowly until they met behind her, lifting and massaging her mounds of flesh. And she moaned, first soft and low, then with a begging that made me harder. Her hands stroked my back up and down, then slid around to the seething place between us and clasped together in a soft tunnel that rubbed me gently, pulling me forward, pushing back, slowly forward, slowly back, now squeezing me slightly. My mouth left hers and I raised a hand to lift her breast to me, kissing its top and then drawing her nipple between my lips. It grew and hardened, swelling and pulsating now as her moans rose from deep within her. Then we melted to the ground, every part of us pressed together as I took her other breast in my mouth and felt my center slide deeply into hers.

44

THEN BOB EDWARDS SAID "GOOD MORNING!" AND READ THOSE HEADLINES about Clinton and the abortion clinic shooting and Dale Evans' birthday. A few minutes later — I was peeing in my hose at the time, you may remember — he crushed the notion that I'd built up the night before with all that furious writing, the illusion that I have an infinitesimal particle of control in this soap opera.

"Since becoming the primary victim of the so-called 'eco-sabotage' designed to stop logging in the Pacific Northwest," Bob read, "John Gilliam, Jr. has been recuperating in his family home in the tiny town of Lewis Falls, Oregon, with a 24-hour security detail buffering him from media and public attention. Yesterday Gilliam made his first public comments in weeks. He told the Alternative Radio Network he doesn't think the FBI's main suspect in the incident is the right man."

The next voice, like I said back at the beginning, was mine. What I said over millions of radios at that moment was

> ...Zenith doesn't know anything about the spiking. Jesus, is the whole world ready to chew the guy up because he's a little strange? I can see why the big timber boys would want to but if you believe a single one of *them* you're a seriously disturbed individual.

"Comments by tree-spiking victim Jack Gilliam," Bob Edwards said, "provided by Lars Thorndyke of the Alternative Radio Network."

Nothing I've been through has been as bizarre as listening to myself say something I never said to a country full of people. But I heard it. I got about one second to start figuring it out before Bob said, "Identifying Oregon's tree-spiker isn't the only challenge facing authorities in this ongoing drama. A related investigation has just become more difficult with the death last night of Ray Swerdlow. Swerdlow was an unemployed logger who may have played a key role in the recent escalation of Oregon's war in the woods. But as Colin O'Toole of member station KOAR reports, the *meaning* of Ray Swerdlow's role is not quite clear."

The voice changed to Colin's, the guy you hear most on the statewide public network:

> Two weeks after the crippling of 43-year old logger Jack Gilliam rocked the Pacific Northwest and then the nation, a new-age grocery store nearby was burned to the ground. According to a note left at the scene, the arson fire was intended to retaliate against environmentalists for the spiking incident. Two days later Ray Swerdlow, another Lewis Falls resident with long-standing ties to the spiking victim, was arrested for the fire after reporting to an area hospital with severe burns over most of his body. Swerdlow has remained in a coma for the past week. Last night at ten o'clock Pacific time, according to hospital spokesperson Marilee Diskin, Ray Swerdlow died.
>
>> "We just weren't able to reverse the effects of the infection that took hold before the patient entered the hospital. The trauma aggravated other conditions that Mr. Swerdlow had apparently been experiencing for some time in a combination that just overwhelmed his system."
>
> Speculation had grown in recent days that Swerdlow was hired to set the fire, possibly by someone connected with the Lewsco company itself. But FBI spokesman Todd Whittaker gave that theory no credence at a news briefing over the weekend.
>
>> "We have no reason to believe anything but that Mr. Swerdlow acted alone in this matter. You'll hear all kinds of assertions from all kinds of people around here about conspiracies and this and that and the other thing, but we prefer to stick with real evidence and pursue this matter accordingly."

With the death of Ray Swerdlow, it's not clear how much more real evidence will be forthcoming. For National Public Radio, this is Colin O'Toole in Port Douglas, Oregon.

I felt like all of me, from the waist up, too, was paralyzed. Part of it was the jarring feeling that always comes with the death of someone I know — the Ray who was, the Ray whose face I could picture and voice I could remember, now isn't. Within seconds that feeling was gone and all I could think of was Lars Fucking Thorndyke.

I reached for the phone and dialed information for the number of the public radio station on the South Coast College campus. Their tape said the office opened at 8:00 a.m. so I left a message. At 7:45 the phone rang and a male voice that sounded like it wasn't quite finished changing said he was the news director and it would be great, just unbelievable, if we could do just a short little interview right there on the phone. Maybe later, I told him, but I had to hear the tape of what I said on *Morning Edition*.

When he hung up with a promise to call me right back I realized I'd given our number out to a reporter. We'd get another one. Four minutes later he was back on. "Ready?" he said. There was a metallic click, and then my voice on tape.

> .... Zenith doesn't know anything about the spiking. Jesus, is the whole world ready to chew the guy up because he's a little strange? I can see why the big timber boys would want to but if you believe a single one of *them* you're a seriously disturbed individual.

I asked him to rewind and play it again, then a third time and a fourth. By then I could hear it. It wasn't obvious, nothing anyone else would pick up as the story streamed by, but it was there. The word "but" rushed up against "if" a hair's breadth too quickly. Those two words were not next to each other when they came out of my mouth. I've never been raped, but I will bet it feels like this.

"You mind if I run a tape," said the news director, still waiting on the line, "and we could, you know, talk? I know you're really busy and everything, I don't want to bother you, but I was just thinking since we're talking already, I could turn on the tape maybe and ask you a question?"

"Turn it on," I said.

"Yes! Okay, just a second...just a second...just a second...okay! Now, Mr. Gilliam, when you were actually sawing the tree..."

"This is Jack Gilliam, and I want to say that I don't know about the guilt or innocence of anyone in the events that have happened, and any reports that say that I do aren't true. I think everybody should calm down a little bit and let the authorities do their job. That's it."

"And when you were cutting the tree right before it happened..."

"That's it. Thank you." I pressed the little button to hang up and picked the receiver up again without knowing who I'd call. I sat there at the table with a fourth cup of coffee and a plate of Mom's eggs barely touched in front of me, trying to slow my breath. I knew who I wanted to call. I wanted to call every person listening to *Morning Edition* to tell them what it was I actually said. I had to do it fast, because even as I sat there they were probably rushing to their offices, or calling their friends after the kids left for school, saying "Did you hear what Jack Gilliam said? Yes, he finally broke his silence! Did you hear what he *said*?"

I knew I was raving. This was out of my league. I needed help to keep from making mistakes, maybe big ones. I found the number Will had given me and dialed it. After a few rings it kicked over to a switchboard and I left a message. He called back thirty minutes later.

"What do you think?" I asked him.

"Well, I'm sorry about it," he said. "It's a bum deal. But from a practical standpoint, we weren't going to get any more from him anyway."

"What?" I said. "From who?"

He hesitated. "From Swerdlow. Who are we talking about?"

"Oh. Yeah." Normally I would have been embarrassed. "There's something else, Will. Did you hear what I said this morning?"

"What do you mean?"

I told him. Once I got started the whole Lars story flooded out. The only sound I heard him make, a little gust of breath, was when I told him Lars got in by sawing a hole in the floor while everybody was at the ballgame. "I can't believe I was this stupid," I said at the end.

"Well, those things look more stupid afterwards than they do at the time. Listen to me: this doesn't mean it has to be come one, come all for interviews now. You didn't need to do that little statement for the radio station this morning."

"But how else do I get the record straight?"

"You don't, Jack," he said. "And if you try you"ll probably screw it up more. Your friend Lars isn't the only one out there who will get creative for a good story. It'll straighten out eventually, but not by you rushing out with a load of explanations. You have to let it be for now. And if you want more security to keep away whoever wants to one-up Lars, we can do that."

"I don't," I said. "But tell me something else: the hippie van behind Zenith's place? Is that true?"

"I don't know," Will said. "I know they found something up there that keeps them looking at Zenith. Otherwise they'd have released him by now. Like I said, they keep us in separate boxes so nobody knows more than they need to. My box is the fire."

I believed him. "Your box just got harder, huh?"

"Well, I was still hoping Ray would pull out of it. From what I hear he liked to talk."

"But what's the business about him probably acting alone?"

"Where did you hear that?"

"That was the other thing this morning on the radio. That there's no evidence that he wasn't acting alone."

"That's for the news," he said. "We have to play it that way. We need a break to figure out this thing, Jack. The more we say publicly the less chance there is that somebody lets something slip, something they know that they have no reason to know. That's what we need."

"So until then you're stuck? Nothing's moving at all?"

"I didn't say that. Ray's death got his wife talking non-stop, like she finally believes she's safe. You remember the bandanna she found with all the cash in it?"

"Yes."

"She saw Ray pick it up out of the engine compartment of an old junked truck in their front yard the morning before the PDEC fire. She was watching through her kitchen window and saw him rummaging around under the hood and then pick it out like some kind of prize. She asked him what it was when he walked back in but he just mumbled something and keeps walking back to a closet with a loose floorboard where he kept whatever he didn't want her to know about, magazines, mostly. Then there was the fire, and the day after that Ray was laying in bed covered with wet rags, and yelling at her to go out and check in the junk car for another package. He got angrier and angrier when she couldn't find anything and kept sending her back out until she was almost afraid to go inside. He accused her of finding something, he wouldn't tell her what, and stealing it. Then he tried to get out of bed and couldn't. 'Luckily' he couldn't, she said. She was scared to death of him. When he calmed down enough for her to come near him she wrapped him up and drove him down to the hospital. She says the whole way he kept asking how he could be idiot enough to trust a guy who talked like a faggot on the phone. From what Ruth told us I think he was talking about some kind of British accent."

"Probably," I said. "Up here we're wise to those British guys."

"But what does that tell you, Jack? Who would sound like that on the phone?"

"According to Ray Swerdlow? The world-renowned scholar on speech patterns and their origins? Henry Higgins Swerdlow? You know, I'm sorry, but fooling Ray Swerdlow over the phone wouldn't be heavy lifting."

"What about Mel Raines?" Will said. "Can you see him trying a British accent?"

"Why?"

"That's who you thought of the other day," Will said. "You told me to talk to Mel."

"Yeah, when you kept pushing for anything that crossed my mind," I said. "I didn't accuse Mel of anything. He's just who crossed my mind."

"In my experience," Will said after a little pause, "it usually doesn't turn out to be as random as that. We think of people for a reason. Why did you think of Mel, Jack?"

I really did want to be able to answer that one. Did I know, really know, that giving Mel's name had nothing to do with taking a swipe at her and Steve, at least to make Steve's life a little more complicated? If that was the purpose I was being stupid about it — using the wrong tools, Nielsen would probably say. When Steve gets more troubled, Holly's nurturing side can't resist him. Add to that another force working in the same direction, her disgust if she found out that Mel's name came from me, and I'd probably weld her to Steve permanently.

Then again...then again, then again. It never ended, this lifetime of jumpy calculation about what she'd probably think about this, about that, about whatever I did. The prime mover of my life since I could walk had been What Holly Would Probably Think. It was moving me at that moment, as Will waited for me to answer, to back-pedal from what I'd told him before, to tell him now that I didn't really think Mel had anything to do with Ray Swerdlow and the fire. It moved me thirty years ago to smudge up my face on my way down to the Falls after a day setting choker, because she might be there. And my choice to go back into the woods after the buy-out — I know now it's true — that, too was about What Holly Would Probably Think. About pretending I it didn't drive me anymore. I couldn't make a good pretense with any old wimpy gesture of defiance, no, I had to go and start cutting the last big trees on the Range. And just look how nicely that worked out.

Now, though, I was done. I had to be done. "I'll tell you why," I said. "Mel Raines is the about the nastiest prick I ever met. And whatever he wants done up here he can get done. He could get PDEC torched in thirty seconds if he wanted and it wouldn't bother him a bit. Anyone up here would tell you the same thing, if they weren't scared to death of him."

Will waited to see if I was done before he spoke. "Now, that's interesting to hear, Jack," he said. "Let me tell you what happened when I

268 • Jeff Golden

went back to the Spot Saturday right after I saw you. It was early and Sam was there alone doing books, except for the older man in the wheelchair. Fife?"

"Fife Burgess."

"So I had Sam do one more walk-through of the night Swerdlow was carrying on, who said what to who. We pulled the list of names out again. He put it down on the bar and Fife picked it up. Just as I started to leave, Fife said "Mel was here, too, you don't have him on the list.' At first Sam said he was wrong, that it was a night after the fire that Mel was in, and the two of them talked about it until Sam agrees that Fife was probably right. He thinks Mel might have been in that night off at the corner table by the bathrooms."

"But he doesn't know? Sam knows these things."

"He says he thinks Mel drank two beers and left without talking to anyone. But he could have been there when Ray was on the soapbox. Then I called a couple others who were there, the ones who have tried to be helpful. They couldn't stop coming up with details before. They know how many of which brands everyone at the bar drank that night. But when I asked if Mel might have been there it was like they were having trouble recognizing the name."

"What a surprise," I said.

"I'm seeing him this afternoon at his office," Will said. "We set it up yesterday. I called him at home and he said he was just on his way out to church. He said he'd meet me even though it was a waste of my time — all he knows about the fire is what he's read in the paper."

"Nice of him to worry about wasting your time."

"He was low-key about it. Other than that all he said was tree-huggers are hypocrites to pretend they're shocked about the fire; what did they expect, once they start spiking trees?"

The middle of my back was beginning to cramp. I wanted to lie down. "What do you think, Will?"

"I think Mel Raines had better keep our appointment," he said. "I'll talk to you later."

45

I DIDN'T LIE DOWN. I DIDN'T WANT THAT MUCH QUIET AROUND ME. I rolled over to Mom's stereo cabinet, a pecan-colored coffin that had anchored one end of the living room longer than I can remember. NPR was playing a long story about the international variations of Halloween. I turned the volume knob most of the way up to fill the place.

I was alone. Mom had left just before I started talking to Will, grabbed up by Betty Sulkin for a PD trip. Betty's excuse was that their baked goodies — in Mom's case, the same pumpkin walnut cookies punched out into little pumpkin shapes she'd made for probably fifty years — weren't slick enough for tonight's trick-or-treaters. "It's criminal, I know it, Lois, you don't have to tell me, what the kids are eating today, but they just love those miniature little chocolate bars, and Halloween only comes once a year." It was an excuse, of course. If all they wanted was little candies they could get them at Sam's. I think getting Mom away from me and out for a couple of hours on her own has become a permanent community project.

I rolled into the kitchen to find the cookies. There on the chrome-trimmed yellow formica table in the center of the room was one of the lumpy pumpkins that Holly had brought to Mom, hollowed out with the top-plug sitting askew like a cheery little cap. Leaning against it was a clean carving knife. It didn't just happen to be there; Mom's fanatical about having the kitchen spotlessly clean and perfectly picked up whenever she leaves the house.

269

You have to understand about Lewis Falls and Halloween. When I was growing up you'd have trouble finding a front porch without two or three jack-o'-lanterns. Some folks lined up extended pumpkin families, from little grapefruit-sized babies with dots for eyes and triangular pug noses, through jagged-tooth Big Daddies to even bigger Grandma 'n Grandpas with wrinkles and sometimes tufts of cotton-hair to show how very old they were.

We'd have two. Mom and I would pick out one together, then work it over on newspapers spread out across the kitchen table. The actual carving work moved slowly from her to me over the years until at about ten years old I was in charge. I worked in the classic style: triangular eyes and nose, teeth like the profile of a big cross-cut saw. At first it was the only way I could do it. Later on, I didn't see any reason to change.

The other pumpkin was Dad's, which he would find on his own somewhere. Two nights before Halloween he would disappear into his workshed in back until long after I was asleep. The next day while he was at work the shed's door would be padlocked closed, with the blankets hung inside the two windows so I couldn't see inside. I tried. When that night, Halloween Eve, turned dark, he'd go back into the shed. I'd stand by the shed door for as long as I could before Mom's bursting whisper came from the back porch, calibrated so I'd hear it and Dad wouldn't, "Jack! You get back in here!"

I would be asleep before Dad came in. At 5 or 6 the next morning I was on my feet before I was really awake, tumbling out the front door barefoot to find a masterpiece on the porch railing, facing out to the center of town.

They weren't like anybody else's. It was the way every notch and curve came together so that if you looked at it through the corner of your eye and then slightly away you'd swear it was moving, yawning or maybe rolling its hollow eyeballs, behind your back. Dad favored two pumpkin personalities and alternated them from one year to the next. The first was maniacal, with eyebrows pointing sharply up in the middle, eyes blazing and mouth stretching in a silent laugh greeting some calamity you couldn't imagine. It looked like Jack Nicholson at his most deranged. The second was like Rodney Dangerfield, or an old Walter Matthau, all jowls and bulbous nose, heavy bags under sad eyes, everything sagging with the weight of life's meanness. These guys didn't scare you the way the Nicholsons did, but they stick more strongly in my memory.

There hadn't been more than half a dozen jack-o'-lanterns on Mom's porch since Dad died. I'd punched out a couple for her years ago — triangular eyes, crosscut smiles — and the others were gifts from neighbors. I'd never made one for my own place.

Now I picked up the knife and slowly worked its tip into the hard yielding shell. After the first resistance and an awkward minute it felt almost as if the blade were grabbed and pulled from inside by something I didn't control. When I stopped thinking about Holly, about her and Steve, about Will and Mom and Mel Raines, a face grew out of the pumpkin.

It must have been like this for Dad. Release and exclamation, forward motion instead of doubt. This is why he did it every single year, why for the thirty hours before every Halloween it was the center of his life. For the second time I felt like I grasped something from his center. The first was the glimpse he gave me on his last day, as if tipping back the lid of a barrel packed with writhing snakes. I don't know everything he was trying to tell me then. He probably didn't either. I know he was frightened, and not because death was so near. I think it was a fear that if he couldn't make me understand about hanging in, I might waste my life as he was sure he'd wasted his.

He had made me understand. But how about now, Dad? This isn't baseball. How do you hang in there in a fucking wheelchair? If he were here and knew the answer he probably wouldn't tell me. I'd probably have to watch him die again for that.

OF COURSE MOM LOVED THE JACK-O'-LANTERN. THE DEAL SHE MADE over it (after denying that she'd set up the pumpkin and knife to get me going) lasted for most of an hour after Betty dropped her off. At first her excitement seemed silly, but slowly it moved me off my pissiness and gave me some energy. Holly is right about the way Mom manufactures happiness out of absurdly small things. That shouldn't rankle me the way it sometimes does.

Mom saw how her praise brightened me up. She recruited me to set up the pumpkin cookies and a bowl of chocolates — miniature Mr. Goodbars, Baby Ruths and Snickers — on a side table in the entryway. She answered the door the first time it rang while I was here writing in the bedroom. I heard her gasping in fright at the ghouls she saw, then the rustle of goodies hitting the bottoms of paper bags.

With the next ring I put the notebook away and rolled to the living room. When I opened the door I was facing two-thirds scale versions of Bart Simpson, Hillary Clinton, Ken Griffey, a princess and two cosmic warriors. Hillary and Bart were closest. They thrust their bags toward me and started to speak, but the only voice that got out a full "trick or treat!" came from someone behind them too short to see. They stared silently and their arms slowly lowered until their bags touched the ground.

Mom came up behind me with handfuls of candy. "Oh, my goodness, what do we have here? Charlie Brown?" I eased my chair back and to the side to give her a clear shot at them. Their arms went back up, bags pointed towards her, but their little masked heads swivelled to keep watching me.

46

THE MORNING AFTER HALLOWEEN, YESTERDAY MORNING, WAS WARM, ONE of those renegade days that makes you wonder if we've scrambled the natural cycle for keeps — late summertime temperatures on the first of November. Mom pulled the white plastic table and chairs out of the shed and onto the back porch, where she served me a massive egg breakfast with leftover pumpkin-shaped pumpkin cookies (Betty Sulkin had been right about what trick-or-treaters did and didn't want) on the side.

We were talking about Dad. I asked her how many times she could remember that he seemed to be talking about things that really mattered to him, and she was taking time to think carefully when we heard a knock on the door. Mom went in and then I heard Holly's voice. There was a long throaty *rrrrrr* that had to be part of a hug. Then Holly came onto the porch with a package, a thin cylinder wrapped in butcher paper and a puffy red ribbon. She handed it to me, kissed me on top of my head and sat down.

"You have to have this," she said. "I called around until I found it in Grants Pass." I pulled off the wrapping and started unrolling the poster as Mom came out, setting a cup of coffee in front of Holly and making pleased little noises for me. It was a black-and-white photo from *The Wizard of Oz*. The wizard was handing the gift of courage to the cowardly lion.

"Next time I go to town I'll get it framed for you, " she said. "You had it inside you all the time, didn't you, little lion?" She swept one side of

273

her hair behind her ear. "I knew it, too. That finally some things are more important to you than being the nice guy."

I wasn't sure I got it. "This is about what I said on the radio?"

"It most certainly is." She sipped from the coffee cup. "It was great. A tiny bit late, but so what? It was right on."

"I didn't say it, Holly." I got it out fast. If I didn't, if I stayed quiet, I could fall back into another silent crazy-making struggle about what she Would Probably Think, which, I of course don't do anymore. I stepped straight into the pitch. "It was on the radio, but I didn't say it."

Operating on radar, Mom disappeared into the house. Holly swept back the other side of her hair and narrowed her eyes. "What do you mean?"

I told her. I told her all about Lars, the whole story minus the rusty van. She had a dazed look when I finished, staring at me a few seconds before saying anything. Then she took a slow breath and pressed down on the table with both hands. "That's...well, I need to find this guy and find out what he knows. But still the point is what you said on the radio, or the way he made you say it, is true. Believing what big timber guys say *is* nuts."

"Holly, look," I said. "Ben Tyler was a big timber guy. Was your Dad nuts to believe what he said? Was mine? They trusted Ben completely."

"Oh, Jack, please. James Nielsen and his thugs aren't Ben Tyler. If they were none of this would have happened."

"Okay. What about Steve? He's way up there now, big enough that people listen when he talks. You don't seem to have much trouble believing what he tells you."

Her face made me wonder if we'd lurch towards the same meltdown we had two days before. "Are you playing games with this, Jack, or are you serious?"

"I'll tell you what's a game, Holly. It's a game to get on the soapbox and say all timber guys are liars. Even if it revs people up and does great things for your membership..."

"I don't have a membership anymore."

"...but I won't say it because it's not true and because it makes everyone nuts. Timber guys who hear it, I mean the little guys we grew up with, they hear it and they go 'Bullshit. Steve's not a liar, or George Wilson who runs the eastside shows isn't a liar, and I'm not a liar, and if those fucking tree-huggers say we are then they're the liars.' And how hard is it for them to find an enviro sleazeball who's lied or screwed someone over, so there's their proof? Like, maybe some former bosses you could name might possibly fill the bill?" She looked down into her coffee with her mouth twisted tight. "So that leaves us with what? Wherever you stand, everybody on the other side's a liar and an asshole, right? Tell me where it is we're supposed to go from there."

"So we're back to 'Can't we just all get along'?"

"I don't get it, Holly," I rolled the poster back up and tapped the table with it. "Look at you and me. You have everything you have, all the brains and health in the world, great experience, great contacts, a great reputation, better now than when you were doing Stanton's shit-work. What don't you have? You come out of this whole thing with twice the offers and opportunities you had before. *I* come out of it..." I paused, trying to veer away from something too pathetic, and touched my lap with the poster "...like this. You've got it *all*, Holly — how come you're the one who sees the whole thing as Good versus Evil?"

She sighed deeply. Other than the low hum of a car idling in the neighborhood and the buzz of a big out-of-season insect, it was the only sound. The late morning felt still and strange in the low-angled sunlight. "Jack," she finally said, quietly, "there are so many ways we can talk ourselves out of standing up. They're endless, especially when you're smart. I know, I use them myself."

The screen door to the house opened and we both turned towards it. The first thing I saw was a pair of sharp knees in blue jeans, then the front of a wheelchair pushing out onto the porch. Then I heard Mom's voice: "Jackie, you have a visitor." Then Holly and I were looking at Fife Burgess.

I don't know how long it had been since I'd seen Fife. At least a few days before the accident, maybe weeks, and then it wouldn't have been more than half a glance walking past his nook at the Spot. The last time we had anything you could call a conversation was when we heard the buy-out was going through.

Once Mom had him across the threshold Fife rolled himself over to me until our knees almost touched. His face looked years, not months, older than I remembered. The old leather had lost its hard substance, sagging down to blur the creases that had crisply matted his cheeks and forehead for so long. His blue eyes were turning to milk like two tiny jellyfish on a cold beach.

Fife's hand shook as he reached into the frayed pocket of his denim shirt and pulled out a pack of Lucky Strikes and a kitchen match, which he lit with a flick of his thumbnail. He pulled hard on the ciga-rette until the tip glowed. Then he looked at me sideways with an uncertain smile. "How's it with you, Mr. Jack?" he said. The effort pulled a rattling cough from him that lasted a few seconds.

Mom brought him out a cup of coffee and went right back inside. Fife held the cup close to his chest with both hands and stared inside as if it held life's deepest secret. Then he looked up, briefly at me and a moment longer at Holly, then all around the yard until his gaze stopped on the cedar fence that separated my family's backyard from Holly's. A smile came slowly to his face and spread wide. "Damn fine lookin fence you got there," he said. "Fellas built that fence, they musta known what they was doin."

Holly and I laughed softly. Holly stepped over and hugged Fife's head to the hollow of her side, then bent over and kissed him on a rough cheek. She pulled a chair over next to him and we sat quietly for a minute in the odd warmth. Fife finished his cigarette and crushed it out on the chrome rim of his chair. "I shoulda come seen you before this, Jack," he said, looking at the last shreds of tobacco in his hand. "Shoulda come sooner. I…don't get around much, cept for Sam's. You know?"

"Sure. That's fine, Fife. I'm glad you came now."

"Don't get around much," he said again, satisfied that he'd said it exactly right. He reached into his pocket for another cigarette and started to light it. With his tremble I didn't know if he could pull it off. I leaned forward to try to help. Holly was already there, striking a match and trying to touch it to the end of the moving cigarette. I remember years ago how Holly would scream at her Dad and chide mine for smoking, and I wondered if she'd lit anybody's cigarette since then.

"I got somethin to say," Fife said after a deep smoky drag. He looked at Holly, then at me and back again at her. "I don't think you wanta hear this, little girl."

Her forehead wrinkled into a tiny peak above her eyes. "Why not, Uncle Fife?"

"Some things is just hard, Holly. Just kind of hard to hear."

Holly didn't move. Both of them looked at me. "It's okay, Fife. Really. What do you want to say?"

Slowly, mostly looking at the cigarette in his shaky hand, Fife began the story. He'd been at Sam's the night before until it closed, watching the place thin out after midnight until five people were left: Fife, Sam's niece Dot who usually closes up for him, a young truck driver whose name Fife didn't know and, sitting at the corner table behind Fife's nook, Steve and Mel. They'd come in at about 10:00 and except for a couple of runs to the john hadn't left the table since. Dot was taking them a new pitcher about twice an hour. What seemed strange to Fife was that they never said a word to him all night. "There's nobody friendlier than the two o' them, 'specially the boy," Fife said, "but last night it was like nobody else was livin on Earth."

Fife couldn't hear what they were saying, only the sound of their voices behind him as the hours passed ("Sides which I don't make a practice of listenin in on other folks' business, period.") A little before 2:00 a.m. Dot yelled out last call for Mel and Steve's benefit and laid a final Blitz and V-8 in front of Fife. She walked to the other end of the bar, said something to the truck driver, then walked through the door to the storage area that separates the Spot from the general store. The trucker walked around the bar and through the same door. Fife didn't see either one of them again.

Now Steve and Mel were talking faster and louder than before. Fife still couldn't make out the words. Then he heard a fist come down on the table behind him and a chair scrape backwards.

"From then there wasn't no trick hearin them. It was all Mel doin the talkin and he was full of juice as I ever heard him. He says to Steve 'you're a goddamn nitwit or maybe just a coward whichever's worse, you can't see what's happenin in front of your goddamn eyes. Since you gotta know every goddamn thing,' he says, 'wasn't the goddamn tooth fairy spiked that tree. Wasn't Santa Claus or the Easter bunny. Was me,' he says. 'That's right, daughter, just plain old me. I slid her in way up above the top of the mark so's she'd be out of the way. I had it all set up perfect, had the timin right down to where they'd find it when they was unloadin in PD,' he says, 'cept I didn't figure in how you'd get your part 100 percent blue-ribbon fucked up.'"

Fife took a heavy drag on the Lucky and pushed down a cough so he could go on. "That's what Mel says straight to Steve last night, sittin right there behind me. He says 'Scuse me for thinkin your fallers would know what the goddamn hell they were doing, for not guessin you'd hire goddamn Albert Einstein who couldn't hack it way back when, but now all of a sudden he can. Instead of just gettin the goddamn cut in you had to start up a charity for your goddamn loser friends and now I guess that's my fault, says you.'" Fife stopped suddenly. I think he was worried how take this last little nugget would sound to me. "I mean, that's not…that's…" Holly squeezed him with the hand she'd been resting on his arm.

"I know." I nodded carefully to him. "I know, Fife."

He nodded back. "So then he's sayin 'Or maybe you think we all should have stuck our thumbs up our ass and waited for them to take away everything we ever had, laughin while they do it? You'd do it that way, lamb chop, but I guess you don't run everythin yet, do you?' And he's about yellin by now, y'know. All of a sudden he stops and there's not a sound and I know they're starin right at my back, they coulda been smackin me with a axe handle I was feelin it so strong. And it keeps bein quiet, and I just sit there not movin, kinda hunched over low like I get when I'm outa steam, until I hear one of 'em walk right by me and on out slammin the door closed. I can't figure which one and I ain't about to look and then I hear Mel's big V-8 Ram fire up outside, and he's down the road just about leavin rubber. Then nothin for a little till Steve gets up and packs it to the door, then his Explorer fires up and heads out like another bat outa hell, and then there's nothin but me sittin there, not a sound but that grindy Rainier clock over the door. Just like that."

None of us moved for a minute. Then Holly stood up and hugged Fife tightly around his shoulders. Without a word she walked into the house. I heard the front door close behind her. At the sound Fife looked up from his lap and reached into his pocket for a cigarette. I rolled my chair next to his and took the matchbook to help him light up. After a long pull he took it from his mouth and raised his eyes to look squarely into my face. His eyes had a shiny film. "I try to tend my own business," he said. It sounded like a question.

"You do, Fife." Whether or not he knew it he was tossing me a life-line: I could tend to his upset, at least for a minute, rather than feeling the blow of his news all at once. I took it. "People in this town think they have to have their nose in everything, but you're not like that," I said. "That's why people trust you. You had to tell someone. Had to. There's no way this could stay under the rug." His eyes seemed to throb as he looked at me. "It's good you told me, Fife. I mean it. You did the right thing."

We sat for a while longer without talking, swirling in separate currents. When Fife cleared his throat to go it startled me. I thanked him again, told him to go home and not to tell anyone else what he heard. That suited him. He rolled across the deck to the back door, looking back at me as his wheels crossed the threshold. Then he was gone. I sat and watched the pale sunlight on the cedar fence between our place and Holly's turn to shadow.

47

EARLY IN THE EVENING I WAS STARING AT A BLANK NOTEBOOK PAGE AT the dining room table, trying to find words for what this feels like, when Holly came back. She walked through the front door without knocking — Mom was back in her bedroom — and across the entry way to me. Following behind her was Steve.

Holly pulled out a chair at the end of the table and sat down. Steve took off his ball cap, bright orange with a stylized STIHL and an embroidered 2-inch chainsaw above the peak, and tucked it under an arm. He stayed standing. "Hello, Jack," he said.

"Steve," I nodded. "Sit down." He hesitated a moment and then stepped around to take the seat across from me. The cap went on the table with the little saw pointed my way.

Holly took her hands from her lap and laid them flat on the table. "We thought we better talk about things," she said.

I looked at Steve. There was no way he'd slept in the last 24 hours. His face had a gray pastiness, a preview of old age. His hair and eyebrows were rumpled and his eyes, chips of blue set down in two bruise-colored pockets of moist skin, were locked onto some point near my left elbow.

Five seconds passed with no words. What things? Making this easier wasn't my job. For a change. As the silence lengthened, I felt myself relax, actually letting more weight settle in the leather sling of the wheelchair. If they wanted to sit all night without a word, we would do that.

"I didn't think he could," Steve said, his eyes lifting to meet mine and then falling again. "I mean, I thought of all kinds of things with him, because he *says* all kinds of things, stupid things, but I always figured so what? He's a yay-hoo with a big mouth." He looked at me more steadily. "That's who he is. But I swear, I know it sounds stupid, I was sure he'd never really do it."

"You were wrong, Steve," Holly said. She closed her fist in front of her and tapped it on the table. "We can sit and talk all we want about what you thought would happen and wouldn't happen, then you know what? Then we're stuck with a few little facts." Her index finger sprang out from her fist like a darting animal and pointed at me. "One: you hit the spike and it crippled you. There's no way to fix that. Two," shooting out the middle finger, "Mel did the spiking. Three: he did it on his own, probably. There are too many dribble-mouths up here to keep it quiet if it was some kind of committee project. And if he did it on his own, the Company's not going to back him up. That leaves just Mel."

As Holly slowly uncurled her pinky to mark a fourth point, Steve jumped in. "Four is he's completely whacked out about this," he said. "After we fought at the Spot he went home, all the way down the hill to the house on the river and locked himself in the den with the lights out. Mom says he won't open the door. What I'm thinking about is that if everyone finds out…," he shook his head and let out a gust of air. Then as if just startled awake he fixed all his attention on me. "And five, Jack, it's hard to say this to you but it's the truth, five is that he didn't mean to hurt anybody. It was all for propaganda. He had it set up so the spike would travel in the log in a load that he'd be able to monitor, then he'd tip off the mill while the truck was on the road, and they'd find it unloading, on its way to the barker. It just all fucked up."

Steve's hands were out in front of his shoulders now, palms turned up like two small offerings. He was waiting for a reaction he could do something with. I stared back at him. I had just been told that what paralyzed me wasn't supposed to hurt anyone. I almost felt myself brace for a surge of anger, but it didn't come.

What I felt was something like relief. If I'd been alone with him, hearing him saying there was no fault here, that it's just kind of the crummy way things go, having to listen to one more verse of the song he's sung for forty years, that would have driven me batshit. But we weren't alone. Holly was sitting to my right, his left, between us. She heard every word, saw every gesture. Finally. Finally it's all laid out, right here on Mom's kitchen table where you can't miss it. Who he is. Who I am. She couldn't not see it now.

As Steve stared at me I turned to her. Now that everything was clear I was looking to her to make things right. Which, I realized as I watched her watch Steve with the concentration of a lab scientist, was exactly the same thing she was looking for him to do. Which was exactly what he, leaning half his weight over the table, straining to hear from me a word of forgiveness, the shred of a laugh, something, was looking for me to do. I think it's called a Gordian Knot, and as we sat there in silence I realized Steve wasn't going to be the one to cut it. Neither would Holly; that would be giving up on him. Maybe I should, just to show her one more way that he and I are different. If he was waiting to be told what to do, I could do that. But why the goddamn *hell* should that be up to me? I'm not already carrying my share of the goddamn load? Plus, this is the part I keep forgetting, I'm done proving things to Holly. I am. Right?

I lifted my head from my hand and stared squarely at him. "There's a number six, too, Steve," I said. "Because of what Mel did, Zenith' getting rigor mortis in a jail cell downtown, and we can't get him out."

Steve looked at Holly; they'd talked about this. "Okay," he said. "What if we could figure out a way to spring Zenith without turning my Dad in?"

What was this, another assignment for me? "How do you propose to do that?"

Steve rubbed his forehead and eyes hard with his fingers, then slid his hand down over his mouth. "I don't know," he said. "I need time to think."

"Like what kind of time?" Holly asked. "You saw Zenith, too, Steve. We don't have to tell you."

Steve sighed, a quick strong gust, and stood up. He pulled his cap on and looked at us for a moment before he walked out the door. Holly kept watching it after it closed.

"You're not going with him?" I said.

"It's not my business." She sounded like she was trying hard to mean it.

48

I'D THOUGHT THAT WHEN I FOUND OUT WHO THE SPIKER WAS I'D START sleeping better. I didn't. I lay there hours past midnight playing out the three possibilities I could think of. Either Mel would turn himself in with some pushing from Steve, or Steve would turn Mel in, or they'd try to keep the whole thing quiet.

Unless I had Mel completely wrong, the first one was fantasyland. The second was easier to picture, but not much. Holly's right when she says Steve's figured out that Mel's not God. But ignoring Mel's order to stay clear of me and turning Mel in on a serious felony were two different things. Could Steve do it? As his Best Friend I should be able to answer that. I lay in bed wondering, and wondering if Holly was lying in bed right then asking the same question. He's not so jaded that he'd actively try to bury the truth, but he's weak enough to leave to someone else, to Holly or to me, the crappy chore of revealing it. Steve could easily decide that Fife's report to Holly and me lets him off the hook; if we think nailing Mel is so important, we're free to do it ourselves.

And doesn't that sound like a lot of fun. On one side you'd have the bitter spiking victim, who's already condemned the timber industry on national radio as a pack of liars, the ex-assistant and girlfriend of America's most obnoxious environmental celebrity, and the village idiot of Lewis Falls. And that's assuming that we're willing to push Fife into the public spotlight; even if I were, Holly's not. So that leaves two accusers basing their case on a fragment of conversation they didn't actually

282

hear. On the other side stands Mel Raines, timber's crown prince in Southern Oregon, shaking his head at these silly charges. He'd have us for lunch. The only way to protect ourselves would be to stay silent. Is that how Steve will let it happen?

THE ROOM WAS FULL OF SUNLIGHT WHEN I WOKE UP, FULLY ALERT IN the first second. Someone was knocking on the front door. I heard Mom open it and greet Holly. I used my pee tube, wrapped a robe around me, swung into the chair and rolled it out to the living room.

She stood at the TV cabinet flicking through the channels. "Steve called a few minutes ago," she said when she noticed me. She kept cycling through programs. *Good Morning America,* cartoons, some commercials, *Sesame Street,* an aerobics class, *Today,* a full-screen hand showing off a sparkling ring. Then we were looking at the celebrity news face from the Grants Pass station, lots of hair and chin and a camel hair blazer, talking to the camera with the courthouse steps behind him. Holly backed away and sat down in the easy chair next to me. "He told me if he doesn't do it this way he can't be sure he'll do it." She looked at me for a second and then back at the screen.

The camera tilted up from the reporter to an empty podium on the top step. Then Steve walked into the picture and stepped behind it. The camera zoomed into his face, big and smoothly shaven now, crumpled with fatigue. He took a piece of paper from his pocket and dipped his head towards a cluster of microphones. "I have something I want to say and then I don't think there needs to be any questions," he said.

He smoothed the paper out in front of him and started reading it like a precise legal document. "My name is Steve Raines. I work for the Lewis Corporation as Operations Manager for the Lewis Falls District. My father is Mel Raines who is Senior Vice President for General Operations of the Lewis Corporation. He has worked for the Lewis Corporation for forty-one years and in that time has done many good things for his employees and to make Southern Oregon a better place to live. I placed a call to him this morning to discuss this announcement but was unable to make contact. However I feel confident that in taking the step I now take I am living out the principles of the upbringing that Mel Raines himself gave to me..."

A FEW HOURS LATER, JUST AFTER NOON TODAY, MEL AND STEVE WALKED together into the Lewis County Courthouse. That was on TV too, though neither of them said anything. The only one who did was Sheriff Smith, who used the same podium Steve used this morning. One question he answered was whether he thought Mel was also linked to the PDEC fire. "Too early to say," he said, wrinkling his forehead seriously. "We have a lot to talk about with Mr. Raines in the next few days." Close to him, on the edges of the screen, I thought I recognized some of the same characters that had squatted in our yard for so long.

For the first time I can remember, Mom sat down to watch with me empty-handed, no dustrag, no needle work, nothing. She made little gasping sounds when Mel was mentioned, sad enough to draw me towards her. I held her hand.

Though the camera didn't show her I knew Holly was down there somewhere. After his morning press conference Steve had come back up the hill and stopped at her house. Holly's mom called over here to tell her. As Holly left she said she'd call later to let me know what was happening, and after a couple of hours she did. They'd put Mel in a segregated wing of the jail and a little while later a pair of lawyers who flew in to the tiny PD airstrip were let in to see him. "Funny," Holly told me, "but they don't seem to have the same time limits visiting Mel that we did visiting Zenith."

Zenith is finally free. Or if he's not, he will be any minute now. When Holly and I hung up she still had some forms and some other kind of dance to go through with the sheriff. "At first they didn't want to let him go, if you can believe that," she said. "I went in to get him while Steve was still with Mel, and they were saying we need some kind of supervision plan for Zenith before they'd let us have him. Only the difference this time is that I had Jenny Naylor with me, which is what we should have done from the beginning. She's a lawyer who did Endangered Species Act stuff for us at WRDC and I called her Sunday, before we knew about Mel. She got here last night, and you should have seen her rip when they came up with the 'supervision plan' horseshit. Remind me to tell you about her and Smith and the D.A. going at it. Oh, and I have to tell you about this van they found tucked away up at Zenith's, which now they say is the reason they held him all this time, which they somehow forgot to mention to anyone before. It's completely bizarre."

"So what's happening right now?"

"Well, I'm in the outer lobby of the jail and Jenny's inside with the Sheriff. They're waiting for the County shrink to come check Zenith out before we take him. At first we said forget that, but then she and I went in to see Zenith for a few minutes. And the thing is, Jack, they kind of have a point worrying about Zenith. He is really strange."

"Zenith?" I said. "Strange? You're kidding."

"No, it's different now. It used to be he could definitely keep himself together from day to day. Now," she paused, her voice cramped. "Now I don't know what we do. God."

We talked for another minute before she had to go. She said as soon as they released Zenith she and Steve would pick him up and get some dinner. Then they'll come back up the mountain. She'd talked to Sam about putting Zenith in one of his guest cabins tonight, and tomorrow we'll get together — her, lawyer Jenny, Steve, and me if I want — to figure out a longer-term plan. I told her I'm in, though (this I didn't say) I don't know what I have to add. She said they'll come by here sometime around ten tomorrow morning.

We hung up around 4:00. Mom and I watched national news at 6:00. Dan Rather's first two stories were on us. The first was a mix of stuff we'd already seen, the punchline part of Steve's statement this morning, Steve and Mel walking up the Courthouse steps, the ancient snapshot of me up at Bounty, re-used video of me getting lifted into a van in front of the house. Then they did a Bigshot Reaction story. Dee Dee Myers says the President is following developments closely, hoping we can soon put this horrible incident behind us and move forward to a lasting solution of this troubling and complex issue. Senator Hatfield is deeply saddened and more committed than ever to an open dialogue emphasizing the common values we share as Oregonians.

From Hatfield it went back to Rather. "And in Oregon itself the spiking and its investigation has become the centerpiece of a hard-fought Congressional race that will be decided next Tuesday."

Arthur Lane appeared, caught in mid-sentence in front of the entrance to the Grants Pass Super-Mall. "Well, the arrest today tells me it's time to take a deep breath and stop throwing careless accusations around. And also that maybe this great step towards modernization that we're supposed to be so grateful to Oklahoma Oil and Mr. James Nielsen for might not be everything it's cracked up to be. Before they came on the scene I don't remember honest working people like Jack Gilliam getting crippled just trying to do their jobs."

The picture changed to Gina Arnstead. "I just happen to believe in a little thing we have in this country called innocent until proven guilty," she said, "and as I understand it nobody's been proven guilty of anything yet. But no matter how this particular case turns out, I think it would be a mistake if we forgot who it was who brought the climate of violence to the forest in the first place, with their inflammatory speeches and threats of sabotage with the avowed purpose of stopping perfectly legal timber sales that have already met all the strict environmental tests, which I support, that all logging has to meet. That's why I want to go to Congress, to make sure that this climate of violence isn't allowed to continue, so that tragedies to honest working people like John Gilliam won't happen again." People around her clapped and she nodded.

Mom got up and went to the kitchen. I turned off the set a couple of minutes later and followed her. Normally when I watch her cook she buzzes away with a steady line of conversation. A couple of five-word questions keep her going until she sets the food on the table. Tonight she was silent. While I grated carrots for her carrot and raisin salad she plodded around the room as if slogging through a task she hated. "It's a pretty strange deal, isn't it?" I said.

She made no sign that she heard me. She was rolling pork cutlets in flour and laying them in a sizzling skillet. She set down the last one and covered it with a lid. "The only good thing is that your father didn't have to see this."

But I wonder what he'd think if he had. He'd be watching everyone's front foot to see who hung in. Steve? Probably. Dad had always appreciated Steve's form. Mel? No. It's possible Dad could forgive the spiking itself. He might have understood the stakes and why Mel did what he did. What Dad would hate is how Mel let somebody else take the fall. And if it turns out Mel did set up the PDEC fire — well, that whole thing would have made Dad throw up, whoever did it. What about Holly? No. In Dad's world women didn't have the muscles to hang in.

And me, Dad. Have I hung in? If all this is supposed to mean something, is that what it means? That when you hang in the world works right? The bad guys get caught. The unjustly accused go free. The clouds lift from the mind of the fair maiden. Except that right this second, five or six hours since I talked to her, the fair maiden is probably sitting next to Steve on her mission of mercy, awed by the transforming courage he showed today. Finally. Is she thinking it was worth the wait? Or else they've already dumped Zenith at Sam's cabin and the two of them are relaxing, you could say, at the end of a hard day together saving the world. She could be dropping exhausted onto his fake leather couch, kicking off her shoes. He's rattling through the cupboards hoping the good bottle of wine someone brought over months ago is still around. He makes a joke about it and she laughs. He dims the lights as he heads for the couch and that makes them laugh, too.

Okay. Whatever there is to figure out it's obvious I won't figure it out tonight. I started writing when Mom and I finished dinner hours ago and just plowed on, seeing a chance to catch up with the story . Now I have. I've finally written it all down. All the facts, anyway. Pretty soon, if Will's right, which he will be, I'll be able to add the fact of who had PDEC destroyed. The last of the facts we've been so busy uncovering. Then all that will be left, from now on, is me and this fucking chair.

Christ, I'm tired. Sam has a saying he stole from God knows who about the way some of us can drown in the tiny ponds of ourselves. The point being that's not how it has to be. Maybe tomorrow I'll read some Ram Dass. He's a good lifeguard for that kind of thing.

EPILOGUE

49

I READ THIS MANUSCRIPT OVER THREE TIMES BEFORE LETTING IT OUT into the world, because I wanted to feel sure about what Jack would have wanted. But even now I am not sure. He said at the very beginning of course that he had to tell the real story. But on the other hand he really had a jumble of feelings about being known. I think he was bothered more by the way fame appealed to him than by fame itself. Like it was flaky to want fame when fame comes to people for such flaky reasons, which he sort of says in the part where he says he will be chosen one of the most fascinating people of 1994. He thought people should get to be famous for doing ordinary things, too. It almost never happens that way but it happened to him that way.

In the end I think I decided to have this published because I want people to know Jack not just because of what happened to him. I want people to know at least a little about who he was. Maybe it is a good decision and maybe not. It is the best one I know how to make.

He would be amazed that I am the one making the decision. The obvious person for that duty was Lois. But she told me to do whatever I thought Jack would want. I could have told her that reading this has made me less sure I knew much about Jack than I was before. Instead I just said I would take care of it. Right now, complicated questions are something she does not need.

The manuscript was hand-printed on every other line of a set of spiral notebooks. They were found on the floor of his bedroom but not by me. I have not gone in there. When two men came to pick up his rented hospital bed the notebooks were underneath. That would not have been where he kept them because there was no way for him to reach down there. He must have had them wedged between the bed and the end table where no one else would see them.

They are amazing. Some of it I obviously knew. I remember the Timber Carnival he writes about when we walked around and talked about the War like it happened yesterday. When he wrote about the card with the peace sign and not being able to remember what he wrote in it I knew exactly the one he meant. I went to the file cartons in my mother's attic and found it. It says

Dear Holly,
    Maybe there was somebody I was less expecting to see walking around the Bounty carnival, but I don't know who it would be. Jackie Kennedy, maybe? Frank Sinatra? Elmer Fudd? But once we started talking it made perfect sense you were there. The years you've been gone almost melted away. The powerful clippings you sent show me how much I have to learn... things you already know. With your patience, maybe I can catch up.

It was signed Your Redneck Logger Admirer.

I remember what I felt when I got that card. I hoped he was just trying to say he approved of me and what I was doing but I knew that was not the main reason he wrote. It was one of the times I realized the differences between what he wanted and what I wanted and that I owed it to him to be careful. Now when I read how he wrote and re-wrote and rewrote that card to make it right I can barely stand it.

In fact the only hard parts to read are the ones about me. I kept thinking this is not me he has all these feelings for, but some image of me. An idea of me that has built up in his mind. I wish I could talk to him about it. He put himself through so much unnecessary pain. On that last night when he was hurting from imaginings of Steve and me on the couch we were not even together. We had been earlier when we picked up Zenith to drive him back up the mountain. The three of us rode in Steve's truck with me in the middle. We stopped once (at the Chuckwagon in Port Douglas) to get dinner. Zenith brought back heaping plates from the salad bar five times. The family at the next table was staring so hard they stopped eating.

When we got back into the truck it was almost dark. Zenith turned to stare out his window, and I did not see him move during the whole ride. As we left PD and started up the hill Steve began talking. He talked about the guilt he felt about Mel. Like everybody else he sat back and watched Mel do anything he wanted for years, hostile things smaller than this, but now Steve saw how they led to this. It was like a holy war for Mel where none of the usual rules applied to him and no one told him otherwise. Steve said maybe if he had started standing up years ago when Mel would go too far it never would have reached this point. I said I thought that was being pretty rough on himself and to remember he was the child and Mel was supposed to be the parent. Then he said (sarcastically) I should tell Jack that his buddy Steve was being too rough on himself.

I asked him to say more about what he was thinking about Jack and it was obviously hard for him. He said he started praying again for the first time since we were little. There is only one thing that he wants and it keeps coming back to him again and again. He wants to be able to turn back the clock one time so he could go back two months when he asked Jack to come back to work falling. He said he is not even sure why he asked. He needed Jack's help less than he pretended to. It was just a wild hair about doing something together like old times (but I think it was more a way to feel Jack was not judging him too harshly). And he said he really did not expect Jack to say yes. If he could have one thing in the world it would be to turn back the clock to the day he stopped at Jack's shop and to drive right by instead.

Then I said if you are going to be rolling clocks back why not go farther back to before Oklahoma Oil bought out the Company and change that. I know it made a lot of money for his family and it made things more comfortable for my mother too, but that money was obviously too expensive. Steve said no, it was not the buy-out that did it, the buy-out could work out fine in a few years if it gets a chance. I guess he was talking about his idiotic super-seedlings again and the miracle of modern forest management. But it was not a time to argue.

The next thing he said was the one that mattered. Will and the other agents kept after me to try to remember exactly the words Steve used. I think they were these: "Once we start in on things we'd change if we could it's probably a long list. But to me it all revolves around Jack. He is the symbol of this whole thing if you think about it. The whole story, how things were when we were growing up and now how they are today. At the center of the whole thing, there is Jack." When Steve was interviewed he said that was mostly right, but he thinks he used the words "when you think about it, the whole mess boils down to Jack."

We will never know the words exactly and at this point it makes no difference. Whatever they were, I looked over at Zenith about then and he showed no sign of hearing anything. He had no reaction at all. It was like he was frozen stiff staring out the window with his face turned away from us.

That was almost all we said until we arrived in town. Steve parked next to the Spot and went in to find Sam while I waited with Zenith in the truck. I put my hand on his arm and asked him what it felt like to be home. He did not respond or look at me. He sat facing forward with his eyes closed.

Steve came back with the key to the cabin and the three of us went in and turned on the bulb hanging from the ceiling. It only had a cot, two metal folding chairs, an old dresser, a sink and rough plank counter and miniature refrigerator in one corner. An outhouse for all three cabins was a few feet away from the front door. I almost said something about how similar it probably was to where Zenith just came from. I took Zenith by the hand and sat down on the bed with him. I made sure that he understood that we would be back early the next morning to take him to breakfast and to talk about what happens next. I told him we were glad to have him back and that everything would be all right. He nodded but would not look at me. I thought it was because Steve was standing there.

Steve and I got back in the truck and he drove me the two blocks to my mother's. There was not the barest thought (for me and I think for him) that he and I would go off somewhere. Even if we were not both exhausted there would not have been. That is what makes it hard to read what Jack was thinking, and writing fifty yards away, at maybe the same moment that I was getting out of Steve's truck. Steve and I agreed to meet at Sam's at 7 o'clock to get breakfast with Zenith and then go over to Jack's to talk.

I set my alarm for 6:15 and went straight to bed. It seemed like a minute later when I woke with a startled feeling, almost like you would in a earthquake. From the gray light I knew it was morning. I turned over and saw that the clock said 5:58. This will sound strange but as I lay there I knew something was wrong. Then I heard the most terrible sound I have ever heard. It was a scream full of horrible madness.

I was out of the house before I could think. I ran barefoot across the gravel in my tee shirt and panties towards the screaming. Towards Jack's. On the front porch on her knees was Lois, rocking back and forth with her hands over her ears. She was wailing at the top of her lungs and then coughing for breath, rocking back and forth with her whole face squeezed shut except her mouth. Her hands and her robe were smeared with blood. Scurrying around her looking baffled was a County deputy, the last one they had keeping watch over there. As I rushed up to grab Lois he went into the house. I kneeled at Lois' side and held her tight with both arms. I was trying to gentle her rocking and soften her screams before they tore her apart. She probably did not know I was there. When she gasped for breath to scream again I could hear the deputy shouting something into the telephone in the living room behind us. Then he came out and stared down at us. I stayed with Lois another minute and then got up to go inside but he slid over to the door to block my way. I was shouting and trying to push over him and around him but he braced himself in the door jamb and shook his head. That is the instant I knew. I backed up and slid down to be next to Lois without trying to comfort her anymore. The next I remember a sheriff's patrol car, an ambulance and a fire rescue van were all in the front yard with blue and red lights flying everywhere through the air.

Then Lois and I were being lifted to our feet and led away from the house. I struggled and twisted away and tried to run back in. Two men in white shirts caught me (one on each arm) and took me into the ambulance. They sat me down on the bed and made me drink water. I kept saying I wanted to go in and they said no, I did not. When I started yelling one of them put his hands on my shoulders to quiet me and told me what everybody in the world would find out a little while later. Jack was lying on his bed with his skull in two pieces.

There was no mystery to solve. Sometime about 4:00 or 4:30 in the morning Zenith left Sam's cabin and walked to Lois' house. The deputy who was posted by the front door says he was awake the whole time and saw nothing. One way or another Zenith let himself in the back gate and through the kitchen door and into Jack's room. He apparently did not find it right away because his fingerprints were on most of the door knobs. But he was quiet enough. They think Jack was asleep until the last second. They say there was a big slice out of his hand where he probably threw it up as a reflex. I am going to keep thinking that was all it was, a quick scare like you get in dreams sometimes before you actually wake up.

Within an hour of when Lois found him (probably while they were trying to calm me down in the ambulance) a patrol car coming up the hill from Port Douglas found Zenith. He was slowly walking west on the highway shoulder towards the Stagestop Store. He was drenched with blood. He was dragging behind him the double-bladed ax that Sam keeps on the back porch of the Spot to split wood for the big cast iron stove.

I am the one who worked the hardest to get Zenith freed. For weeks it was basically all I did. It was not just about helping Zenith who was innocent and suffering for somebody else's crime. It was obviously for me too. It let me focus on one clear thing instead of having to think about what happened to Jack and what our campaign against OO might have had to do with it. Focusing on something I could work on let me cope. We succeeded in getting him out. If we had failed Jack would still be here. Now that is what I have to cope with.

Coping is not possible when I think about the whole thing all at once. The only way is one little piece at a time. Getting Jack's notebooks out to be read is one piece. Being there for Lois is another (even if I wonder if she notices or not). There was one more piece: the PDEC fire. He wanted it solved more than he let on, especially because of the Jack's Avengers part. Having his name on that note really got to him.

Two days after Jack died I went to see Will Hayama. It was easy to see what Jack was saying about him. He has this very calm way that is very focused at the same time. He answered the questions I had from reading Jack's notebooks like he had all the time in the world. The big one obviously was about the so-called hippie bus behind Zenith's that stole the ceramic spike. Will said Mel admitted giving $200 to two teenage brothers who work summers for the Company to take the bus up there and put it in the ditch (since the arrest Mel was answering all questions without playing games, according to Will). He gave them both soft leather gloves to wear to prevent any fingerprints. All he told them was that it was a practical joke some people wanted to play on Zenith. Knowing the family I can believe the brothers would accept that without any questions and that for $200 they would have been happy to do far worse to someone like Zenith and to keep quiet about it forever. Will says there will probably not be any charges against them.

After we talked Will let me read his notes. I was not allowed to copy them or take them out of the building but I sat in a little room inside the Federal Building in Grants Pass reading them for two hours. His last entry was from talking to Mel about that night at the Spot with Ray Swerdlow. Mel admitted he was there that night for a little while. He said he drank two beers and listened to Ray's tirade. He obviously must have enjoyed hearing how well his plan to get things riled up was working. At least it was in the Spot. The notes said Mel did not talk to anyone that night or hear anything that would help discover who hired Ray. Will told me he was going back the next day to interview Mel again. I asked him if I could come. He said that was too far outside the rules, but if someone else who was permitted to see Mel invited me to come along there was nothing anyone could do about that. Will obviously knew that the only people allowed to visit Mel other than lawyers and investigators are Mel's family.

I called Steve. He said he would set up a visit with Mel after dinner that same night. We met at the jail and they took us to a private room on a different floor from where we used to visit Zenith. There was no glass separation. It was just Mel, Steve and me sitting at a little table with a guard standing by the door watching us.

I was nervous going in. I knew what Mel thought about me and with what happened to Jack I was unsure what I would say to him. But the moment they brought him in I could see it was a different person than I knew before. He looked exhausted and very old. When he spoke his voice was quieter than before. Coming into the room he looked at me without any surprise or upset. He and Steve talked for a few minutes about how Steve's mother is doing. Then Steve asked if Mel was willing to talk again about the night at the Spot before the PDEC fire. Mel said he was. Then he told us the same things I had read in Will's notes.

When he stopped Steve looked at me so I just started asking questions. I asked him again if anybody other than Ray stuck out in his mind that night. He said no. I asked him again if he talked to anyone. He said no, other than to order beer. I asked him to try to break down the time he spent there minute by minute: what he remembered about walking in the door, who he passed walking to his table, when he ordered the first beer, how it was brought to him, when he ordered the second, what he was doing when Ray got so loud. He seemed to think carefully about everything I asked before he answered and he did think of one or two more little details. I asked him if anyone came in while he was there. He said nobody he could remember. I asked if anyone had left.

He started to say no. Then he stopped and said there was something else. When he finished his second beer he went to the bathroom. He went in and saw somebody was at the urinal. He had on a beige felt cowboy hat and sunglasses and Mel thought he was one of the TV reporters. Rather than wait Mel opened the door to the toilet stall and went in.

Then the cowboy at the urinal started talking. How's it going? he said. Mel didn't say anything. Quite a hero we have out there, the cowboy said. Mel knew he meant Ray because Ray was doing all the talking. Sounds like he plans to make the world safe for clearcutting again all by himself, the cowboy said. Then Mel said something about the spiking getting everybody upset because Jack was one of their own, so people feel the spike attacked all of them. Then the cowboy said the accident was too bad but something like that was bound to happen when greed starts running wild. Mel says he felt himself start to get mad but decided not to say anything because there was no point. A hotshot reporter from a TV news network or wherever he was from would obviously not be interested in the facts.

Then as the cowboy was washing his hands he said something else to Mel. He said it was so crazy, the forest stripped, one man crippled, this whole town headed down the tubes. All of it just so James Nielsen can keep his polo ponies in premium oats.

I asked Mel to repeat what he said. He did, exactly the same way. He was sure of those words in particular because they almost made him jump the cowboy then and there. The idea that the TV people who told everybody else what to think would boil everything down to an ignorant smartass remark like that was nearly more than he could take. But it was not a time to draw attention to himself so Mel was quiet and the cowboy walked out.

Only one person uses that particular smartass remark. It was fresh in my mind because I had just read it in Jack's notebooks, from the media event we did at the top of the Falls road when the cutting was at its peak and the one who said it was Stanton. Then I remembered him using it in a WRDC fundraising letter a few months ago. It was pure Stanton. It was one of those magic button-pushing phrases that he loves to hear coming out of his mouth. I guess what Jack said about Ray Swerdlow's being like Henry Higgins was not so far fetched after all. To someone from Lewis Falls the way Stanton talks, with a tight jaw like William Buckley, would sound funny.

I said nothing to Mel or Steve. As soon as I left Steve I called Will to see if he would meet me back at my mother's in an hour. He did and I told him. The cowboy hat and sunglasses fit the description of one of the two people that nobody could name on the list of people at the Spot that night. Will asked me what motive Stanton would have for burning down PDEC and I told him. He asked where I would be the next day. I said right there, my mother's house. I have not quite figured out how long I'm staying here and where I will go when I leave. Will said he would call me in the morning.

The next morning he asked if I would help them get Stanton. It would mean calling him on a tapped phone and getting him to say something that proved that he gave Ray money to set the fire. Will wanted Stanton to say something so clear that no defense attorney could confuse a jury about what it meant. I asked how I would know when he had what he needed. He said I would make the call from his office where he could sit with me and listen. I asked Will if I could have the rest of the day to think about it and he said of course and to call him back that night.

It makes me a little sad that I thought I needed time to decide. But Stanton was someone in my life. We shared things that are important. He showed me sides of himself that other people have never seen. I could go on but none of it comes close to mattering as much as what happened to Jack and the part I played in it. I called Will back ten minutes after we hung up and said yes.

It turned out to be simple. I went down to the Federal Building in Grants Pass the next morning, the day before yesterday. There was an electronic unit that looked like a briefcase on Will's desk and he had me sit in his chair. I dialed the WRDC number and Cheryl answered. She sits at the front desk and for the first month I worked there I slept on her couch. She wanted to talk but I said I was on the road using the private phone in a little store and maybe we could do it the next day. She said fine and told me Stanton was in a meeting. She asked me if I wanted her to interrupt him. Will shook his head no. I said no and that I'd call back in half an hour. We talked for a few more minutes (she is too nice to work there) before hanging up.

I walked around the building three times trying to focus on what I would say. When I went in and called again Cheryl put me through to Stanton. He was in a friendly mood and sounded glad to hear from me. He said he was really shocked about Jack. He asked me if I had received his card about it and when I said no he said oh, there it was on the corner of his desk under some papers, he must have spaced out about mailing it and he would mail it today. That made what I had to do easier. There was no card on his desk. He would write one after we got off and put it in the mail. I have seen him do the exact same thing to other people on the phone and laugh about it afterwards.

Will had told me that the best way to do this was with the least deception possible. I told Stanton that I had just met someone who saw him at the Spot the night that Ray Swerdlow was threatening massacre to get even for the spiking. He asked me who Ray Swerdlow and what the Spot was. I said I was sure he knew already. There was a pause and then he asked why I called. I told him I thought he should know he had been seen so he could have answers together if the FBI called him. He asked if I thought they would call. I said all I know is that they were sure somebody hired Ray to burn PDEC but still did not know who. He said nothing.

After a few seconds I just said why did you do it? He said what makes you think that I did? I said it was the way he talked about the spiking after it happened, how hurting their own side was the only thing the timber dogs could do that would turn things around for them. I said he almost sounded jealous of them for thinking of it. I said I remembered how he felt about stealing good tactics wherever we found them. In the conference room at Western Resources there is a white board where people write good quotes across the top. I told him I remembered when he posted one saying plagiarism is the sincerest form of flattery.

That is true, he said. He sounded like an Oxford professor. I told him so and said it was unbelievable how blasé he sounded after setting something up that killed one person directly and helped stir the pot that eventually killed somebody else. He said it was unbelievable how naive somebody who knew as much as I did about the nature of the timber industry could be. I said that this showed he had the same kind of nature.

That sent him off. He said to me you are always talking about standing for something and how the problem with the world is that not enough people do it. So you stand for something and you tell everybody what it is and why it is so important. And they look at you and say Holly's so brave and idealistic. Here's what I say, he said: so what? After you stop talking about your noble truth of the week the only thing that's changed is that people know your opinion about it. What he's figured out, he said, is that the people who talk the most about standing up for something are the ones most frightened to go the next step and do something for what they supposedly believe in. They are hypocrites, he said, worse than the mass of people who at least do not pretend to believe in anything.

I pushed down all I wanted to say to that and said so you have no regrets. He said I have one: nobody had to die. I should not have picked the biggest moron in Oregon to torch the store. If there had been more time I would have found someone with half a brain and we would not be having this conversation. That was when Will nodded at me and clasped his hands together over his head.

An hour later the FBI in San Francisco arrested Stanton. They walked right into the office and led him away in handcuffs. A picture of them coming out of the building lobby was in yesterday's *Oregonian*. They still have to decide what the charges will be but Will says Stanton will be much older when he gets out. I thought about it today when my mind wandered during Jack's memorial service, wondering what he thought the right punishment for Stanton would be, and for Mel, too. I think he would say put them in the same cell together for a month or two and that would be plenty.

The service started at noon down at the Falls and about twenty people came. There would have been more but we kept it a secret so no reporters would come. I had asked Steve to take charge of it. First he said no. I said all he had to do was get it started and ask if anyone had anything to say and then at the end thank everyone for coming. I said I was sure Jack would appreciate it and he looked at me like he would argue but then he nodded.

He opened the ceremony as we stood under the trees by the trail that led to the Elders. That was the closest we could be to the Falls and still hear each other speak. We are here to honor my friend, Steve said. Everyone here can say that, I know. Now he is inside of me and he always will be and that makes me better than I was.

Peter Thomas got up and said the difference between Jack and him was that Jack did not go around trying to make people think he was deep, he just was. Then I got up and said Jack was my teacher in seeing people in three dimensions and though I have a long way to go I plan to end up his star pupil. When I finished I saw Fife moving his chair forward and asked him if he wanted to speak. He nodded his head and cleared his throat but he couldn't get anything out.

Dougy Ferrin got up and said one thing we should not forget was how funny Jack was. He told a story about a spontaneous conversation between Jack and Sam for the benefit of a group of hunters who were sitting in the Spot all decked out in brand new Eddie Bauer outfits. Their eyes got wider and wider as they listened to those two make a plan to fight the state's decision to cut off funds for the reform school for the elk that loitered on the highway. By the time Dougy finished the story almost everyone was laughing, some so hard they leaned against each other. Even Lois was smiling. I stood next to her with my arm through hers.

Then Sam recited about half of "The Road Less Traveled," only he did not mention Robert Frost, he made it prose instead of poetry and he changed about a third of the words. When he finished he said, At least that's the way I see it and knowing Jack I believe he did, too.

When everyone who wanted a turn had spoken, Steve picked up an old cedar box that Jack's father made a long time ago. Jack's ashes were inside. We walked to a spot just above the Falls and he attached it to a double cable rigged to cross the river. Someone on the other side pulled on a line until the box was over the middle of the river. Then Steve pulled on another line that turned the box upside down. Chunky powder (from the shore it looked like just a handful) fell into the water. I saw the water turn milky where it hit. The stain held together for a moment, floating toward the Falls slowly and then faster. The current drew it towards a crease in the Falls where the ledge bent in on itself. That funneled an extra portion of river into a single spot. The little patch of water still had a little ashy whiteness when it rose over the shoulder where the water gathers and then down into the mass of crashing water. It was gone.

We watched silently for a minute. Then Annette Ferrin from the Church choir started singing *Amazing Grace* (that was the one thing that Lois asked for) and it was over.

Steve came up and asked me if I wanted a ride back up to the church. My mother and Betty Sulkin had organized a gathering there. When I said no he nodded and turned away. After all the cars left I walked back to the beach and sat on the same log that Jack wrote about, the old one we used as a backrest all those summer days. You can feel from its softness now the puffy rot inside.

As I looked into the Falls I remembered the part I liked best in Jack's notebooks. It was when he was looking into the Falls and realized he saw exactly what Benson Lewis saw all those generations ago, rounding a corner in the stream not knowing what he would find. Like Jack I wonder what he thought that first moment, standing and staring as the mist sprayed over him and his band of trappers. Was he one of those husky heroes who thought his "discovery" made a place real for the first time? Or did he look into the Falls and realize he was seeing exactly what someone long before (maybe an ancestor who died in the Crusades or a Babylonian soldier) would have seen if they had somehow walked around that bend in the river? Not just that they would have seen water fall over the ledge in the same way it does now. That they would have seen the same water. The same water falling over the ledge on its 1,000,001st trip to the sea.

From now on when it returns to fall he'll be in it. He will come back to the Falls again and again and again before I die, no matter what I do or where I go, then another million times after that.

As I walked up the road back to town I decided to stay around here for a while.